# TYNDALE OLD TESTAMENT COMMENTARIES

## VOLUME 25

TOTC

# JOEL AND AMOS

# Tyndale Old Testament Commentaries

## Volume 25

Series Editor: David G. Firth
Consulting Editor: Tremper Longman III

---

# Joel and Amos

## An Introduction and Commentary

## Tchavdar S. Hadjiev

Academic
An imprint of InterVarsity Press
Downers Grove, Illinois

Inter-Varsity Press, England
36 Causton Street, London SW1P 4ST, England
Website: www.ivpbooks.com
Email: ivp@ivpbooks.com

InterVarsity Press, USA
P.O. Box 1400, Downers Grove, IL 60515, USA
Website: www.ivpress.com
Email: email@ivpress.com

Inter-Varsity Press, England, publishes Christian books that are true to the Bible and that
communicate the gospel, develop discipleship and strengthen the church for its mission in the world.

IVP originated within the Inter-Varsity Fellowship, now the Universities and Colleges Christian
Fellowship, a student movement connecting Christian Unions in universities and colleges throughout
Great Britain, and a member movement of the International Fellowship of Evangelical Students.
That historic association is maintained, and all senior IVP staff and committee members subscribe
to the UCCF Basis of Faith. Website: www.uccf.org.uk.

InterVarsity Press®, USA, is the book-publishing division of InterVarsity Christian Fellowship/
USA® and a member movement of the International Fellowship of Evangelical Students. Website:
www.intervarsity.org.

Unless otherwise stated, Scripture quotations are from the NRSV. See pp. xiii–xiv for Bible
acknowledgments.

First published 2020

Set in Garamond 11/13pt
Typeset in Great Britain by CRB Associates, Potterhanworth, Lincolnshire

UK ISBN: 978–1–78359–970–7 (print)
UK ISBN: 978–1–78359–984–4 (digital)

US ISBN: 978–0–8308–4272–8 (print)
US ISBN: 978–0–8308–4277–3 (digital)

**British Library Cataloguing-in-Publication Data**
A catalogue record for this book is available from the British Library.

**Library of Congress Cataloging-in-Publication Data**
A catalog record for this book is available from the Library of Congress.

# CONTENTS

# GENERAL PREFACE

The decision to completely revise the Tyndale Old Testament Commentaries is an indication of the important role that the series has played since its opening volumes were released in the mid 1960s. They represented at that time, and have continued to represent, commentary writing that was committed both to the importance of the text of the Bible as Scripture and a desire to engage with as full a range of interpretative issues as possible without being lost in the minutiae of scholarly debate. The commentaries aimed to explain the biblical text to a generation of readers confronting models of critical scholarship and new discoveries from the Ancient Near East while remembering that the Old Testament is not simply another text from the ancient world. Although no uniform process of exegesis was required, all the original contributors were united in their conviction that the Old Testament remains the word of God for us today. That the original volumes fulfilled this role is evident from the way in which they continue to be used in so many parts of the world.

A crucial element of the original series was that it should offer an up-to-date reading of the text, and it is precisely for this reason that new volumes are required. The questions confronting readers in the first half of the twenty-first century are not necessarily those from the second half of the twentieth. Discoveries from the Ancient Near East continue to shed new light on the Old Testament, while emphases in exegesis have changed markedly. While remaining true to the goals of the initial volumes, the need for contemporary study of the text requires that the series as a whole be updated. This updating is not simply a matter of commissioning new volumes to replace the old. We have also taken the opportunity to update the format of the series to reflect a key emphasis from linguistics, which is that texts communicate in larger blocks rather than in shorter segments such as individual verses. Because of this, the treatment of each section of the text includes three segments. First, a short note on *Context* is offered, placing the passage under consideration in its literary setting within the book as well as noting any historical issues crucial to interpretation. The *Comment* segment then follows the traditional structure of the commentary, offering exegesis of the various components of a passage. Finally, a brief comment is made on *Meaning*, by which is meant the message that the passage seeks to communicate within the book, highlighting its key theological themes. This section brings together the detail of the *Comment* to show how the passage under consideration seeks to communicate as a whole.

Our prayer is that these new volumes will continue the rich heritage of the Tyndale Old Testament Commentaries and that they will continue to witness to the God who is made known in the text.

David G. Firth, Series Editor
Tremper Longman III, Consulting Editor

# AUTHOR'S PREFACE

My interest in the Minor Prophets goes back to my time as an undergraduate student in theology and what seemed at the time to be a fairly random and insignificant event. One summer my sister-in-law Mimi Furnadjieva asked me to put my newly acquired theological skills to some use and write a Bible study on Amos for her church in Bansko, Bulgaria. As I worked my way through the text I was fascinated. In spite of the vast chronological chasm, the more I read this prophecy the more relevant it seemed; it felt both foreign and familiar. Consequently, I gave Amos the next ten years of my life, writing a study on it in Bulgarian and eventually doing a D.Phil. on its redactional history at Oxford. During that period I also developed a special link to the Tyndale Commentaries on the Old Testament. With the help and support of Colin Macpherson, I was involved in organizing the translation and publication of the entire series in Bulgarian. That was a long project full of many challenges as well as some incredible encouragements, chief of which was the long-lasting friendship with my former colleague Marty Raichinov, who was the driving force behind it.

I am grateful to David Firth and Philip Duce for inviting me to contribute the new iteration of Joel and Amos to the series, and to Lindsay Brown for the initial encouragement to do so. Many thanks to David Firth for his insightful suggestions and observations which helped to improve the quality of my work. Above all, I would like to gratefully acknowledge the debt I owe to my teachers, especially Chris Jack from Romsey House, Cambridge, the late Martin Selman from Spurgeon's College, and my doctoral supervisor Hugh Williamson from Oxford. They did not just pass information on to me but inspired me to learn, challenged me to wrestle with Scripture and broadened the horizons of my vision and understanding. As I seek to teach others I hope that at times I may be able to do the same.

Tchavdar S. Hadjiev
Belfast

# CHIEF ABBREVIATIONS

| | |
|---|---|
| AB | Anchor Bible |
| *ABD* | D. N. Freedman et al. (eds.), *The Anchor Bible Dictionary*, 6 vols. (New York: Doubleday, 1992) |
| ANETS | Ancient Near Eastern Texts and Studies |
| ATD | Das Alte Testament Deutsch |
| AYB | Anchor Yale Bible |
| BEATAJ | Beiträge zur Erforschung des Alten Testaments und des Antiken Judentums |
| BHQ | Biblia Hebraica Quinta |
| *BHS* | K. Elliger and W. Rudolph (eds.), *Biblia Hebraica Stuttgartensia*, 5th edn (Stuttgart: Deutsche Bibelgesellschaft, 1997) |
| BIS | Biblical Interpretation Series |
| BZAW | Beihefte zur Zeitschrift für die alttestamentliche Wissenschaft |
| *CBQ* | *Catholic Biblical Quarterly* |
| CD | The Damascus Document |
| CHANE | Culture and History of the Ancient Near East |
| *COS* | W. W. Hallo and K. L. Younger, Jr. (eds.), *The Context of Scripture: Canonical Compositions, Monumental Inscriptions, and Archival Documents from the Biblical World*, 3 vols. (Leiden/Boston: Brill, 2003) |
| CSHB | Critical Studies in the Hebrew Bible |

| | |
|---|---|
| *DCH* | D. J. A. Clines (ed.), *The Dictionary of Classical Hebrew*, 9 vols. (Sheffield: Sheffield Academic Press, 1993–2016) |
| *DDD* | K. van der Toorn, B. Becking and P. W. van der Horst (eds.), *Dictionary of Deities and Demons in the Bible*, 2nd edn (Leiden: Brill, 1999) |
| *DOTP* | M. J. Boda and J. G. McConville (eds.), *Dictionary of the Old Testament Prophets* (Downers Grove: InterVarsity Press; Nottingham: Inter-Varsity Press, 2012) |
| EVV | English versions |
| FAT | Forschungen zum Alten Testament |
| GKC | *Gesenius' Hebrew Grammar*, edited and enlarged by E. Kautzsch, translated by A. E. Cowley (Oxford: Clarendon Press, 1910) |
| *HALOT* | L. Koehler and W. Baumgartner, *The Hebrew and Aramaic Lexicon of the Old Testament: The New Koehler-Baumgartner in English*, 5 vols. (Leiden/New York/Cologne: Brill, 1994) |
| ITC | International Theological Commentary |
| *JBL* | *Journal of Biblical Literature* |
| *JHS* | *Journal of Hebrew Scriptures* |
| JSOTSup | Journal for the Study of the Old Testament Supplementary Series |
| *JTS* | *Journal of Theological Studies* |
| KAT | Kommentar zum Alten Testament |
| LAI | Library of Ancient Israel |
| LHBOTS | Library of Hebrew Bible/Old Testament Study |
| LXX | Septuagint (pre-Christian Greek version of the Old Testament) |
| MT | Masoretic Text (the standard Hebrew text of the Old Testament) |
| NAC | New American Commentary |
| NCBC | New Century Bible Commentary |
| *NEAEHL* | E. Stern (ed.), *The New Encyclopedia of Archaeological Excavations in the Holy Land*, 4 vols. (Jerusalem: Israel Exploration Society, 1993) |

| | |
|---|---|
| *NETS* | A. Pietersma and B. G. Wright (eds.), *A New English Translation of the Septuagint* (Oxford: Oxford University Press, 2007) |
| NICOT | New International Commentary on the Old Testament |
| *NIDB* | K. D. Sakenfeld (ed.), *The New Interpreter's Dictionary of the Bible*, 5 vols. (Nashville: Abingdon Press, 2006–9) |
| *NIDOTTE* | W. A. VanGemeren (ed.), *New International Dictionary of Old Testament Theology and Exegesis*, 5 vols. (Grand Rapids: Zondervan, 1997) |
| NSKAT | Neuer Stuttgarter Kommentar Altes Testament |
| OAN | Oracles Against the Nations |
| OBO | Orbis Biblicus et Orientalis |
| OT | Old Testament |
| OTL | Old Testament Library |
| OTS | Oudtestamentische studiën/Old Testament Studies |
| *RB* | *Revue Biblique* |
| SCS | Septuagint Commentary Series |
| SGOT | T&T Clark Study Guides to the Old Testament |
| SHBC | Smyth & Helwys Bible Commentary |
| *SJT* | *Scottish Journal of Theology* |
| SOTSM | Society for Old Testament Study Monographs |
| TOTC | Tyndale Old Testament Commentaries |
| *VT* | *Vetus Testamentum* |
| VTSup | Vetus Testamentum Supplement |
| WAW | Writings from the Ancient World |
| WBC | Word Biblical Commentary |
| WMANT | Wissenschaftliche Monographien zum Alten und Neuen Testament |
| *ZAW* | *Zeitschrift für die alttestamentliche Wissenschaft* |

## Bible versions

| | |
|---|---|
| ESV | The ESV Bible (The Holy Bible, English Standard Version), copyright © 2001 by Crossway, a publishing ministry of Good News Publishers. Used by permission. All rights reserved. |

# SELECT BIBLIOGRAPHY

Ahlström, G. W. (1971), *Joel and the Temple Cult of Jerusalem*, VTSup 21 (Leiden: Brill).

Albertz, R. (1994), *A History of Israelite Religion in the Old Testament Period*, trans. J. Bowden, OTL (Louisville: Westminster/ John Knox Press).

Allen, L. C. (1976), *The Books of Joel, Obadiah, Jonah and Micah*, NICOT (Grand Rapids: Eerdmans).

Andersen, F. I. and D. N. Freedman (1989), *Amos*, AB 24A (New York: Doubleday).

Assis, E. (2013), *The Book of Joel: A Prophet between Calamity and Hope*, LHBOTS 581 (New York: Bloomsbury).

Barker, J. (2014), *From the Depths of Despair to the Promise of Presence: A Rhetorical Reading of the Book of Joel*, Siphrut 11 (Winona Lake: Eisenbrauns).

Barré, M. L. (1986), 'The Meaning of *l' 'šybnw* in Amos 1:3 – 2:6', *JBL* 105: 611–631.

Barstad, H. M. (1984), *The Religious Polemics of Amos: Studies in the Preaching of Am 2, 7b–8; 4, 1–13; 5, 1–27; 6, 4–7; 8, 14*, VTSup 34 (Leiden: Brill).

Bartlett, J. R. (1989), *Edom and the Edomites*, JSOT Sup 77 (Sheffield: JSOT Press).

Barton, J. (1980), *Amos's Oracles against the Nations: A Study of Amos 1:3 – 2:5* (Cambridge: Cambridge University Press).

—— (2001), *Joel and Obadiah: A Commentary*, OTL (Louisville: Westminster John Knox Press).

────── (2012), *The Theology of the Book of Amos* (Cambridge: Cambridge University Press).

Bergler, S. (1988), *Joel als Schriftinterpret*, BEATAJ 16 (Frankfurt am Main: Peter Lang).

Boer, R. (2015), *The Sacred Economy of Ancient Israel*, LAI (Louisville: Westminster John Knox Press).

Campos, M. E. (2011), 'Structure and Meaning in the Third Vision of Amos (7:7–17)', *JHS* 11, art. 3.

Coggins, R. J. (2000), *Joel and Amos*, NCBC (Sheffield: Sheffield Academic Press).

Cook, S. L. (1995), *Prophecy and Apocalypticism: The Postexilic Social Setting* (Minneapolis: Fortress).

Crenshaw, J. L. (1995), *Joel*, AB 24C (New Haven/London: Yale University Press).

Dahmen, U. (2001), 'Das Buch Joel', in U. Dahmen and G. Fleischer (eds.), *Die Bücher Joel und Amos*, NSKAT 23.2 (Stuttgart: Verlag Katholisches Bibelwerk), pp. 11–113.

Davies, P. R. (2006), 'Amos, Man and Book', in B. E. Kelle and M. B. Moore (eds.), *Israel's Prophets and Israel's Past* (London/New York: T&T Clark), pp. 113–131.

Eidevall, G. (2017), *Amos*, AYB 24G (New Haven/London: Yale University Press).

Faust, A. (2012), *The Archaeology of Israelite Society in Iron Age II* (Winona Lake: Eisenbrauns).

Firth, D. G. (1996), 'Promise as Polemic: Levels of Meaning in Amos 9:11–15', *Old Testament Essays* 9: 372–382.

Fleischer, G. (2001), 'Das Buch Amos', in U. Dahmen and G. Fleischer (eds.), *Die Bücher Joel und Amos*, NSKAT 23.2 (Stuttgart: Verlag Katholisches Bibelwerk), pp. 115–292.

Fleming, D. E. (2010), 'The Day of Yahweh in the Book of Amos: A Rhetorical Response to a Ritual Expectation', *RB* 117: 20–38.

Garrett, D. A. (1997), *Hosea, Joel*, NAC 19A (Nashville: B&H).

Gelston, A. (2010), *The Twelve Minor Prophets*, BHQ 13 (Stuttgart: Deutsche Bibelgesellschaft).

Gillingham, S. (1992), '"Who Makes the Morning Darkness": God and Creation in the Book of Amos', *SJT* 45: 165–184.

Glenny, W. E. (2009), *Finding Meaning in the Text: Translation Technique and Theology in the Septuagint of Amos*, VTSup 126 (Leiden: Brill).

—— (2013), *Amos: A Commentary Based on Amos in Codex Vaticanus*, SCS (Leiden/Boston: Brill).

Goff, M. (2008), 'Awe, Wordlessness and Calamity: A Short Note on Amos v 13', *VT* 58: 638–643.

Goswell, G. (2011), 'David in the Prophecy of Amos', *VT* 61: 243–257.

Hadjiev, T. S. (2007), '"Kill All Who Are in Front": Another Suggestion about Amos ix.1', *VT* 57: 386–389.

—— (2008), 'The Context as Means of Redactional Reinterpretation in the Book of Amos', *JTS* 59: 655–668.

—— (2009), *The Composition and Redaction of the Book of Amos*, BZAW 393 (Berlin/New York: Walter de Gruyter).

—— (2020a), *Joel, Obadiah, Habakkuk, Zephaniah: An Introduction and Study Guide*, SGOT (London: Bloomsbury T&T Clark).

—— (2020b), 'A Prophetic Anthology Rather than a Book of the Twelve: The Unity of the Minor Prophets Reconsidered', in L.-S. Tiemeyer and J. Wöhrle (eds.), *The Book of the Twelve: Composition, Reception, and Interpretation*, Formation and Interpretation of Old Testament Literature/VTSup (Leiden: Brill), pp. 90–108.

Hagedorn, A. C. (2007), 'Looking at Foreigners in Biblical and Greek Prophecy', *VT* 57: 432–448.

Hamborg, G. R. (2012), *Still Selling the Righteous: A Redaction-Critical Investigation of the Reasons for Judgement in Amos 2.6–16*, LHBOTS 555 (New York/London: T&T Clark).

Hammershaimb, E. (1970), *The Book of Amos: A Commentary* (New York: Schocken Books).

Hayes, J. H. (1988), *Amos the Eighth-Century Prophet: His Times and His Preaching* (Nashville: Abingdon Press).

Hopkins, D. (1996), 'Bare Bones: Putting Flesh on the Economics of Ancient Israel', in V. Fritz and P. R. Davies (eds.), *The Origins of the Ancient Israelite States*, JSOTSup 228 (Sheffield: Sheffield Academic Press), pp. 121–139.

Houston, W. J. (2008), *Contending for Justice: Ideologies and Theologies for Social Justice in the Old Testament* (London/New York: T&T Clark).

—— (2010), *Justice: The Biblical Challenge* (London/Oakville: Equinox).

—— (2017), *Amos: Justice and Violence*, SGOT (London: Bloomsbury T&T Clark).

Hubbard, D. A. (1989), *Joel and Amos*, TOTC (Leicester: Inter-Varsity Press).

Hundley, M. B. (2013), *Gods in Dwellings: Temples and Divine Presence in the Ancient Near East* (Atlanta: Society for Biblical Literature).

Irwin, B. (2012), 'Amos 4.1 and the Cows of Bashan on Mount Samaria: A Reappraisal', *CBQ* 74: 231–246.

Jeremias, J. (1998), *The Book of Amos*, OTL (Louisville: Westminster John Knox Press).

—— (2007), *Die Propheten Joel, Obadja, Jona, Micha*, ATD 24.3 (Göttingen: Vandenhoeck & Ruprecht).

Koch, K. (1974), 'Die Rolle der hymnischen Abschnitte in der Komposition des Amos-Buches', *ZAW* 86: 504–537.

Koenen, K. (2003), *Bethel: Geschichte, Kult und Theologie*, OBO 192 (Freiburg: Universitätsverlag; Göttingen: Vandenhoeck & Ruprecht).

Kratz, R. G. (2015), *The Prophets of Israel*, CSHB 2 (Winona Lake: Eisenbrauns).

Linville, J. R. (2008), *Amos and the Cosmic Imagination*, SOTSM (Aldershot: Ashgate).

McLaughlin, J. L. (2001), *The* marzēaḥ *in the Prophetic Literature: References and Allusions in the Light of the Extra-Biblical Evidence*, VTSup 86 (Leiden: Brill).

McNutt, P. M. (1999), *Reconstructing the Society of Ancient Israel* (Louisville: Westminster John Knox Press).

Malamat, A. (2001), 'Amos 1:5 in the Light of the Til Barsip Inscriptions', in A. Malamat, *History of Biblical Israel*, CHANE 7 (Leiden: Brill [originally published 1953]), pp. 366–369.

Mazar, A. (1990), *Archaeology of the Land of the Bible 10,000 – 586 BCE* (New York: Doubleday).

Möller, K. (2003), *A Prophet in Debate: The Rhetoric of Persuasion in the Book of Amos*, JSOTSup 372 (Sheffield: Sheffield Academic Press).

Moughtin-Mumby, S. (2011), '"A Man and His Father Go to Naarah in Order to Defile My Holy Name!" Rereading Amos

2:6–8', in A. C. Hagedorn and A. Mein (eds.), *Aspects of Amos: Exegesis and Interpretation*, LHBOTS 536 (New York/London: T&T Clark), pp. 59–82.

Müller, R. (2010), 'Der finstere Tag Jahwes: Zum kultischen Hintergrund von Am 5,18–20', *ZAW* 122: 576–592.

Nissinen, M. (2003), *Prophets and Prophecy in the Ancient Near East*, WAW 12 (Leiden/Boston: Brill).

—— (2017), *Ancient Prophecy: Near Eastern, Biblical, and Greek Perspectives* (Oxford: Oxford University Press).

Nogalski, J. D. (2011), *The Book of the Twelve*, SHBC (Macon: Smyth & Helwys).

Noonan, B. J. (2013), 'There and Back Again: "Tin" or "Lead" in Amos 7:7–9?', *VT* 63: 299–307.

Nwaoru, E. O. (2009), 'A Fresh Look at Amos 4:1–3 and Its Imagery', *VT* 59: 460–474.

Paas, S. (2003), *Creation and Judgement: Creation Texts in Some Eighth Century Prophets*, OTS 47 (Leiden/Boston: Brill).

Paul, S. M. (1991), *Amos*, Hermeneia (Minneapolis: Fortress).

Petersen. D. L. (1981), *The Roles of Israel's Prophets*, JSOTSup 17 (Sheffield: JSOT Press).

Plöger, O. (1968), *Theocracy and Eschatology*, trans. S. Rudman (Oxford: Basil Blackwell).

Pomykala, K. E. (2004), 'Jerusalem as the Fallen Booth of David in Amos 9:11', in J. H. Ellens at al. (eds.), *God's Word in Our World*, vol. 1, JSOTSup 388 (London: T&T Clark), pp. 275–293.

Radine, J. (2010), *The Book of Amos in Emergent Judah*, FAT 45 (Tübingen: Mohr Siebeck).

Redditt, P. L. (1986), 'The Book of Joel and Peripheral Prophecy', *CBQ* 48: 225–240.

Riede, P. (2008), *Vom Erbarmen zum Gericht: Die Visionen des Amosbuches (Am 7–9\*) und ihr literatur- und traditionsgeschichtlicher Zusammenhang*, WMANT 120 (Neukirchen-Vluyn: Neukirchener Verlag).

Rudolph, W. (1971), *Joel, Amos, Obadja, Jona*, KAT 13.2 (Gütersloh: Gerd Mohn).

Schmidt, L. (2007), 'Die Amazja-Erzählung (Am 7,10–17) und der historische Amos', *ZAW* 119: 221–235.

Seitz, C. R. (2016), *Joel*, ITC (London: Bloomsbury).

Simkins, R. (1991), *Yahweh's Activity in History and the Nature of the Book of Joel*, ANETS 10 (Lewiston: Mellen).

Smith, G. V. (1988), 'Amos 5:13: The Deadly Silence of the Prosperous', *JBL* 107: 289–294.

Soggin, J. A. (1987), *The Prophet Amos* (London: SCM).

Stökl, J. (2012), *Prophecy in the Ancient Near East: A Philological and Sociological Comparison*, CHANE 56 (Leiden/Boston: Brill).

Strawn, B. A. (2013), 'What Is Cush Doing in Amos 9:7? The Poetics of Exodus in the Plural', *VT* 63: 99–123.

——— (2016), 'Material Culture, Iconography, and the Prophets', in C. J. Sharp (ed.), *The Oxford Handbook of the Prophets* (Oxford: Oxford University Press), pp. 87–116.

Strazicich, J. (2007), *Joel's Use of Scripture and the Scripture's Use of Joel: Appropriation and Resignification in Second Temple Judaism and Early Christianity*, BIS 82 (Leiden/Boston: Brill).

Stuart, D. (1987), *Hosea–Jonah*, WBC 31 (Waco: Word).

Sweeney, M. A. (2000), *The Twelve Prophets*, Berit Olam (Collegeville: Liturgical Press).

Troxel, R. L. (2013), 'The Problem of Time in Joel', *JBL* 132: 77–95.

——— (2015), *Joel: Scope, Genre(s), and Meaning*, CSHB 6 (Winona Lake: Eisenbrauns).

Waard, J. de (1977), 'The Chiastic Structure of Amos V 1–17', *VT* 27: 170–177.

Weinfeld, M. (1995), *Social Justice in Ancient Israel and in the Ancient Near East* (Jerusalem: Magnes Press; Minneapolis: Fortress).

Williamson, H. G. M. (1990), 'The Prophet and the Plumb-line: A Redaction-Critical Study of Amos vii', in A. S. van der Woude (ed.), *In Quest of the Past: Studies on Israelite Religion, Literature and Prophetism*, OTS 26 (Leiden: Brill), pp. 101–121.

——— (2016), 'History and Memory in the Prophets', in C. J. Sharp (ed.), *The Oxford Handbook of the Prophets* (Oxford: Oxford University Press), pp. 132–148.

Wolff, H. W. (1977), *Joel and Amos*, Hermeneia (Philadelphia: Fortress).

Wood, J. R. (2002), *Amos in Song and Book Culture*, JSOTSup 337 (Sheffield: Sheffield Academic Press).

# JOEL

## INTRODUCTION

### 1. Structural patterns in the book of Joel

The book of Joel is often divided into two main sections, but interpreters disagree as to where the decisive turning point is. Some who are guided primarily by formal criteria identify 2:18 as the watershed. In 1:2 – 2:17 the prophet calls his people to lament their circumstances and to turn to the Lord for help. From 2:18 onwards we have God's response to the congregation and a description of his intervention on their behalf. According to Bergler (1988: 69–130), the book is carefully constructed as an imitation of a lament liturgy. Two parallel depictions of disaster, followed by calls to the people to pray (1:4–20 and 2:1–17), lead to two parallel oracles of salvation (2:18–27 and 2:28 – 3:21 [MT 3:1 – 4:21]).[1] The first oracle

---

1. Chapter and verse divisions are different in English and Hebrew for the second half of Joel. The MT treats what in EVV is 2:28–32 as chapter 3 (comprising five verses altogether) and consequently takes what is 3:1–21 in EVV as 4:1–21.

(2:18–27) provides an answer to the first lament (1:4–20), while the second, eschatologically oriented oracle (2:28 – 3:21 [MT 3:1 – 4:21]) corresponds to the second disaster, with its apocalyptic flavour and imagery (2:1–17). Assis (2013: 53–54) offers a modified version of this division based on the understanding that Joel deals with two different but interrelated problems: a locust infestation and a military calamity. The first part (1:2 – 2:17) is the prophet's call to the people, imploring them to turn to God. It culminates with a priestly prayer which brings to the fore the dual problem: natural calamity and political trouble (2:15–17). God's answer (2:18 – 3:17 [MT 2:18 – 4:17]) falls into two parts, each dealing with a discrete issue: a promise to save the people from the locusts' invasion (2:18–27) and from the foreign conquerors (2:28 – 3:17 [MT 3:1 – 4:17]). The last verses provide a conclusion which summarizes the message of agricultural (3:18 [MT 4:18]) and political (3:19–21 [MT 4:19–21]) redemption.

The alternative is to see 2:28 (MT 3:1), not 2:18, as the book's pivot (Barton 2001: 5–14; Jeremias 2007: 3–4). The guiding criterion in this case is subject matter, rather than form. The first part of the book deals with a 'this-worldly' problem, an agricultural crisis which threatens the survival of the community (1:2 – 2:27). This is a didactic work calling the elders to pass on to future generations the memory of a spectacular divine intervention in the life of the community (1:2–3). It begins with two parallel descriptions of the calamity (1:4–14 // 2:1–11), followed by calls to cry out to God (1:15–20 // 2:12–17). The second prayer (2:17b) brings the book to a climax. Its resolution comes in God's answer with the promise of divine restoration (2:18–27). The narrative provides future generations (1:3) with a model of how to act when faced with similar challenges.

The second part of the book (2:28 – 3:21 [MT 3:1 – 4:21]) has a different temporal perspective and a different focus. It no longer deals with economic difficulties and natural disasters but concentrates on the world of politics, international relations and war. The chief adversaries of God's people are the nations, not the locusts. The resolution is not the removal of plagues and the provision of abundant rain, as in 2:20–27, but the radical transformation of nature (3:18 [MT 4:18]) and the annihilation of attackers (3:13–17

[MT 4:13–17]). It sounds like a description of the end of history as we know it.

The two parts of Joel are closely interconnected. Agricultural and military imagery are mixed throughout the book. At the start the locusts are compared to an army (1:6; 2:1–11), while at the end the defeat of the enemy nations is described as a harvest (3:13 [MT 4:13]). Both the locust infestation (1:15; 2:1–2, 11) and the final battle (3:14 [MT 4:14]; 2:31 [MT 3:4]) are identified as *the day of the LORD*. The apocalyptic language is not confined to the second half but appears in the first as well. The sun, moon and stars are darkened and the world trembles and shakes in 2:10, and then again in 2:31 (MT 3:4) and 3:16 (MT 4:16). Finally, there are numerous verbal and thematic parallels between the two major sections of the book (Assis 2013: 26–30). The links suggest that the locust plague is a Day of the Lord and an anticipation of the final and climactic manifestation of that day. The eschatological imagery applied to the locusts (2:10–11) draws out the theological significance of that event. The book moves from natural and military crises that can be experienced and reversed in the course of history to the final crisis which will constitute the end of history.

Table 1 on page 4 presents the most important cases of words that are repeated in Hebrew in the two halves of the book, even though they may sometimes be rendered differently by English translations.

To conclude, there are two different structural patterns operating simultaneously in the book. One is the structure of a lament liturgy (Wolff 1977: 9). The people are called to lament in the face of a disaster (1:2 – 2:17), and God responds to their cry (2:18 – 3:21 [MT 2:18 – 4:21]). Alongside this liturgical pattern operates a separate narrative structure, governed by 1:2–3 and 2:18–19a (Wolff 1977: 9; Troxel 2015: 51–71). Right at the very start of the prophecy the audience are called to tell the future generations a story about a great calamity that overtook them and the great deliverance that followed. The turning point of the narrative, its resolution, is found in 2:18–19a. God heard the cry of the people and redeemed them from their troubles. This is the message the elders and all the inhabitants of the land are to pass on to their children.

Table 1 Key words and phrases repeated in the Hebrew text

| 1:5 | *sweet wine* | 3:18 (MT 4:18) |
|---|---|---|
| 1:9, 13, 14 | *the house of the Lord [your God]* | 3:18 (MT 4:18) |
| 1:14; 2:15, 16 | *call* and *sanctify* | 3:9 (MT 4:9) |
| 1:15 | *the day of the LORD is near* | 3:14 (MT 4:14) |
| 1:19 | *cry to/call on [the name] of the LORD* | 2:32 (MT 3:5) |
| 1:20 | *the watercourses/stream beds* | 3:18 (MT 4:18) |
| 2:1 | *Zion, my holy mountain* | 3:17 (MT 4:17) |
| 2:3 | *nothing escapes/there shall be those who escape* | 2:32 (MT 3:5) |
| 2:7 | *warriors . . . soldiers . . . come up/scale* | 3:9 (MT 4:9) |
| 2:10 | *the heavens and the earth shake/tremble* | 3:16 (MT 4:16) |
| 2:10 | *The sun and the moon are darkened, and the stars withdraw their shining* | 3:15 (MT 4:15) |
| 2:11 | *the LORD utters his voice* | 3:16 (MT 4:16) |
| 2:11 | *the great and terrible day of the LORD* | 2:31 (MT 3:4) |
| 2:24 | *the vats overflow* | 3:13 (MT 4:13) |
| 2:27 | *you shall know . . . the LORD your God* | 3:17 (MT 4:17) |

The two structures coincide and support one another, but they work best when applied primarily to 1:2 – 2:27. The final section of the book (2:28 – 3:21 [MT 3:1 – 4:21]) builds on them but takes the book in a slightly different direction. The liturgical structure is, by and large, preserved intact, only the divine oracle is extended so that it finely balances the lament. In terms of the narrative, the effect of 2:28 – 3:21 is more complicated. Although these verses continue the future orientation of the divine speech in 2:19b–27, from the perspective of the implied reader – that is, the future generations of 1:3 – there is an important temporal shift. The verbs of 2:19b–27 describe events that are future to the elders of 1:2; 2:15–17, but past from the point of view of the readers (1:18–19a). On the other hand, the verbs of 2:28 – 3:21 (MT 3:1 – 4:21) refer to actions of God that are future for everybody, the elders and the implied readers alike. Thus, the concluding section takes the lessons learned from divine intervention in history and applies them to the end times. The Lord's intervention in the locust crisis became the pretext for and context of a revelation for his plans on a grander scale.

## 2. The date of the book

Unlike most other prophetic books, Joel contains no information on dating in its superscription. Its most likely historical context is the Persian period (Crenshaw 1995: 21–29; Barton 2001: 15–18; Nogalski 2011: 202), although the evidence for this is not as clear as we might wish. Allusions to historical situations provide the starting point. The 'scattering' and selling into slavery of the people of Judah, accompanied by the appropriation of their land by foreign nations (3:2–3 [MT 4:2–3]), probably refers to the Babylonian exile (587 BC). The use of Edom in parallel to Egypt (3:19 [MT 4:19]) as one of the chief enemies of Judah also presupposes a date after the sack of Jerusalem. From that point onwards Edom, which assisted the Babylonians in their attack on Judah (Hadjiev 2020a: 45–47), often appears as a representative or symbol of the enemy nations.

The first part of Joel takes for granted the existence of the Jerusalem temple (1:9, 14, 16; 2:17). This pushes the date of the book after the rebuilding of the temple (515 BC).[2] The internal conditions presupposed by the prophecy fit well with this general period. The calls assume the existence of a community small enough to gather at the temple (2:16–17). Its leaders are priests and elders, with no king in sight (1:2, 13–14). The *grain-offering and the drink-offering* (1:9, 13; 2:14) refers to the *tamid* sacrifice, the daily offering at the temple (see below, 1:8–10), mentioned only in post-exilic texts.

Stuart (1987: 266–267) attempts to undermine the post-exilic date of Joel by suggesting that in 3:1–3 (MT 4:1–3) the Assyrian deportations of 722 or 701 BC could be in view. Alternatively, he suggests 'the sort of smaller deportation following the capture of Judean troops in border wars'. This is unlikely given the references

---

2. Recently Assis (2013) has argued against this widely accepted conclusion. According to him, Joel was composed during the exilic period when the temple was in ruins. For evaluation see Hadjiev (2020a: 20).

to foreigners 'passing through' Jerusalem (3:17 [MT 4:17]) and
dividing the land of Judah (3:2 [MT 4:2]), which are most naturally
taken in connection with the events of 587 BC. The rest of the
arguments for Persian dating, when taken on their own, are not
particularly strong. The lack of a mention of a king is an argument
from silence. There are plenty of texts from the monarchic period
that do not refer to the king (Rudolph 1971: 27 cites Isa. 1 – 5 as an
example). The suggestion that the calls to assemble imply a small
community is based on an unnecessarily literal reading of those
calls. The elders may be mentioned because of their age, not their
political role, and the priests are naturally present in a speech that
deals with cultic actions and temple worship. The reference to the
*tamid* sacrifice does not exclude a pre-exilic date since 'some such
offerings must have formed a feature' of pre-exilic temple worship
(Coggins 2000: 31).

However, while on their own none of these points is strong
enough to establish the case, their cumulative effect needs to be
considered. A few other considerations also need to be added into
the mix. Joel 2:32 (MT 3:5) quotes the exilic text of Obadiah 17 and
so cannot be earlier than the sixth century BC. In addition, the
language of Joel is thought to contain some late elements. Wolff
(1977: 5) lists *šelaḥ* ('missile'; 2:8), *sōp* (*rear*; 2:20) and *ṣaḥănă* (*foul smell*;
2:20) as words that occur only in indisputably late texts. To this list
Crenshaw (1995: 26) adds some expressions that are not exclusively
post-exilic but become more common in later times: the short form
of the first-person personal pronoun *'anî*, the phrase *Judah and Jerusalem*, *we'im* ('or') and *běnê-ṣiyyôn* ('sons of Zion'). Ahlström's (1971:
1–22) detailed investigation allows for a late pre-exilic dating of the
language of Joel, but it still lands on the early post-exilic period as
the most likely time.

On the other hand, there is little evidence that demands an
early date for Joel. Garrett (1997: 286–294) opts for a seventh-
century BC setting simply on the basis that the arguments for a
Persian dating, taken in isolation, are not convincing enough.
There is no positive indication that Joel should be situated in the
monarchic period apart from a general bias towards earlier dating.
The cumulative evidence, meagre as it is, points in the opposite
direction.

The post-exilic context is helpful in terms of understanding chapter 3 (MT 4) in particular, but also the references to shame and mockery in 2:17, 19, 26. While the deliverance from the locust plague provided the Judean community with relief from one significant threat to its existence, the larger problem of defeat, powerlessness and subservience to other nations that originated with the Babylonian conquest remained a constant reality throughout the Persian period. The book of Joel has a starting point in a particular crisis occasioned by the natural calamity but then gradually moves to address the larger problem of foreign dominion as well.

## 3. Joel and the 'Book of the Twelve'

Canonical tradition locates the book of Joel among the twelve so-called Minor Prophets whose books are shorter than the Major Prophets Isaiah, Jeremiah and Ezekiel. The MT, followed by modern English translations, places Joel in second position, between Hosea and Amos. The LXX, on the other hand, has a different order for the first six books of the Minor Prophets: Hosea, Amos, Micah, Joel, Obadiah, Jonah.

In recent decades an increasing number of scholars have argued that the Minor Prophets should not be seen as independent works. Instead, they must be read as constituent parts of a single composition – the 'Book of the Twelve', as it is referred to in Jewish tradition (cf. *DOTP* 806–807). Joel plays an important role in this hypothesis, since it is thought to have been written specifically for its current literary context between Hosea and Amos. If this were true, then the wider literary context of the twelve would be crucial for determining the meaning of individual passages and verses in Joel. Conversely, Joel would play an important role in the larger composition. It would anticipate later developments in the rest of the twelve and serve as a hermeneutical key to the whole (Nogalski 2011: 211–213; Seitz 2016: 63–64). This approach assumes that the MT order of the Minor Prophets is primary. Sweeney (2000: xxvii–xxxix), however, argues that the LXX arrangement is original. In it the fate of the Northern Kingdom was seen as a paradigm for the fate of Judah (Hosea–Micah), and Joel opens a new section

(Joel–Obadiah–Jonah–Nahum) that deals with the foreign nations and the threat they pose to Jerusalem.

In fact, it is highly doubtful that an independent and self-contained 'Book of the Twelve' ever existed in antiquity. There is no evidence that Joel was composed for its current context between Hosea and Amos. The different canonical arrangements of the MT and the LXX are likely the product of chance and bear no interpretative significance. Therefore, it is best to read the book of Joel first and foremost on its own, as an independent composition. If a recourse to the wider biblical context is needed, there is no reason to restrict that to the Minor Prophets alone. The prophetic corpus as a whole and then more broadly the rest of Scripture is Joel's primary canonical context (see further Hadjiev 2020b; 2020a: 6–10).

## 4. Joel and intertextuality

A striking feature of the book of Joel is the numerous literary connections with other parts of the Old Testament (see Table 2 on p. 9). These links can be explained in several different ways (Hadjiev 2020a: 27–28). On some occasions we likely have stock phrases that came to the prophet from common tradition, or widespread liturgical formulas that appear independently in other Old Testament texts (Barton 2001: 23–26). In some instances, Joel may be the earlier text (Rudolph 1971: 27). However, we cannot rule out the possibility that at least some of the literary connections are due to deliberate literary allusion on Joel's part. In an important study Bergler (1988: 344) argued that the book was conceived as a literary product right from the start, aiming to interpret, apply and actualize earlier texts for its own time. According to him, the drought, which was the real problem that the community was facing, was interpreted by the prophet with the help of allusions to the exodus narrative as a 'locust-type' plague. Strazicich (2007: 1–3) defines Joel's method as 'appropriation and resignification'. Joel takes up earlier traditions but transforms their original meaning as he uses them to fashion his own message. Two types of hermeneutics are operative in Joel's use of Scripture. In the first half of the book Scripture is utilized for the purposes of prophetic critique. Texts, images and motifs that originally pointed to enemies of

Table 2 Literary connections in Joel with other parts of the Old Testament

| | |
|---|---|
| *Alas for the day!* <br> *For the day of the LORD is near,* <br> *and as destruction from the Almighty it comes* (1:15) | Isa. 13:6; Ezek. 30:2 <br> (Obad. 15; Zeph. 1:7) |
| *Even the wild animals cry to you* <br> *because the watercourses are dried up* (1:20) | Ps. 42:1 (MT 2) |
| *a day of darkness and gloom,* <br> *a day of clouds and thick darkness* (2:2) | Zeph. 1:14–15 |
| *Before them the land is like the garden of Eden,* <br> *but after them a desolate wilderness* (2:3) | Isa. 51:3; Ezek. 36:35 |
| *all faces grow pale* (2:6) | Nah. 2:10 |
| *he is gracious and merciful,* <br> *slow to anger, and abounding in steadfast love,* <br> *and relents from punishing* (2:13) | Jon. 4:2; Exod. 34:6 |
| *Who knows whether he will not turn and relent* (2:14) | Jon. 3:9 |
| *Why should it be said among the peoples,* <br> *'Where is their God?'* (2:17) | Ps. 79:10 |
| *the LORD has done great things!* (2:21) | Ps. 126:3 |
| *I, the LORD, am your God and there is no other* (2:27) | Isa. 45:5, 6, 18, 22; 46:9 |
| *before the great and terrible day of the LORD comes* (2:31 <br> [MT 3:4]) | Mal. 4:5 (MT 3:23) |
| *for in Mount Zion and in Jerusalem there shall be those* <br> *who escape* (2:32 [MT 3:5]) | Obad. 17 |
| *and cast lots [for my people]* (3:3 [MT 4:3]) | Obad. 11 |
| *I will turn your deeds back upon your own heads* (3:4, 7 <br> [MT 4:4, 7]) | Obad. 15 |
| *Beat your ploughshares into swords,* <br> *and your pruning-hooks into spears* (3:10 [MT 4:10]) | Isa. 2:4; Mic. 4:3 |
| *The LORD roars from Zion,* <br> *and utters his voice from Jerusalem* (3:16 [MT 4:16]) | Amos 1:2 |
| *So you shall know that I, the LORD your God* (3:17 <br> [MT 4:17]) | Ezek. 36:11 |
| *the mountains shall drip sweet wine,* <br> *the hills shall [flow with milk]* (3:18 [MT 4:18]) | Amos 9:13 |

Israel are now applied to Joel's audience. Thus, a parallel is established between God's people and various foreign nations under judgment. In the second half of the book Scripture is used differently, to proclaim a message of salvation and restoration (Strazicich 2007: 30–31).

It is very difficult, if not impossible, to decide with certainty whether a certain allusion was intended by Joel. Fortunately, our inability to come to firm historical conclusions on that matter does not impede our ability to read the text as we now have it with the richness of the intertextual links in the background. Joel is now a part of the biblical canon and is read by contemporary communities of faith within the context of that canon. Therefore, it is inevitable for the modern reader to hear the echoes of Scripture and understand the text of the prophecy in that light.

## 5. The setting and genre of the book

Joel cares deeply about temple worship. His main worry, in connection with the locust plague, is the lack of provisions to maintain the temple cult and offer sacrifices (1:9, 13, 16). He often mentions the *priests* and *the ministers of the altar* (1:9, 13; 2:17). The temple itself is of paramount importance in his prophecy. Mount Zion is a *holy mountain* (2:1; 3:17 [MT 4:17]), a place of safety and refuge (2:32 [MT 3:5]), a source of life-giving waters (3:18 [MT 4:18]) and the dwelling place of the Lord (3:17, 21 [MT 4:17, 21]). A strikingly similar concentration of motifs appears in Psalm 46, showing the proximity of Joel's thinking to the theology of the Jerusalem temple. Joel calls the people to engage in cultic actions: to gather at the temple to fast, weep, lament, dress in sackcloth and cry out to God (1:13–14; 2:12–17). At the same time, some of his language and imagery resembles that of later apocalyptic works. The darkening of the skies and the shaking of the cosmos (2:10–11; 2:30–31 [MT 3:3–4]; 3:15–16 [MT 4:15–16]) in the context of an all-out onslaught by an apocalyptic army (cf. Ezek. 38 – 39; Zech. 14) is followed by the renewal and transformation of the world (3:17–18 [MT 4:17–18]).

This link between cultic and proto-apocalyptic language has puzzled scholars. An influential attempt to explain it by completely separating the two comes from Plöger (1968: 98–117). He argues that the first part of Joel was a cultic text originating from circles associated with the temple, while the second part consists of a series of apocalyptic additions that came from marginal groups opposed to the establishment. The two different genres are explained by reference to two different sociological groups, one at the centre and the other at the periphery of society (cf. Redditt 1986). The problem is that the cultic and apocalyptic traits cannot be pulled apart so neatly. Apocalyptic imagery appears already in 2:1–11, and Zion theology plays a prominent role in chapter 3 (MT 4). Wolff (1977: 11–12) accepts the unity of the book and reconciles its diverse features by downplaying the cultic aspects of Joel's thought. In his view Joel was a 'literary' or 'learned' prophet who belonged to an eschatological group critical of the priestly hierarchy. This, however, is based on an anti-ritualistic bias which reads into the text an ambivalence towards temple ritual that is simply not there (Barton 2001: 65–66).

At the other end of the spectrum, Cook (1995: 188) suggests that 'the cult prophet Joel wrote apocalyptic literature'. In his view, the book 'reflects the course of the actual proceedings of a lament liturgy in the central cult' (1995: 199) led by Joel, an important member of the priestly establishment. The liturgy was designed as a response to a real-life natural calamity that threatened the survival of the community. The calamity is couched in apocalyptic terms because it is seen as a harbinger of eschatological events. In the same vein, the deliverance from it prefigures the final salvation at the end of time (Cook 1995: 180–184, 196–199). Cook makes an important contribution to the debate by pointing out that apocalyptic thinking is not confined to marginal groups. However, the proposal that the book is the text of an actual liturgy goes a little too far. As Barton (2001: 21) rightly notes, Joel could be read during a liturgy but it is not designed to function as an 'order of service'.

The book of Joel is a didactic work made up of a complex mix of genres (Hadjiev 2020a: 24–30). It imitates a liturgy of lament but fundamentally consists of a didactic narrative that is incorporated into a proto-apocalyptic vision of the end of the world. Its primary aim is to teach the audience how to act in crisis situations in the light of the Lord's past actions in history and his decisive future intervention. The liturgical forms and the apocalyptic language are heuristic devices that correspond to its dual focus on the present and the future (see next section).

## 6. The message of Joel

### a. The didactic narrative: the goodness and mystery of God (1:2 – 2:27)

The prophecy of Joel begins with a theological interpretation of a past historical event. The locust infestation that overran Judah at some point during the Persian period was a Day of the Lord (1:15; 2:1, 11). Yet the locusts are mentioned explicitly only twice (1:4; 2:25). The description of the disaster employs a variety of images, so much so that at certain points the reader may begin to wonder whether the prophet is still talking about the locusts or has moved on to something else. The language of 1:8–20 implies a drought, while 1:6 and 2:1–11 speak of a military attack. To make things even more confusing, the deliverance in 2:19–27 addresses all these problems: God repays the years eaten by the locusts, sends rain, drives the northern army into the sea and puts an end to the nations' mockery. The liberal use of metaphors distances the experience as much as possible from its concrete historical shell and allows the story to address the future generations of 1:2–3 in a variety of ways. The communities to come do not need to suffer from a locust plague in order to identify easily with the anguish of Joel's calls; the text can speak into situations of crop failure, drought or military defeat just as easily. The central point is that the current crisis, whatever its precise contours, is caused by the arrival of the Day of the Lord. To the people undergoing that ordeal it felt like the end of the world. The sun may still have been shining in Egypt and Mesopotamia, but to the inhabitants of Jerusalem it was as if the primal darkness of chaos had fallen upon the land and creation itself had been undone (2:10–11).

The audience is not told why the Day of the Lord has arrived. Joel talks neither about divine anger, nor about Judah's transgressions, nor about demands for a changed lifestyle. This is not to say that the people are necessarily innocent, just that the question of guilt is not discussed, and the prophet offers no explanation for God's actions. This vagueness aids continuing application of the prophecy. If the future generations need to repent of something, they will have to find that out for themselves. A faithful reading of Joel requires creative thought about the reader's present. More importantly, Joel assumes the possibility that an explanation giving the reasons for the disaster may not be forthcoming at all. This is a powerful and striking affirmation of the mystery of God and the inexplicability of the world. It says something about the limitations of prophecy. Prophetic insight does not always afford a complete picture and clear answers. There are dark corners of human experience that will remain in the shadows even after God's mouthpiece has delivered the divine message. Yet faithful living in the present does not always require the acquisition of intellectual answers. The community can respond to the crisis and deal with their current circumstances without addressing the burning question 'Why is this happening to us?'

The solution to the crisis is to be sought at a practical, rather than on a purely intellectual, level. To protect themselves from the Day of the Lord the people must *Return to the LORD* (2:12–14). Other prophets emphasize the ethical dimensions of this return. For Amos, to 'seek the LORD' means to practise justice (Amos 5:4–6, 14–15). Joel's perspective is radically different. A return to the Lord involves a public expression of grief and an engagement in liturgical actions (1:13–14; 2:12–17). These two approaches are sometimes seen as mutually exclusive, that is, merely external action is set against authentic internal disposition. However, they do not need to be so. Ritual does not preclude ethical action and true spirituality. In fact, when read in its canonical context, the theological value of Joel consists precisely in his ability to complement the preaching of the other prophets on this specific point. Return to the Lord should be a communal enterprise, and communities need rituals to express their collective grief, longing and plea. This is precisely what Joel calls them to do.

We are left to assume that the prophet's audience heeded his call and matched the urgency of the summons to a sacred assembly (2:15–17) with an equal urgency of action, because the next thing we hear is that the Lord *had pity on his people* (2:18). He speaks and promises a complete reversal of the misfortunes (2:19b–27). The restoration of prosperity brings with it a new revelation of God. There is an indissoluble link between *eat[ing] in plenty and [being] satisfied* (2:26) and knowing God (2:27). The blessings of God experienced in the present show that God is good and he cares for his people. In this way Joel validates the theological importance of present reality. What happens in history matters, not least because it shapes human understanding of God. It is legitimate, normal, even commendable, to seek to experience blessing and to rejoice in the good gifts that God lavishes upon his people. This is the default position of human existence. When this position is disrupted for reasons that are beyond current knowledge, the community of faith is called not to abandon the Lord but to seek him even more earnestly.

### b. The proto-apocalyptic vision: God's plans for the future (2:28 – 3:21 [MT 3:1 – 4:21])

The present is not the only reality that matters because history is not a cyclic repetition of crises and deliverances. It is heading towards a final showdown when the Lord will confront the forces of chaos and renew the world. The experiences of the various days of the Lord – the locust infestation (1:4 – 2:11), the sack of Jerusalem (3:2–3 [MT 4:2–3]), the attacks of neighbouring nations (3:4–6 [MT 4:4–6]) – point towards that last confrontation and find their ultimate resolution there. That last Day of the Lord is depicted in a variety of ways: as a military attack of the combined forces of the nations on Judah (3:9–11 [MT 4:9–11]; 2:30–32 [MT 3:3–5]); as a judgment scene in the valley of Jehoshaphat (3:2, 12 [MT 4:2, 12]); as a harvest (3:13 [MT 4:13]); as a cosmic disturbance of the natural order of the world (2:30–31 [MT 3:3–4]; 3:15–16 [MT 4:15–16]); and as a divine attack on Edom and Egypt (3:19 [MT 4:19]). All of these are symbols of a future reality, accessible to the reader only via metaphors. The canonical context of Joel pushes this line even further. The transformation of nature which is still depicted within the familiar framework of agricultural abundance (3:17–18 [MT 4:18–19]) in fact points to a radical renewal of the world and to a new creation (Rev. 22:1–2). The encounter in the valley of Jehoshaphat (3:12) points to the final judgment of the living and the dead (Rev. 20:11–15).[3]

---

3. Interestingly enough, Garrett (1997: 387–391) wants to read into Joel 3:12 (MT 4:12), which talks about the nations 'arousing [themselves]'

These trajectories, already present in Joel (note, for example, the symbolic use of names like Jehoshaphat, Shittim, Egypt, Edom) and amplified by its incorporation into the canon of Scripture, require us also to 'denationalize' the picture of ethnic conflict in chapter 3 (MT 4). On a Christian reading, Zion and Jerusalem symbolize the 'new Jerusalem' (Rev. 21:2; Heb. 12:22–24), the bride of Christ, to which all nations will bring their gifts (Rev. 21:24–26). The spirit of God is poured out on *all flesh* (2:28 [MT 3:1]), and *everyone who calls on the name of the LORD* (2:32 [MT 3:5]) is invited into the security of this new and glorious city. The New Testament applies these promises to the coming of Christ and the gift of the Holy Spirit (Acts 2:16–21; Rom. 10:13). So Joel, read in the light of the New Testament, anticipates the work of Christ who triumphed over the powers of wickedness through the cross (Col. 1:13; 2:15) and who will destroy every ruler, authority and power, even death, the last enemy, at his second coming (1 Cor. 15:24–26). The Day of the Lord, therefore, is not a partisan vindication of one group of people against another. It is the eradication of the forces of wickedness (3:13 [MT 4:13]), the redemption of humanity (2:28–32 [MT 3:1–5]) and the purification and transformation of the world (3:17–18 [MT 4:17–18]). A particularistic hope of vindication is dissolved into a universal vision of reconciliation and redemption.

Taken as a whole, the book of Joel invites its readers to interpret their present experiences in the light of the past and future actions of God, and to live in accordance with that understanding. It sees the world as a dangerous and mysterious place, riddled with insecurity, ambiguity and threat. The only way to navigate this complex reality is to constantly turn to the Lord: to rejoice in his goodness in times of plenty, and to lament and cry out to him in times of disaster. The story of the elders teaches the reader that on

---

or 'waking themselves up', the notion of the resurrection from the dead from Rev. 20:11–13. It is very hard to argue, as Garrett seems to want to do, that this idea is already latently present in Joel in some shape or form. It is much better to admit that this, originally foreign, idea is *introduced* into Joel on the basis of the new canonical context where the book of Revelation plays a decisive role.

some occasions it is possible to experience an immediate and decisive change of fortunes. God is active in history. However, at other times the divine intervention may not be so readily forthcoming. Still, the reader is assured that a time is coming when the uncertainty, scarcity and conflict of this world will come to an end with the dawn of a new creation. The call to return to the Lord with all your heart (2:12–14) continues to have validity. Ultimately all these experiences can and should lead the community of faith to a more authentic and real knowledge of the Lord (2:27; 3:17 [MT 4:13]), to a better appreciation and a deeper understanding of his goodness, power, inscrutability and greatness.

ANALYSIS

## 1. INTRODUCTION (1:1)

## 2. GOD'S GRACE DURING PAST CRISES (1:2 – 2:27)
 A. The first call to lament (1:2–20)
  i. Gather all the inhabitants of the land to weep (1:2–14)
  ii. Alas, for the Day of the Lord is near (1:15–20)
 B. The second call to lament (2:1–17)
  i. The army of the Lord approaches (2:1–11)
  ii. Return to the Lord (2:12–17)
 C. The Lord's response (2:18–27)

## 3. GOD'S GRACE IN THE CRISIS TO COME (2:28 – 3:21 [MT 3:1 – 4:21])
 A. The outpouring of the spirit (2:28–32 [MT 3:1–5])
 B. The crimes and judgment of the nations (3:1–8 [MT 4:1–8])
 C. The last battle (3:9–21 [MT 4:9–21])

# COMMENTARY

## 1. INTRODUCTION (1:1)

The formula *The word of the LORD that came to [name of prophet]* is identical to the opening words of Hosea, Micah and Zephaniah. The similarity is not the result of any literary interdependence and is not an invitation to read these texts as parts of a larger literary work. The book of Joel simply uses a well-known expression to stress the divine nature and origin of the prophetic oracles. The coming of the word of the Lord may be a vision (Gen. 15:1), an auditory revelation (1 Sam. 3:1–11) or perhaps a dream (2 Sam. 7:4), but most often the way the revelation happens is not specified (1 Kgs 16:1; 17:2). Crenshaw (1995: 79–80) translates the 'word entrusted to Joel' and thinks the phrase has a nuance of commissioning. According to him, the revelatory event included not just the initial word or vision but also the prophet's reflection on and proclamation of that word. The *word of the LORD* always comes to a specific individual. This is *Joel*, of whom we know nothing apart from the name of his father, *Pethuel*. There is no information as to the date of his ministry, which gives the text a timeless quality and invites application to different situations (Seitz 2016: 51–52).

## 2. GOD'S GRACE DURING PAST CRISES (1:2 – 2:27)

### A. The first call to lament (1:2–20)

#### i. Gather all the inhabitants of the land to weep (1:2–14)
*Context*

The passage consists of five stanzas. The first (1:2–4), with its invitation to hear and tell future generations, introduces 1:2 – 2:27 and anticipates the deliverance in 2:18–27. The other four stanzas open with variations on the call to lament and are arranged in an alternating A-B-A-B pattern. The second (1:5–7) and the fourth (1:11–12) have a similar outline, while the third (1:8–10) and the fifth (1:13–14) explore the effects of crop failure on the cult and share a lot of common vocabulary. The literary pattern emphasizes the connection between agriculture and temple worship. The exodus tradition stands in the background of this section. The eighth Egyptian plague was an infestation of locusts (Exod. 10:1–20), and there are a number of connections between the narrative in the book of Exodus and the text of Joel: both events are described as incomparable (1:2; Exod. 10:6, 14), in both cases there is an injunction to teach the children and grandchildren (1:3; Exod. 10:2), and ultimately both plagues are said to result in knowledge of the Lord (2:27; Exod. 10:2; cf. 8:22). The plague narrative which ends with the hardening of Pharaoh's heart (Exod. 10:20) also prepares the reader for the call to the people later in Joel to rend their hearts (2:13).

## Comment

**2–4.** The call to *Hear* and *give ear* is often used at the start of new sections in prophetic books (Isa. 1:2; Mic. 1:2), probably because it was a standard way of beginning a speech (Judg. 5:3; Job 33:1; Ps. 49:1; Hos. 5:1). The *elders* were the community leaders but here the focus is on their age. As guardians of the community's memory, they are best qualified to answer the question

> *Has such a thing happened in your days,*
> *or in the days of your ancestors?*

The injunction to *Tell your children of it* seems initially to refer to the disaster that is about to be described, and the four generations in verse 3 correspond to the four types of locusts in verse 4. However, as Jeremias (2007: 12) rightly observes, the motif of telling the future generations about the mighty deeds of the Lord is common in Old Testament literature (Pss 22:30–31; 44:1; 48:13; 78:1–4). It plays an important role in the exodus tradition (Exod. 12:26–27; 13:8, 14), especially in the narrative about the locust plague (Exod. 10:2). The point of remembering what God has done in the past is to develop an attitude of trust, obedience and adoration (Deut. 6:20–25; Pss 22:4–5; 79:13). Therefore, what is to be passed onto the children is the story of how the community turned to the Lord with weeping (2:12–17) in a time of great suffering (1:4 – 2:11) and how God delivered and blessed them (2:18–27). See further on 2:18–19a below.

The disaster is a locust infestation which has destroyed the entire vegetation of the land. It is described with the help of three tightly structured lines. In Hebrew each has exactly four words, the first of which is *yeter* (*what . . . left*) and the third *'ākal* (*has eaten*). We are not sure what is the precise nuance of the four different terms for locusts used here (and repeated in 2:25). One possibility is that they refer to different stages of the life cycle of the desert locust (Wolff 1977: 26–28; *NIDOTTE* 1.492) but this is unlikely (Simkins 1991: 103–107). The translation *cutting, swarming, hopping* and *destroying locust* relies on the possible etymology of the various terms and is to be preferred. If the locusts are understood primarily as symbols, then the four different types might refer to four successive empires that dominated the people of Judah (Nogalski 2011: 218–219). It is best, however, at this point to remain on the literal level and think primarily of a natural disaster (see vv. 6–7). The piling of near synonyms combined with the skilful use of repetition creates the overall impression of the enormity of the locust plague, a disaster of breathtaking magnitude.

**5–7.** The structure of this oracle is the same as that of verses 11–12. (1) Calls to *weep/be dismayed* and to *wail* (*hêlîlû*) are followed by (2) the object of lament (*sweet wine/wheat and barley*), introduced by the preposition *over* (*'al*) (vv. 5, 11). Then (3) a description of the agricultural catastrophe comes, introduced by *for* (*kî*) (Crenshaw 1995: 100). *Weep* and *wail* introduce the major theme of this chapter – lamentation caused by harvest failure. The cutting off of the *sweet wine* is the first representative example of the wider agricultural catastrophe that is going to occupy the attention of the reader for the rest of the chapter. The *drunkards* and *wine-drinkers* are mentioned not to criticize the ills of alcohol abuse (see Crenshaw 1995: 94); they are simply the most appropriate people to mourn the loss of wine, which is the cause of the general withering of joy in the parallel verse 12.

The catastrophe is attributed to the advance of a mighty *nation* against the land of Judah. In describing the *powerful and innumerable* army, the focus is not on the soldiers' weapons or tactics but on their *teeth*, compared to the *fangs of a lioness*. The end result of their conquest is the laying *waste* of *vines*, the splintering of *fig trees* and the stripping of the trees' *bark* (presumably by chewing it) so that the branches become *white*. This suggests the army in view is not a human enemy, but a metaphorical description of the locusts already mentioned in verse 4. The *vine* and the *fig trees* appear together as a proverbial image of security and blessing (2 Kgs 18:31; Mic. 4:4) which is here reversed. Three times the first-person singular pronoun appears (*my land, my vines, my fig trees*). The speaker could be God, but more likely the pronoun refers to the prophet who is identifying himself with his audience and their plight (see the first-person singular in v. 19).

**8–10.** The command *Lament* is feminine singular, in contrast to the masculine plurals of the surrounding verses, and is not followed by an addressee. This could be either the result of damage to the original text,[1] or a deliberate literary technique that sets verses 8–10 apart from the surrounding context. The implied addressee must be 'daughter Zion', the city of Jerusalem symbolizing the community as a whole. The image of *a virgin* lamenting *the husband of her youth* is explicable against the background of ancient Israelite marriage practices. It alludes to the time of betrothal when the man has already paid the bridal price but has not yet taken his fiancée to his house. During that period the woman was still a virgin but was already considered legally the wife of her future husband (Deut. 22:23–24; Wolff 1977: 30–31). Losing a husband during the time of betrothal is an apt metaphor of a grievous tragedy, and a cause of a most intense and bitter form of lament.

The tragedy in view is the devastation of the *fields* leading to a shortage of *grain, wine* and *oil*. This in turn adversely affects the cult as *the grain-offering and the drink-offering are cut off* [cf. v. 5, *sweet wine . . . cut off*] *from the house of the LORD*. A grain offering of flour and oil and a drink offering of wine were presented alongside a lamb each morning and evening as part of the daily sacrifice of the temple (Exod. 29:38–42; Num. 28:1–8). The crop failure has led to the suspension of daily temple worship and because of that the *priests*, described also as the *ministers of the LORD* and later *ministers of the altar* (v. 13), *mourn*.

**11–12.** The fourth stanza follows the structure of the second (vv. 5–7) and repeats from it the pair *vine/fig tree* (vv. 7, 12). After verses 8–10 it takes us away from the temple precincts and back to the *field* with its *crops* and *trees*, where *farmers* and *vine-dressers* work.

---

1. LXX 'wail to me' (*thrēnēson pros me*) may reflect a slightly longer Hebrew text. Wolff (1977: 18) proposes a reconstruction of the original Hebrew which is too drastic and speculative to be convincing.

At the same time it is linked to the preceding unit by means of repetition and wordplay around the two Hebrew verbs 'to be dismayed/ashamed' (*bôš*) and 'to dry up' (*yābaš*): *hôbîš tîrôš* (*the wine dries up*, v. 10; cf. *DCH* 2.131, *fails* from *bôš*); *hôbîšû 'ikārîm* (*Be dismayed, you farmers*); *haggepen hôbîšâ* (*The vine withers*); *kol 'aṣê haśśāde yābēšû* (*all the trees of the field are dried up*); *hôbîš śāśôn* (*joy withers*). The verb 'dry up' (*yābaš*) reappears at the end of the chapter in verse 17 (cf. ESV; *failed*, NRSV) and in verse 20 where a drought is in view. After verse 10 mentioned the grain (*dāgān*; cf. 1:17), wine and oil, this section continues to pile up agricultural terms in order to convey the extent of the disaster: *wheat, barley, the crops of the field, the vine, the fig tree, pomegranate, palm, apple, all the trees of the field* (cf. 1:19). Everything and everyone is affected. Simkins (1991: 129) notes that during a 1958 locust infestation in Ethiopia the locusts consumed 167,000 tons of grain and destroyed the natural vegetation.

The verb *bôš*, *Be dismayed* ('Despair', NIV), is better translated 'Be ashamed' (ESV, NKJV). The farmers' shame is the failure of their efforts to secure an abundant harvest. A similar picture emerges from Jeremiah 14:1–6 where drought causes suffering and mourning, but also an intense humiliation. Just as honour and glory result from victory and success, so shame is often the outcome of a public display of one's weakness or lack of effectiveness. The farmers' shame is compounded by the fact that such failure also implies that they have been abandoned by God (*DOTP* 334). See further below at 2:17.

**13–14.** The final stanza brings the whole passage to a conclusion and climax. The call to *wail* points back to sections 2 (v. 5) and 4 (v. 11), while the mention of the *elders* and *all the inhabitants of the land* (cf. v. 2) serves as an *inclusio* and brings together all the various groups that have been addressed in the preceding sections. However, the strongest links are with the third unit, from which almost all the key terms are picked up and repeated: *ḥrg* [*Put on/ dressed in*] *sackcloth* (vv. 13, 8); *grain-offering and drink-offering* (vv. 13, 9); *priests* and *ministers* (vv. 13, 9); *house of the LORD* (vv. 14, 9). Thus, both the centre and the conclusion of the passage focus the attention of the reader on the cult. The magnitude of the disaster is measured by its effects on temple worship; the way out of it is in the performance of cultic actions. The *priests* are called to *Come* to the temple and *pass the night in sackcloth* and prayer (cf. 2 Sam. 12:16). A *fast* accompanied mourning, weeping (2 Sam. 1:12) and wearing of sackcloth (1 Kgs 21:27; Ps. 35:13) to signify grief or remorse. For a communal fast people gathered at the temple (Jer. 36:6, 9) in response to a natural (Jer. 14:1-12) or a military (Judg. 20:25-26) disaster. This is what Joel is inviting the people to do in response to the locust plague. On *solemn assembly* see Amos 5:21.

*Meaning*
The effect of Joel's opening section relies on the extensive use of repetition of terms, phrases and structural patterns, and on the piling up of words from the same semantic field. The locusts have destroyed everything. The devastating effects of the plague are felt by everyone everywhere. Consequently, everybody is invited again and again to come, weep and lament. Together the five stanzas paint a comprehensive picture of an extremely severe natural disaster. Its tragic nature stems not primarily from the loss of wealth, but from the adverse effects on worship. There is no missing the importance of cultic ritual in this prophecy. The people are called to lament not just the threat to their own existence but their inability to serve God at the temple. The allusions to the exodus narrative imply that, for some unidentified reason, Judah has now taken the place of Egypt. There is only one proper response to such a tragedy: a ritual of lament at the temple. Paradoxically, when poverty makes proper cultic worship impossible there is one final route open to the people: a liturgy of grief that requires only sackcloth and tears.

## ii. Alas, for the Day of the Lord is near (1:15-20)
*Context*
The preceding section concludes with a call to the leaders and the people to gather at the temple and cry out to the Lord. In 1:15-20 the content of their prayer is given (Barton 2001: 58). It elaborates the theme of agricultural disaster from 1:4-14 and picks up some of the key vocabulary from there. Yet it also introduces new emphases: a focus on the fate of the animals, a depiction of famine caused by drought, and notably the topic of the Day of the Lord. Just as the intertextuality behind 1:2-4 suggests that what is

happening to Judah is a repeat of the Egyptian plagues from the exodus, so 1:15 invites a comparison between the current disaster and the Lord's war against Babylon in Isaiah 13.

## Comment

**15.** The substance of this verse is identical to Isaiah 13:6. While the phrase *For the day of the LORD is near* is common in prophetic literature, the continuation *and as destruction from the Almighty [kĕšôd miššadday] it comes*, with its characteristic wordplay, is unique to Isaiah and Joel. The opening cry *Alas for the day!* conveys terror, dismay and despair (Judg. 11:35; 2 Kgs 3:10). Followed by a similar statement about the nearness of the Day of the Lord it appears also in Ezekiel 30:2–3 where the Day of the Lord brings judgment upon Egypt. It is difficult to know whether Joel is here making a deliberate literary reference to Isaiah and Ezekiel, or simply relying on traditional language familiar to him from oral tradition and temple worship (Hadjiev 2020a: 27–28). In any case, the canonical context invites us to compare the situation of Judah with those of Babylon and Egypt. The people of God are in the same position as the world empires who stood under divine judgment (Strazicich 2007: 104–110).

The key question is whether the Day of the Lord refers to the agricultural disaster lamented in 1:4–14 or points to a separate, future event. Since Joel proclaims that the day is *near*, it is possible to see a distinction between it and the current crisis. The locust plague would then be a harbinger of the impending eschatological judgment (Cook 1995: 183; Barker 2014: 99). It is better, however, to take the expression *the day of the LORD* as a reference to the disaster that is in view in chapter 1 (Barton 2001: 58–62; Seitz 2016: 142).[2]

---

2. The Hebrew could be translated to support either interpretation. NJPS has: 'Alas for the day! For the day of the LORD is near; it shall come like havoc from Shaddai.' On the other hand, Barton (2001: 57–58, 62) suggests: 'Alas for the day! For a day of YHWH has drawn near, and as destruction from Shaddai it is coming.' The imperfect *yābô'* could refer to the future ('will come'), or convey a present continuous action, like the imperfects in 1:19 (*I cry*) and 1:20 ([*the animals*] *cry*).

The nearness of the day conveys its imminence and immediacy (Pss 22:11; 85:9). In Joel 3:14 (MT 4:14) the phrase *the day of the LORD is near* clearly describes a reality which from the point of view of the text is present, not future. Just as Amos (5:18–20) saw the fall of Northern Israel to the Assyrians and Zephaniah (1:14–18) saw the capture of Jerusalem by the Babylonians as manifestations of the Day of the Lord, so Joel identifies the locust plague as another Day of the Lord. Realizing that today is the Day of the Lord evokes the terrified shriek 'alas for today!'[3] In addition, the allusion to the Day of the Lord against Egypt in 1:15 (Ezek. 30:2–3) connects with the allusions to the locust plague against Egypt in 1:2–4 (Exod. 10) and invites the reader to interpret the locust infestation and the Day of the Lord in close connection to one another.

**16.** The first-person plural (*our eyes*) suggests that the congregation now speak. The passage picks up some of the language from the preceding sections, making it clear that it is a response to the calls found there. The *food* is *cut off* (cf. 1:5) from the people and so too are *joy and gladness* (*śimḥâ wāgîl*) – compare 1:12, *joy* [*śāśôn*] *withers*. The fourth mention of the *house of* [*our*] *God* (1:9, 13–14) draws attention to the connection between the parallel expressions [*the*] *grain offering* [*is*] *withheld from the house of your God* (*nimnaʿ mibbêt ʾĕlōhêkem minḥâ*; 1:13) and *joy . . .* [*is cut off*] *from the house of our God* ([*nikraṯ*] *mibbêt ʾĕlōhênû śimḥâ*). The ears (1:2), mouths (1:5; cf. 1:3) and now the *eyes* of the prophet's audience are involved in the experience of the disaster.

**17–20.** As in 1:11–12, the focus of attention shifts from the temple to the fields where *the grain has failed* ('dried up', ESV). *Storehouses* and *granaries* are abandoned and lie in ruins because there is nothing to store in them. Not just the humans but also the *animals*, both domesticated (*cattle, sheep*) and *wild* ('the beasts of the field', ESV), suffer. They *wander about* aimlessly in search of food, but there is none. The *flocks of sheep are dazed*. The verb *neʾšāmû* ('starving', NAB; 'suffer', ESV, NIV; 'bear punishment', NJB; NKJV) in the simple stem means 'to be guilty' or 'to pay for one's guilt'. The idea would be that the animals suffer on account of the guilt of the congregation

---

3. In Hebrew 'day' with the definite article can mean either 'that day' or 'today' (*HALOT* 2.401).

(*DCH* 1.415). However, the people's guilt is never mentioned in Joel. The alternative is to emend to *nāšammû*, 'desolated' (*BHS*; *HALOT* 4.1564), of which 'dazed' (NRSV; NJPS) and 'starving' (NAB) are interpretations. The LXX 'they are destroyed' (*ēpanisthēsan*) supports that emendation.

The speaker reappears briefly in verse 19. The first-person singular *I cry* (contrast the plural of v. 16) suggests that this is a representative of the community, either the prophet himself (vv. 6–7) or a priest. The direct address, *O LORD*, shows that the whole passage is a response to the summons of verse 14. *Even the wild animals cry to* (*ta'ǎrôg*; 'pant for', ESV, NIV) God, in imitation of the cry of the congregation. Joel echoes Psalm 42:1 where the longing of the psalmist for God is compared to a deer panting/longing (*ta'ǎrōg*) for 'flowing streams' (the same Hebrew expression, translated here as *watercourses*).

The disaster is described with the twice-repeated bicolon *fire has devoured / the pastures of the wilderness* and its parallel *flames have burned / all the trees of the field*. This depicts a drought, as a result of which *The seed shrivels under the clods*[4] and *the watercourses are dried up*. How this drought relates to the locust infestation of 1:4 is not entirely clear, although the connection is stressed by the fact that the fire 'devours' (*'ākělâ*) the fields just as the locusts 'devoured' (*'ākal*) the harvest (1:4). One option is that the passage envisages the next stage of the calamity. The effects of the locust plague, which destroyed the grain harvest in the spring, are compounded by the lack of rain during the hot summer months (Simkins 1991: 149–154). If one understands the locusts as a metaphor for an invading army, then the fire points not to heat but to the scorched earth policy of the invaders (Stuart 1987: 245). Most probably, the language here is stereotypical. A similar juxtaposition of locusts and fire can be

---

4. The translation is uncertain. *Pĕrudôt* could be (1) stored supplies, (2) seeds or (3) figs (*DCH* 6.756); *megrĕpōtêhem* (1) '[their] clods' (NRSV), (2) 'their shovels' (*HALOT* 2.546) or (3) 'their casings' (Stuart 1987: 238). Barton (2001: 58) concludes: 'we are never going to know what this verse means and . . . there is no realistic prospect of restoring the original Hebrew or, if MT is correct, of deciphering it'.

found in Amos 7:1–6 (Jeremias 2007: 19–20). The chapter is a tapestry of traditional images of natural disaster, conflated together so that the prophecy can be read and applied by future generations regardless of their specific circumstances. It is not the concrete historical details but the theological significance of the events that is of paramount importance.

### Meaning

The voices of the congregation, its chosen representative and even the wild animals in the fields join together to cry out to God in response to the injunction of verse 14. The cry expands the description of the disaster by supplementing it with a picture of a drought which, like the locusts, has destroyed the vegetation, and also dried up the rivers. The suffering of the animals comes into view as a further symbol of the danger to the agricultural community. Humans and animals together stand for all creatures living on the land (Dahmen 2001: 54–55), underlying the comprehensive nature of the catastrophe. The whole of creation groans (Rom. 8:19–22) together with the people gathered at the temple and participates in their plight. More importantly, the cry interprets the disaster as a Day of the Lord. At the literary level this magnifies the gravity of the event. Theologically, it identifies it as an act of God, rather than the product of blind chance. There is no indication as to why the Lord has brought this Day upon Judah, apart from the oblique and uncertain reference to the animals' 'guilt' in verse 18. What is important is that in the fire and famine the people recognize God's destructive presence at work and see themselves as Egypt and Babylon who suffered similar encounters with the divine. In the face of such danger the detailed description of suffering is not an indulgence in self-pity; it is part of the ritual of lament which seeks to move God to compassion and alleviate the suffering.

## B. The second call to lament (2:1–17)

### i. The army of the Lord approaches (2:1–11)
#### Context
This passage narrates the arrival of the Day of the Lord, brought about by the onslaught of a supernatural army on Zion. It is debated

whether this army is a human military force, an apocalyptic foe, an amalgamation of traditional motifs or another highly imaginative portrayal of the locusts (Hadjiev 2020a: 31–34). How the passage relates to the calamities of chapter 1 is also unclear. In Hebrew the verbs used in 1:2–20 are predominately perfect (*qatal*), which would normally indicate past events, while the verbs in 2:1–11 are mainly imperfect (*yiqtol*), which would usually look towards the future, a distinction often obscured in English translations. On this basis one can read 1:4 – 2:11 as the description of two different events: a locust plague in the past (1:4–20) and the Day of the Lord still to come in the future (2:1–11) (Wolff 1977: 41–42; Garrett 1997: 333–334). However, even in 2:3–9 perfect and imperfect forms are used together in parallel lines (cf. vv. 3, 6), and it is not at all certain that they are meant to convey time. Troxel (2013: 92–94) suggests that the mixture of the two verb forms is employed to create a picture of the incomparable army of the Lord in the process of attack, not to communicate the time of the onslaught.

It is best to see 2:1–11 as a parallel but heightened description of what has already transpired in 1:4–20 (cf. Barton 2001: 47, 69, 77; Assis 2013: 32). Both events are said to be unique and without parallel (1:2–3; 2:2), just like the locust plague in the exodus narrative (Exod. 10:6, 14). The locusts are already compared to a mighty army in 1:6 (see also 2:25), anticipating the picture of the army's advance in 2:1–11. Isaiah 13 stands in the background of both sections. Isaiah 13:6 is quoted in 1:15, while at the same time many of the details of the army's advance in Isaiah, including the climactic darkening of the skies and shaking of the earth (Isa. 13:10, 13), correspond to those in Joel 2 (2:10–11) (Hadjiev 2020a: 27).

### Comment

**1–2.** *Blow the trumpet* implies war (Jer. 42:14). The trumpet was sounded in order to call people to arms (Judg. 3:27; Jer. 51:27), to start an attack (Judg. 7:18–22) or to call off an attack (2 Sam. 2:28; 18:16). In a city the trumpet was a *sound* of *alarm*, causing people to *tremble* because it signalled the approach an enemy. It invited everybody to take refuge behind the city walls and prepare for defence (Ezek. 33:2–5; Amos 3:6; cf. Judg. 9:34–39). The expression is often used in prophetic literature to announce judgment in the form of a military attack (Jer. 4:5; 6:1; Hos. 5:8). The trumpet was also used in the context of royal celebrations (1 Kgs 1:34) and religious worship (2 Sam. 6:15; Pss 47:5; 81:3; 98:6; Isa. 27:13). Joel exploits well this dual usage later on (2:15).

The speaker is the Lord himself, who appears to want to protect *Zion*, his *holy mountain* where the temple was situated. This initial impression is quickly dispelled as it becomes clear that the alarm is caused by the *coming*[5] of the *day of the LORD* (cf. 1:15). The description *a day of darkness and gloom, / a day of clouds and thick darkness* is taken from Zephaniah 1:15b (see also Amos 5:20), where the Day of the Lord is a 'day of wrath' against the military might of Judah and Jerusalem and a 'day of trumpet blast and battle cry' (1:14, 16). The *darkness*, *clouds* and *trumpet* blast remind the reader of the Sinai theophany (Exod. 19:16–19; Deut. 5:22–23) and invite us to see in the impending doom the presence of God himself.

The *great and powerful army* that comes to attack Jerusalem gradually spreads over *the mountains* as it approaches the city. According to MT it spreads 'like dawn' (*šaḥar*; NIV, NJB); *BHS* repoints to *šĕḥōr = Like blackness* ('soot', NJPS). If this is the correct reading, another allusion to the exodus locust plague might lie behind it (Exod. 10:15; Allen 1976: 68–69). The opening verses contain several allusions to the preceding chapter: *all the inhabitants of the land* (1:2, 14), *the day of the LORD is coming, it is near* (1:15), a *powerful* nation (1:6; cf. 2:5). The assertion of the uniqueness and incomparable nature of the army, with a reference to the past and the future, finds its parallel in 1:2–3 and echoes Exodus 10:6, 14. The links to the preceding chapter and to the exodus narrative are the first hints that in 2:1–11 we might have a heightened repetition of the description of the disaster in chapter 1.

**3–5.** The first two bicola are structured around the contrast between *lĕpānāw* (*in front of/Before*) and *wĕ'aḥărāw* (*and behind them/but after them*), which builds on the contrast between the past (*from of old*) and the future (*wĕ'aḥărāw = after them*) in verse 2. It could be an

---

5. The Hebrew *bā'* could be parsed as a third-person masculine singular perfect verb ('has come') or as a masculine singular participle ('is coming').

allusion to the 'before/after' of Exodus 10:14 (Troxel 2013: 88). This
contrast underlines the army's destructive potential. The *fire* which
*devours* before the army and the *flame* which *burns* after it create
the impression of an almost supernatural foe. The images allude
back to the devouring fire (1:19) and locusts (1:4) of chapter 1 and
strengthen the connection between the two descriptions of the
disaster. The popular trope of the *desolate wilderness* transformed *like
the garden of Eden* through the power of God (Isa. 51:3; Ezek. 36:35)
is here reversed to convey the effects of the army's devastating
march. The comparison of the soldiers to *horses* is the first explicit
indication that the army might be a metaphor for the locust swarm
(cf. 2:25). The appearance of locusts is likened to that of horses
(Rev. 9:7) in a variety of cultures (Barton 2001: 73). The sound
of the locusts' advance is compared to the *rumbling of chariots* and
the *crackling of a flame of fire* to convey the speed and totality of the
approaching devastation.

**6–9.** Just as the waters of chaos (Ps. 77:16) writhe in fear (*yāḥîlû*)
and the earth (Ps. 97:4; cf. Hab. 3:10) trembles (*tāḥēl*) before the
awe-inspiring presence of God, so the *peoples are in anguish* (*yāḥîlû*)
in the face of his army, and their *faces grow pale* (Nah. 2:10). In these
verses it becomes clearer that the army is a metaphor for a locust
swarm. The attackers *charge* and *scale the wall, like warriors* and *like
soldiers*. The statement makes no sense if a human army is in view.
In Ancient Near Eastern texts armies were often compared to
locusts to emphasize their size and power (Crenshaw 1995: 91–94),
but here the simile functions in the opposite way. The locusts are
compared to an attacking army which strikes fear in the hearts of
the besieged. The behaviour of the soldiers fits better with a locust
infestation than with the actions of human warriors. They *leap upon
the city* and *run upon the walls*, and once they are inside the city *they
climb up into the houses* and *enter through the windows*, rather than barging
in through the doors. The rest of the soldiers' description could
conceivably apply to disciplined military personnel:

> *Each keeps to its own course,*
> > *they do not swerve from their paths.*
> *They do not jostle one another,*
> > *each keeps to its own track.*

However, this is also an apt description of a locust swarm. In the hopper phase of their development locusts congregate in groups which march by walking or hopping. Such bands advance without deviating from their course, disregarding any obstacles before them, and their members move at a similar rate with synchronized, parallel movements (Simkins 1991: 113–114, 163–165). *They burst through the weapons / and are not halted:*[6] the locusts are an invincible force that can be stopped neither by high walls, nor by conventional weapons.

**10–11.** These verses form the conclusion and climax of the description of God's advancing force. *Before them, the earth quakes* (*lĕpānāw rāgĕzâ 'ereṣ*), just as 'before them' (*lĕpānāw*) the fire desolates 'the earth' (*hā'āreṣ*; v. 3) and all the inhabitants of the earth 'tremble' (*yirgĕzû*; v. 1). They are 'powerful' (ESV; *'āṣûm*; cf. 2:2) and so have the capacity to 'execute his word' (ESV), that is, to carry out God's command to bring about the *day of the LORD* which is *great* and *terrible* (2:31 [MT 3:4]; cf. 2:1) upon Jerusalem.[7] While at the literary level this repetition of words and motifs brings the passage to a close, at the thematic level there is unmistakable heightening. This is no longer a purely metaphorical description of a locust infestation with the help of military language but an apocalyptic vision of the undoing of creation. The *earth, heavens, sun, moon* and *stars* are all affected (cf. 2:30–31 [MT 3:3–4]). The shaking of the cosmos and

---

6. The meaning of the Hebrew is uncertain. 'Arrows fly, they still press forward, never breaking ranks' (NJB) is based on understanding *haššelaḥ* as 'missile' (*HALOT* 4.1516–1517). Alternatively, the word has been taken to mean a 'canal' (Neh. 3:15) or repointed to *šilōaḥ* (as in Isa. 8:6) which yields the translation: 'they descend into a tunnel' (Crenshaw 1995: 116, 124). The idea would be that the locusts/soldiers attack via the Siloam aqueduct that brought the water from Gihon to Jerusalem (Allen 1976: 72 n. 47). Simkins (1991: 158), 'through Shiloah they attack', thinks the reference is not to Hezekiah's tunnel but to the general region of Shiloah, i.e. the locusts attack from the south. NJPS: 'and should they fall through a loophole, they do not get hurt'.

7. V. 11 picks up the motif of the *voice* (*qôl*) from v. 5 (*rumbling, crackling*). Note also the wordplay in Hebrew between *at the head of his army* (*lipnê ḥêlô*) and *Before them* [*the people*] *are in anguish* in v. 6 (*mippānāw yāḥîlû*).

the darkening of the skies signifies the dissolution of order and the return of chaos. As light is withdrawn from the universe and terrifying darkness engulfs creation, the sound of God's voice pierces the tumult and issues a command to attack. We can no longer see what is going on, but we can hear the numberless multitude of *those who obey his command* and we can remember the vision of them spread across the mountains and advancing relentlessly. It is, therefore, fitting to end this passage with the emotionally charged rhetorical question: *terrible indeed – who can endure it?*

*Meaning*

At its most basic level we have here a metaphorical description of the locust swarm from chapter 1. The description, however, is outlandish and ends on an apocalyptic note, with the cosmos writhing in darkness and fear. The fantastic imagery conveys effectively the dread caused by the locust plague. It offers a theological interpretation of the meaning and significance of a specific natural disaster: the locusts are a manifestation of the terrible Day of the Lord (Allen 1976: 75–76). Simultaneously, the imagery allows the locusts to be interpreted symbolically, as pointing beyond themselves (Assis 2013: 137–138). The text possesses a liturgical dimension which transcends the narrow confines of one particular historical event and addresses a variety of possible future crises. The picture of a natural disaster morphing into a military attack of universal proportions makes that possible. The key is not the precise nature of the enemy but the feeling of weakness and the inability to resist. The relentless advance of a vast unstoppable host draws the gaze of the reader and dominates the passage. Nothing else attracts attention, not even the reactions of the besieged citizens of the holy hill. Transfixed by the march of the attackers, the reader is filled with a sense of complete and utter impotence. Judah has now taken the place of Egypt from the exodus story and Babylon from Isaiah 13. God is about to fight his people in a battle they cannot win.

## ii. Return to the Lord (2:12–17)

*Context*

With 2:12 there is an abrupt change of speaker and theme. We hear, albeit briefly, the divine voice (cf. 2:11) calling the people of Zion to return to God. This call transforms the rhetorical question *who can endure [the day of the LORD]?* (2:11) from a cry of helpless terror to a genuine question that is about to receive its answer. The description of the impending disaster (2:1–11) parallels 1:4–14 and leads up to the extended call to return (2:12–17 // 1:15–20). This invitation is motivated by a confession about the Lord's character and an allusion to his mercy towards the repentant Assyrians in Jonah 3 – 4. The second part (2:15–17) is a carefully crafted mosaic of motifs which have already appeared in the previous material or will play an important role in the second half of the book. As such it functions as an effective conclusion to 1:2 – 2:17 and a bridge to the next sections.

## Comment

**12–14.** The invitation to *return* to the Lord raises the question about the underlying reasons for the approaching calamity. It assumes that the people need to repent for sins they have committed and to seek God's forgiveness (Garrett 1997: 346). Yet the book of Joel contains no specifics about Judah's guilt. The injunction *return to me* and *Return to the LORD, your God* could be taken as a hint that the people have worshipped other gods and are now invited to offer their exclusive allegiance to the Lord. However, it is not wise to over-interpret the pronouns *me* and *your* since nothing in the rest of Joel indicates the presence of idolatrous practices (2:27 is too vague to be considered a hint in that direction).

Another option is to focus on the contrast between the rending of *hearts* and the rending of *clothing*. This can be understood as a criticism of Judah's 'empty ritualism' (Wolff 1977: 49), a worship which focused on the external ritual rather than on the internal spiritual reality. However, this again over-interprets a minor textual detail and as a result imposes on the text a meaning that is not found there. In Joel, liturgical actions are not condemned but embraced. The audience is continually invited to engage in the rituals of *fasting, weeping, mourning* and the tearing of their garments as an outward expression of a deeply felt grief and a longing for God's presence (Sweeney 2000: 165). The rending of the heart is not a substitute for the torn garment but accompanies it. Turning to

God is accomplished through the rituals of lament that express the inner brokenness of the people.

Finally, it is possible that the people's guilt is visible once Joel is read in the context of other Old Testament traditions to which it purposefully alludes (Barker 2014: 150–156). The language of returning to God with *all your heart* echoes passages like Deuteronomy 30:2–10, while verses 13–14 evoke both Exodus 32 – 34 and Jonah 3 – 4 (see below). Perhaps the sin of Joel's community is like the sin of the golden calf (Exod. 32) or the 'wicked ways' of the citizens of Nineveh. However, it is not at all clear why the prophet would opt for such a subtle approach, which leaves room for much uncertainty, instead of stating unambiguously what was wrong with the lifestyle of his audience as all the other prophets before him did. The more reasonable explanation is that Joel did not specify Judah's sins because he was not certain what those sins were. The meaning of historical events is not always fully transparent even to the eyes of the prophet. The emphasis of the text is not on the transgressions from which the Judeans must turn, but on God to whom they are invited to return. Perhaps the disaster itself has alienated the people from God (Assis 2013: 140–141). In any case the audience are called to seek the presence and saving help of the Lord during their troubles (Barton 2001: 76–80). He may be the force behind their disaster, but he is also its ultimate answer.

The liturgical formula *gracious and merciful, / slow to anger and abounding in steadfast love* comes from Exodus 34:6. It appears often in the Old Testament as a confessional summary of God's character which gives people confidence to seek his help in difficult times (Neh. 9:17; Pss 86:15; 103:8; 145:8; cf. Num. 14:18; Neh. 9:31; Nah. 1:3). Joel could be using independently a well-known expression. There is, however, reason to believe that on this occasion the prophet is quoting Jonah 4:2. The last line, *and relents from punishing* (see Exod. 32:12, 14), is found only in the Joel and Jonah iterations of the liturgical formula. On top of that, verse 14 immediately follows it with the rhetorical question *Who knows whether he will not turn and relent . . . ?*, which is taken word for word from Jonah 3:9. By placing Jonah 4:2 and 3:9 together, Joel creates a powerful intertextual connection. If God was willing to show mercy to the wicked city of Nineveh, he would surely be prepared to be gracious towards his own people (Strazicich 2007: 149–153). At the same time the rhetorical question safeguards the freedom of God to punish or forgive by not presuming that divine actions are entirely predictable and under a measure of human control (see the 'perhaps' of Amos 5:15; Zeph. 2:3). On the hope that God might change his mind and *relent* (*niham*) see Amos 7:3, 6 where the same verb is used.

God will *turn* to his people in response to their *return[ing]* to him. This turning finds a very specific expression in the restoration of the *blessing* whose absence occasioned the lament in the first place. The blessing, in typical Joel fashion, is understood in cultic terms: as a *grain-offering and a drink-offering* (cf. 1:9, 13), that is, restoration of temple worship. The fact that the Lord leaves the blessing *behind him* (*'aḥărāw*) contrasts with the devastation which his army leaves in its wake (2:3 *wĕ'aḥărāw* = *and behind them/but after them*).

**15–17.** This unit begins with a seven-plus-one pattern; there are seven verbs in the masculine plural imperative followed by a final verb in jussive, *Let [the bridegroom] leave*. The opening command *Blow the trumpet in Zion* is a verbatim repetition of the beginning of 2:1. The trumpet summons people to a religious ceremony but also reminds them of the military danger which has been the centre of attention so far. *Sanctify a fast; / call a solemn assembly, / gather* comes from 1:14. Everybody is summoned without exception: *the people* and *the congregation* are to include everyone, from *the aged* ('elders', ESV, NIV) right down to the *children, even infants at the breast*. The call to the *bridegroom* and the *bride* to interrupt their wedding night indicates how urgent and extraordinary the situation is. The *room* (*ḥeder*) was the innermost room of the house which afforded maximum privacy to the newlyweds (2 Kgs 9:2; Song 1:4). For *the priests, the ministers of the LORD*, see 1:9, 13; for *weep* see 1:5. The priests are to stand in the open space between the *altar* for burnt offerings, situated in the inner court, and the *vestibule* to the temple (1 Kgs 6:3), an area where sacrifices were made (1 Kgs 8:64). The crimes of idolatry (Ezek. 8:16) and murder (Matt. 23:35) committed on this spot are considered especially odious because of its heightened sanctity. On this holy ground the priests are to utter their prayer (parallel to 1:15–20).

Surprisingly, the prayer contains no reference to the locusts but focuses on Judah's relationship to the *nations*. The disasters have made the community a *mockery* and a *byword* among its neighbours, developing further the idea already present in incipient form in 1:11–12 (cf. 2:19, 26–27). The taunting question *Where is their God?* (Pss 42:3, 10; 79:10; 115:2) implies that God has abandoned Judah. This is grounds for ridicule because to be abandoned means to be publicly declared undesirable and, consequently, lacking in worth (Isa. 54:4–7). The natural disaster suggests that God has no longer an interest in helping his people. The prayer subtly links the humiliation of the people with the honour of the Lord by emphasizing their connection with a series of possessive pronouns: *your people*, *your heritage*, *their God*. The Lord is asked to intervene in order to salvage the reputation of those who worship him and, by implication, to defend his own name (*DOTP* 334–337). *Spare* (*ḥûsâ*) literally means to let your eyes flow with tears for someone (Isa. 13:18), hence, to look upon someone with grief and compassion (*HALOT* 1.298). The same verb appears in Jonah 4:10–11, strengthening further the connection already established by the allusions to Jonah 4:2 and 3:9 in verses 13–14 (see above).

The line *limšol bām gôyim* (*a byword among the nations*) could also be translated 'that the nations should rule over them' (NKJV; cf. LXX; Wolff 1977: 52) because in Hebrew there are two different roots for the verb *māšal*, one meaning 'to recite derisive verses' and the other, 'to rule, have dominion over' (*HALOT* 2.647). The parallel word *mockery* argues strongly in favour of the interpretation of NRSV, but there might be a deliberate ambiguity. The nations will become an important theme in the latter part of the book and so the secondary meaning of this line prepares the reader for what is to come.

### Meaning

With 2:12–17 we reach the conclusion of 1:2 – 2:17 and an important turning point in the book. The extended call to gather at the temple and return to the Lord reiterates the calls with which the book began (1:2–14). The elaborate depictions of disaster in 1:4–20 and 2:1–11 highlight the urgency of this call. The allusions to Exodus 10 and Isaiah 13 placed Judah in the position of Egypt and Babylon who experienced divine judgment. Now the allusion to Jonah 3 – 4 links Judah to another pagan empire, the Assyrians, the recipients of God's mercy. The people are invited to express the inner reality of heartfelt grief and longing for God's presence by weeping and lament. They are invited to return as a community in which everybody, young and old, participates. Their prayer is to convey the pain of their shame and appeal to the compassion and the honour of their God.

## C. The Lord's response (2:18–27)

*Context*

This passage contains God's response to the people and forms the climax of the first part of the prophecy. The opening lines (2:18–19a) point the reader back to 1:2–4 and together with those verses form the narrative frame of the book. The rest is an 'oracle of assurance', a type of prophetic pronouncement in the cult given as an answer to the prayer of the congregation (Wolff 1977: 58). Here it provides the divine answer to the earlier cries of the community (1:15–20; 2:17b). It falls into three subsections: first-person divine speech (vv. 19b–20), prophetic speech containing a string of imperatives (vv. 21–24) and first-person divine speech (vv. 25–27). The oracle picks up many of the key motifs from the preceding material in order to describe a complete reversal of fortune.

*Comment*

**18–19a.** *Then the LORD became jealous . . . had pity . . . said.* There are two main ways of relating these verses to their immediate context. The first is to see them as a promise of restoration, conditional on the people's repentance, and still in some way in the future. The prophet states what the Lord will do if his audience heeds the calls in 2:12–17 (Nogalski 2011: 235; Assis 2013: 164). So the passage provides a further, positive motivation for the preceding exhortation. The verbs are often translated in the past tense but this is taken to convey in prophetic fashion the absolute certainty of the promise (Barker 2014: 173–174). NKJV repoints the verbs as future, and of the ancient versions Theodotion follows a similar path (Gelston 2010: 76).

The alternative is to take this as a straightforward reference to something that has already happened. The difficulty is that the transition between verses 17 and 18 then becomes quite abrupt, since we are not told how the community responded to Joel's preaching. This is not an insurmountable problem – the reader can easily fill the gap after verse 17 (Allen 1976: 86). Hebrew narrative often omits overt reference to actions that are understood to have happened and expects that readers will supply the information themselves. On this view, verses 18–19a point back to 1:2–4 and together form the overall narrative frame. The story begins with the calamity that befell the community, continues with the urgent call to turn to the Lord in the midst of it, and culminates in God's gracious response (Troxel 2015: 51–71).

**19b–20.** The promise to send *grain, wine, and oil* (cf. 1:10) so that his people would no longer be *a mockery among the nations* (cf. 2:17) picks up the language of the earlier material in order to convey the key idea of this passage: God is about to reverse the people's fortunes. He is going to eradicate the agricultural scarcity which lay at the heart of the people's humiliation. The mention of the *northern army* (lit. 'the northerner', ESV, NJPS) builds on the metaphorical description of the locusts as a military force (1:6; 2:25) that is central to 2:1–11. It also widens the applicability of the text beyond the narrow confines of the locust plague. In Canaanite mythology the north (*ṣāpôn*) was the mythical dwelling place of the gods (cf. Isa. 14:13) and in prophetic literature it becomes the place from which enemy armies come to attack Israel (Jer. 1:14; 4:6; 6:1, 22; 10:22; Ezek. 38:6, 15; 39:2). The northerner in Joel is a semi-mythological figure of giant proportions whose body stretches from the *eastern sea* (the Dead Sea) to the *western sea* (the Mediterranean), similar to the sea dragon in the Nile delta of Ezekiel 32:2. The incompatible depictions of the destruction underline the highly poetic nature of the imagery. The northerner is driven into a *parched and desolate land* and at the same time into the *sea*. The desert and the sea were both places of chaos, danger and death. The next line, *its stench and foul smell will rise up*, presupposes a realistic image of a defeated army, and a battlefield littered with corpses left unburied.

The comment *Surely he has done great things!* does not fit the context neatly and may be the result of a dittography from the next verse. If the line is integral to its context, the greatness of the northerner must refer to his arrogance and boasting (Ezek. 35:13; Ps. 35:26).

Alternatively, it could be taken as an introduction to the following: 'For the LORD shall work great deeds' (NJPS; cf. *BHS*).

**21–24.** This passage consists of three units addressed to the *soil* (v. 21), the *animals* (v. 22) and the *children of Zion* (vv. 23–24). Each unit begins with a command followed by a motivation introduced by *for* (*kî*). The first unit, whose two commands *Do not fear* and *be glad and rejoice* are repeated in the second and third unit respectively, serves as an introduction.

The section picks up the language of the first half of the book in order to stress the complete reversal of the disaster. The NRSV obscures this by translating the same Hebrew words differently. The mourning '*ǎdāmâ* (*soil*; ground in 1:10) is called to *be glad and rejoice* (cf. 1:16). The *bahǎmôt śāday* (*animals of the field*; wild animals in 1:20) which used to cry to God in their need are now called not to *fear*. The *pastures of the wilderness*, previously consumed by fire (cf. 1:19), are now covered in *green* vegetation. The *fig tree and vine* which were splintered and withered (cf. 1:7, 12) are now covered in *fruit*. The word *ḥayil*, translated *yield* ('riches', NIV; 'strength', NJPS), means 'power, wealth, army'. It is the same word used in 2:25 and 2:11 to describe the army of the Lord. *Zion*, which was under attack by the Lord's army (2:1, 15) and whose *wine* and *oil* had failed (cf. 1:10) due to the drought, now experiences abundance of rain resulting in *threshing-floors . . . full of grain* and *vats* (cf. 3:13–14 [MT 4:13–14]) that *overflow*. Both nature and human beings were affected by the disaster; now the whole of creation participates in the blessing of restoration.

Three different words for rain are used in verse 23: *abundant rain* (*gešem*), *early . . . rain* (*môreh*) in the autumn and *later rain* (*malqôš*) in the spring; *môreh* is repeated twice so the fourfold mention of rain matches the four types of locusts in verse 25. The strong emphasis on the sending of rain confirms the interpretation of 1:16–20 as a depiction of drought.

The phrase *hammôreh liṣdāqâ* (lit. 'the rain/teacher[8] for righteousness') can be translated and interpreted in several different ways. (1) *He has given the early rain for your vindication.* The intervention of God

---

8. LXX has 'food [*ta brōmata*] for righteousness' and Wolff (1977: 55) emends the MT to *ma'ăkāl* ('food').

on behalf of the people restores their honour and reputation in the eyes of the nations. Alternatively, the rain is a sign that the covenant relationship is renewed and the people are made right with God (Allen 1976: 93). (2) 'He has given you the autumn rains / because he is faithful' (NIV; cf. NJPS 'in His kindness'). The restoration is an expression of the character of God, and of his kindness and faithfulness to his people. Stuart (1987: 259) suggests that righteousness in this case denotes primarily divine generosity. (3) 'He has given you a Teacher for salvation.' The rain sent by the Lord which saves people from deprivation is a teacher that testifies to God's goodness and leads the people to the knowledge of the Lord (Jeremias 2007: 34, 38). (4) Ahlström (1971: 108–110) argues that the promised teacher of righteousness is the cultic and political leader of the community whose righteous teaching will bring prosperity and life.[9] Garrett (1997: 362–363) sees a double entendre here. Behind the announcement of the coming 'rain of righteousness' lurks the promise of the appearance of a 'teacher of righteousness', an eschatological prophet of salvation. (5) The best solution is to recognize that *ṣĕdāqâ* can refer to the right order of the universe established at creation (Simkins 1991: 199–200; Crenshaw 1995: 155). The rain falling in its season functions as an integral part of the created order. God rolls back the forces of chaos and destruction and restores blessing and harmony to his world.

**25–27.** The four terms for *locust* from 1:4 are repeated here, creating an envelope around the first major part of the book. The locusts are called a *great army* (2:11; cf. 2:2; 1:6–7), confirming the interpretation of 2:1–11 as a metaphorical description of the locust infestation. God will *repay* his people for the lost *years* of prosperity and joy by dealing *wondrously* with them and providing for them. The repeated colon *my people shall never again / be put to shame* picks up the theme of 1:11–12 and 2:17, 19. The new age involves not just

---

9. A similar line of interpretation is already present in the earliest Jewish reception of this phrase. In CD and the Qumran commentary on Habakkuk, the 'Teacher of Righteousness' is a title applied to the founder of the Qumran community who was raised by God to teach the faithful the true interpretation of the law.

material provision but restoration of honour and self-respect.
Wrapped in it is the climactic announcement that Israel *shall know*
the Lord. The experience of salvation has a revelatory dimension.
The ultimate goal of the promised prosperity is not self-indulgence
but knowledge of God's goodness and love. To *eat in plenty and be
satisfied* could result in arrogance and forgetting the Lord (Deut.
8:12–14), but equally it can bring people to a deeper fellowship with
God. Two aspects are emphasized in particular: (1) the Lord is *in
the midst of Israel*, that is, his redeeming presence is with his people;
(2) the Lord is God and *there is no other*, that is, he is unique and has
no rival among the gods of the nations that mock Judah (cf. 2:17).
The motif of the knowledge of God plays a key role in the exodus
narrative (Exod. 5:2; 6:3, 7; 7:5, 17; 8:10, 22; 9:14, 29; 10:2; 14:4, 18)
and the recognition formula is frequently used in Ezekiel (34:30;
36:11, 38; 37:6, 13; 38:23; 39:6–7). Acts of judgment and salvation
make the Lord known as Redeemer and Judge, and reveal his
power, goodness and incomparable nature.

*Meaning*
The mocking question of the foreign nations *Where is their God?*
(2:17) has now been answered definitively. God is in the midst of
his people Israel. The blessings he has poured upon them prove
that. Abundance of rain brings plentiful crops and bountiful
harvests. The forces of chaos have been rolled back and creation is
restored to harmony and peace. Deprivation and humiliation are
replaced with jubilation that ultimately leads to a deeper knowledge
of God as Creator, Provider and Redeemer. The material and the
spiritual are closely linked. Israel experience God in the course of
history as a Lord who intervenes, alters circumstances and touches
the everyday realities of their lives. That intervention is a testimony
to the power and care of God, who has no rival and no equal.

# 3. GOD'S GRACE IN THE CRISIS TO COME
(2:28 – 3:21 [MT 3:1 – 4:21])

## A. The outpouring of the spirit (2:28–32 [MT 3:1–5])

*Context*

Formally, this passage is a continuation of the preceding one. The opening *Then afterward* indicates a temporal distance from the events of 2:18–27 but the first-person divine speech invites the reader to see verses 28–32 (MT 3:1–5) as part of the continuing description of God's intervention in world affairs. Thematically, however, the break between verses 27 and 28 (MT 3:1) is clear. The preceding unit deals with the restoration of agricultural prosperity which is the Lord's response to the people's lament. Now we move to another Day of the Lord, a new threat that will bring more devastation. The imagery suggests further cosmic disturbances and military attack. From the perspective of the reader, the events of 2:18–27 are in the past while those of 2:28–32 (MT 3:1–5) still lie in the future. The two Days of the Lord in Joel are distinct but interrelated. The deliverance from the locust crisis serves as a teaching tool (see 2:23 above, where the 'rain for righteousness' could also be a 'teacher of righteousness'). It provides a paradigm of how all future days of the Lord, including the final one, should be handled by the believing community.

*Comment*

**28–29 (MT 1–2).** With the phrase *Then afterwards* we jump forward to an unspecified point in time. There is no indication whether this is the immediate or the distant future. Acts 2:17 ('In the last days') interprets the phrase eschatologically, postulating a long gap between verses 27 and 28 (MT 3:1).[1] *I will pour out my spirit* serves as an *inclusio*. In Isaiah the outpouring of the divine spirit is parallel to the pouring out of water on the dry ground (Isa. 44:2–5) which results in the transformation of nature (Isa. 32:15–17). In Ezekiel 39:25–29 the spirit is linked to the motifs of shame, safety from enemies and knowledge of the Lord. Thus thematically, verses 28–29 (MT 3:1–2) are closely connected to verses 18–27 where the same motifs appear. The divine spirit, operative in the creation of the world (Gen. 1:2), is a life-giving power (Job 33:4; Ps. 104:29–30) that enables individuals to perform certain tasks (Exod. 31:3; 35:31; Judg. 14:6, 19; 1 Sam. 11:6), including the ability to *prophesy* and to receive *dreams* and *visions* (Num. 11:24–30; 12:6; 1 Sam. 10:6, 10). In Joel the outpouring of the spirit brings new life to the people and, through its revelatory power, a deeper, more intimate knowledge of the Lord.

The reference to prophecy could mean that a proclamation of the divine word to other people is also in view (Hubbard 1989: 69). However, nothing in the immediate context supports the idea of a world mission by the people to whom the spirit is given (Wolff 1977: 66–67). The nations are conquered, not converted. The thought of Joel is close to Ezekiel 36:26–27 and 37:1–6 where prophecy and the divine spirit are the power that restores the life of the exiles (Assis 2013: 203–204). On the other hand, the gift of the Holy Spirit in Acts is directly linked to the spreading of the

---

1. Alternatively, but less likely, the phrase could indicate a logical rather than a temporal connection, allowing the passage to be interpreted as parallel to 2:18–27, not subsequent to it (cf. Barker 2014: 202–204).

gospel to all nations. If Joel is read together with Acts, prophecy could also entail proclamation to outsiders. The canonical context brings to the surface a meaning which is only latent in the original text.

The spirit comes on *all flesh*. The phrase could mean all of humanity, but here it must be understood more narrowly as referring just to Israel (cf. the fourfold *your*). Again, however, the canonical context widens this original, more limited meaning of the phrase. In the book of Acts the Holy Spirit comes first on the Jewish believers gathered in Jerusalem for the festival of Pentecost. As the narrative progresses the Spirit breaks forth beyond the ethnic boundaries of Israel to touch Gentile believers as well. This more universal approach is already foreshadowed in the text of Joel which abolishes social and gender hierarchies. *Sons* and *daughters*, *old* and *young*, *male and female*, *slaves* and free, all receive the spirit on an equal basis, and all have the same unmediated access to God. The trajectory points to the Pauline 'no longer slave or free … no longer male and female' and eventually 'no longer Jew or Greek' (Gal. 3:28). The priests who played such an important role in the first part of the book are no longer in view, probably because all people are now prophets.

**30–32 (MT 3–5).** *Portent (môpēt)* is 'an event or object that points beyond itself to some remarkable divine intervention' (Barton 2001: 97). This could be a symbolic action like Isaiah walking naked in Jerusalem (Isa. 20:3), an event which carries theological significance like the enactment of the covenant curses (Deut. 28:45–46) or a miraculous occurrence like the torn altar of Jeroboam (1 Kgs 13:3, 5; cf. Deut. 13:2–3). Most often in the Old Testament the word refers to the exodus plagues (Exod. 11:9–10; Deut. 26:8; Ps. 78:43; Jer. 32:20–21). In Joel it describes meteorological phenomena or historical events that signal the arrival of the Day of the Lord. The *sun* turning to *darkness* and the *moon to blood* could be a reference to an eclipse or a desert storm. *Blood and fire and columns of smoke* are more readily associated with warfare (Judg. 20:40).[2] *Tîmârâ* is

---

2. Sweeney (2000: 174–175) makes the interesting suggestion that they could also describe cultic ritual: the blood of the sacrificial victim

derived from *tāmār*, 'palm', and means 'a palm-like column' (of smoke). The images speak primarily of divine intervention which results in the undoing of creation and the return to primal chaos.

The mentions of the *heavens, earth, sun, moon* and *the great and terrible day of the LORD* point the reader back to 2:10–11. These literary links emphasize the theological connection between the two Days of the Lord in Joel. The locust plague is described with end-of-the-world imagery in 2:10–11 because it is an anticipation of the climactic manifestation of God's destructive power, depicted on the final Day of the Lord here. Acts 2:16–21 interprets Joel's day as an eschatological event: the crucifixion, the second coming, or both.

In the midst of all this trouble are *survivors* who *shall be saved* and *escape* the destructive effects of the Day of the Lord. They will do so not by running or fighting but through their genuine commitment and exclusive loyalty to God. To [*call*] *on the name of the LORD* (cf. 1:19) means to pray to (1 Kgs 18:24–26; 2 Kgs 5:11) and, more broadly, to worship God (Gen. 12:8; 13:4; Pss 105:1; 116:17; Isa. 12:4; Zeph. 3:9). In Psalm 79:6 and Jeremiah 10:25 the phrase stands in parallel to 'knowing' God and in Isaiah 65:1, to 'seeking' him. The canonical context fills this with more precise meaning. To call on the Lord, according to Paul, means to confess Christ (Rom. 10:13). Paradoxically, the people who call on the Lord are at the same time *those whom the LORD calls*. There is a perfect symmetry between human action and divine initiative. *Among* really means 'all (survivors)'; see Daniel 12:2 where 'many' means 'all'. The preposition does not suggest two categories of survivors: those called and those not called by the Lord.

The phrase *in Mount Zion* [*and in Jerusalem*] *there shall be those who escape* is a quotation of Obadiah 17 (see on 3:19 below). If the phrase *as the LORD has said* is an acknowledgment of that reference, Joel regards Obadiah as containing divine speech. In Obadiah the people escape from the onslaught of the nations, symbolized and

---

burned on the altar and going up to heaven in a column of smoke. The temple ritual which served to renew creation is here re-enacted on a cosmic scale and the seeds of renewal are already present in the fires of judgment.

represented by Edom. The intertextual link prepares the reader for the central role the nations will play in the following chapter. The original audience would have understood Zion and Jerusalem as a literal reference to a real geographical location. The New Testament, however, transforms this interpretation by equating Mount Zion with the 'heavenly Jerusalem' to which all followers of Christ have access (Heb. 12:22–24).

### Meaning

The story about the locust plague (1:2 – 2:27) now reaches its goal. In the future a new Day of the Lord will appear. The forces of chaos will be unleashed again and the whole world will writhe in confusion and pain. But those who have learned the lesson of the previous Day of the Lord, and as a result have come to know the Lord and trust in his goodness, will be safe. God will pour his life-giving spirit on them and will protect his true worshippers who have taken refuge on his holy mountain.

## B. The crimes and judgment of the nations (3:1–8 [MT 4:1–8])

### Context

This passage maintains the eschatological perspective of 2:28–32 (MT 3:1–5) but ties it much more closely to historical events. The image of judgment on all nations at the end of history is grounded in specific transgressions that are still alive in the memory of the original audience. This is presented in a general way in 3:1–3 (MT 4:1–3) and then a historical example is given in 3:4–8 (MT 4:4–8). Verses 4–8 stand out thematically and stylistically from the rest of the chapter and are often regarded as an insertion. Be that as it may, the passage is clearly formulated with an eye on verses 1–3 and meant to be understood in relation to those verses. The immediate context suggests that this is all part of the Day of the Lord (2:31 [MT 3:4]; 3:14 [MT 4:14]). Just like the locust plague, military crises and foreign incursions constitute historical manifestations and anticipation of that day.

### Comment

**1–3.** *In those days and at that time* establishes a link with 2:28–32 (MT 3:1–5) but the connection is rather loose. We have another brief glimpse into the future, not a consecutive description of events. For *restore the fortunes*, see below on Amos 9:13–15. Here the meaning is primarily return from exile, since the people of the Lord have been *scattered . . . among the nations* and their *land* is *divided* and controlled by foreign powers. The conquerors *cast lots* (Obad. 11; Nah. 3:10) to divide among themselves the captives who will then be *sold* into slavery for ridiculously small prices: money enough only to pay for a night with a *prostitute* or to buy a bottle of *wine*. God's response to this outrage is to *gather all the nations* to the *valley of Jehoshaphat* and to *enter into judgement with them*. Jehoshaphat in Hebrew means 'the Lord has judged' and so the name of the valley is symbolic (cf. v. 12). We do not know of any valley in Israel with such a name. The interest is in the theological significance of the event, not in its historical or geographical particularities.

**4–6.** The foreigners who oppress Israel here crawl out of their anonymity. They are *Tyre and Sidon*, the two major Phoenician cities on the Mediterranean coast, and the *regions of Philistia* to their south. The Lord turns to address them directly and challenges them for their actions. They have plundered the temple of Jerusalem, taking its *rich treasures*, *silver* and *gold* to their own *temples* (or 'palaces', NJPS), and they have *sold* [cf. v. 3] *the people of Judah and Jerusalem* (cf. v. 1) as slaves to the Ionian *Greeks* who live in Asia Minor. We have no further historical knowledge of this incident, but it is interesting that the Phoenician and Philistine actions parallel the actions of the Babylonians who plundered the temple, carried off the sacred vessels and deported the inhabitants of Judea. Whatever occurrence lies behind this passage, it bears the general marks of disrespect for the Lord and oppression of the weak which characterize the nations' dealings with Israel in verses 1–3. The historical vagueness of the oracle underlines the typical nature of the events.

The rhetorical question *Are you paying me back for something?* suggests that the joint campaign is justified by the attacking forces as a retaliatory response to some earlier grievance. The comment is sarcastic (Crenshaw 1995: 180). Even if the neighbouring nations imagined they had a justifiable cause for their actions, God will still *turn* their *deeds back upon* their *own heads swiftly and speedily*.

**7–8.** The details of the punishment are given. The repetition *I will turn your deeds back upon your own heads* underlines its poetic justice. Judah's fortunes will be reversed as its people are roused to *leave the places* of their captivity. The *sons* and *daughters* of the Phoenicians and the Philistines, on the other hand, will be sold into slavery to *Sabean* merchants (Ezek. 27:22–23; 38:13) in a land that is *far away* (Jer. 6:20), just like the Judean boys and girls before (vv. 3, 6). The *Sabeans* are probably the inhabitants of the kingdom of Sheba in the south-western part of the Arabian Peninsula (*ABD* 5.861, 1171).

### Meaning

The capture of Jerusalem by the Babylonians (587 BC) and the subsequent exile of the people is the experience which ultimately stands behind verses 1–3. This is portrayed in Joel not as a unique historical occurrence but as a typical event that embodies the world's contempt for God and for his defeated people. A later incident involving the Phoenicians and the Philistines is the most recent manifestation of this attitude, as far as the readership of Joel is concerned. God will not tolerate such disregard for his name and abuse of his people. Even now the eschatological confrontation between the oppressors and their divine judge, which will take place in the mysterious valley of Jehoshaphat, breaks into the present as individual acts of aggression are punished and reversed. The community of faith may be defeated and enslaved, but it has hope because it looks to God who intervenes in its history.

## C. The last battle (3:9–21 [MT 4:9–21])

### Context

The military imagery already present in the depictions of the Day of the Lord now takes centre stage. The locusts have disappeared from view completely and foreign armies take their place. The Day is a battle between God and his enemies, followed by a cosmic transformation and a state of unending prosperity and safety. The passage picks up many themes and phrases from the earlier sections of the book, pointing out that the future Day of the Lord is the ultimate answer to all past and present crises. Thus, the section runs in parallel to 2:18–27 and complements it. The earlier promise of extravagant fertility is reaffirmed, and the expectation of victory and enduring safety is expanded and emphasized. The unit does not provide a running narrative of events at the end of history. It is more like a collage where snippets in various hues burst forth to paint a multifaceted picture of triumph and blessing.

## Comment

**9–11.** The unit begins with an extended call to battle. The speaker could be the prophet (Sweeney 2000: 181) but is more likely to be the Lord addressing the members of the heavenly council (Rudolph 1971: 82–83). At first, it sounds as if the angels are commissioned in verses 9–10 to call the people of Judah to prepare for the coming battle. 'Proclaim a holy war!' (NAB) could be a distant reference to Israel's holy war traditions.[3] The enrolment of the *weakling*[*s*] in the army and the conversion of agricultural tools to weapons may suggest frantic, last-minute efforts to mount a defence in the face of an impending invasion. However, it is preferable to see the whole of verses 9b–11a as an ironic call addressed to the nations. Their 'holy war' is against God and his people, but it cannot be won despite all the efforts and resources poured into it. *Beat your ploughshares into swords, / and your pruning-hooks into spears* is a reversal of a widespread proverbial saying (Isa. 2:4; Mic. 4:3). This is not a minor skirmish but total war to which everything and everyone is committed.

As the *nations gather* themselves *there*, presumably in the valley of Jehoshaphat (v. 12), the divine speech is interrupted by a brief prayer, either by the prophet or by a heavenly being: *Bring down your warriors, O LORD.*[4] This could be a reference to the armies of Judah

---

3. *Prepare* [*qaddĕšû*] *war* (Jer. 6:4) is literally 'sanctify war' ('Consecrate for war', ESV). War was seen by monarchic Israel as a religious activity conducted under divine leadership. In Isa. 13:3, which may still be in the background (cf. on 1:15), God's soldiers are called his 'consecrated ones'. However, it is possible that the verb in this phrase has lost this more specific religious connotation by the time of Joel (Crenshaw 1995: 187), hence the rendering of NRSV.

4. The verb is the Hiphil of *nḥt*, either 'bring down' (Rudolph 1971: 77–78) or a technical military term 'launch into battle' (*HALOT* 2.692). The

descending from the surrounding mountains to attack (Jer. 21:13) their enemies (see v. 8 where Judah is the instrument of the Lord's judgment). However, it is better to see here a reference to an angelic army which comes down from heaven (Barton 2001: 103–104). As the nations come against the defenceless people of God, they do not realize that the Lord has another, invisible army up his sleeve which is going to decide the outcome of the confrontation.

The call mirrors the language of the earlier sections. *Proclaim/* 'call' (*qirʾû*) and *Prepare/*'sanctify' (*qaddĕšû*) echo the exhortations to *Sanctify* (*qaddĕšû*) a fast and *call* (*qirʾû*) a solemn assembly (1:14; 2:15). The *warriors* and the *soldiers* who *come up* (*yaʿălû*) remind the reader of the *warriors* and *soldiers* who *scale* (*yaʿălû*) the wall in 2:7.

**12.** The mysterious *valley of Jehoshaphat* appears again and the repeated play on the verb *judge* (*šāpaṭ*) underscores, as in verse 2, the symbolic meaning of the name. The sudden shift in metaphors is another way of emphasizing the symbolic nature of the whole picture. We expect a description of a battle but instead the Lord *sit*[*s*] down, as if in a courtroom, to judge the nations. The reference to Jehoshaphat evokes the memory of the king's judicial reforms in 2 Chronicles 19 as well as the story of God's military intervention on behalf of Judah in 2 Chronicles 20. While verse 2 talks about 'all nations', in this passage the attackers are described twice (vv. 11, 12) as the 'surrounding' nations (ESV). NRSV interprets this as the *neighbouring* nations, restricting the horizons of the event to a more local affair involving just Judah's immediate neighbours. However, the global perspective of the rest of the chapter (though contrast v. 4) should be maintained here. *All around* (v. 11) describes not the place of origin of the nations but their menacing approach from all sides (Jer. 51:2; Lam. 2:22; Ezek. 23:22).

**13–16.** The metaphor changes again. The execution of the divine verdict is depicted with the help of two separate agricultural

---

(note 4 *cont.*) LXX translates this phrase 'let the meek become a fighter' (*NETS*), which probably results from a misreading of the MT (Gelston 2010: 77–78). Many commentators emend the text: 'that Yahweh may shatter your heroes' (Simkins 1991: 229 n. 75); 'he who is frightened must be a soldier' (Stuart 1987: 265).

images: harvesting grain and making wine by treading grapes. On the harvest as a picture of judgment, see below at Amos 8:1–2. The two Iron Age wine presses at Tel Michal illustrate the agricultural installation mentioned by Joel (*NEAEHL* 3.1038). A 2 × 3 m rectangular platform, where the grapes were placed, was connected by channels to two round collection vats, 1.5 and 0.8 m in diameter respectively. People crushed the grapes by walking on them barefoot and the juice flowed through the channels into the vats. This activity, which resulted in red-stained clothes, is an apt image of bloodshed and military violence (Isa. 63:1–6). The reason for judgment is mentioned briefly: *their wickedness is great*, presumably a reference to the nations' actions in verses 2–3 and 19. The wine which the nations received as a payment for their corrupt dealings (v. 3) now becomes the symbol of their demise. The wickedness of the attacking force highlights their role as an embodiment of the forces of chaos that rise against God and seek to destroy his creation and his people (Cook 1995: 177).

The repeated *Multitudes, multitudes*, a word that can mean both 'crowds' and 'noises' (so LXX), conveys a sense of chaos and disturbance. The atmosphere of urgency is accentuated by the repetition of the phrase *the valley of decision*, presumably another name for the *valley of Jehoshaphat* (vv. 2, 12), where the sentence of the divine judge will be announced and executed. The word *decision* (*ḥārûṣ*), which also means a 'threshing-sledge' (Amos 1:3), is another double entendre. It recalls the judicial imagery of verse 12 while keeping in the background the agricultural picture of judgment from verse 13. The complex blend of symbols reminds the reader not to take the description literally.

*For the day of the LORD is near.* This is the last mention of the Day in Joel (1:15; 2:1–2, 11, 31 [MT 3:4]). *The sun and the moon are darkened, / and the stars withdraw their shining* (v. 15) is a verbatim quotation from 2:10b; see also 2:31 (MT 3:4). *The heavens and the earth shake* (v. 16) alludes to 2:10a. The literary connections suggest that all previous Days of the Lord that have taken place in history find their climactic expression in this final event. Creation writhes as chaos returns, because the clash in the valley of decision is a cosmic battle of ultimate significance. In the wake of the apocalyptic shaking, the world is remade (Cook 1995: 176–178).

The Lord, whom we last saw sitting in the valley of Jehoshaphat (v. 12), now suddenly *roars from Zion, / and utters his voice from Jerusalem* (see further on Amos 1:2 below). We are not meant to imagine that he has moved in the meantime, nor should we ask the question why *his people* are flocking to the holy mountain, seeking *refuge* and protection, after what seems to have been a decisive military defeat of their enemies. The rapidly changing pictures are not to be reconciled as pieces of a coherent narrative. The point is that *the LORD is a refuge* and *a stronghold for the people of Israel* throughout the course of history and at its end.

**17–18.** The promise *you shall know*, which in 2:27 concludes the first part of the book, is now repeated at the end of the second. *I, the LORD your God, / dwell in Zion, my holy mountain* is a variation of the earlier statement emphasizing God's presence amid his people (2:27). The divine protection, deliverance and blessing have a revelatory purpose: to help people understand more clearly God's goodness, and to experience more intimately his presence and power.

God's dwelling in *Jerusalem* is manifested in two ways: holiness and prosperity. By taking up his residence on Zion, the Lord will ensure that the holiness of the city is not threatened again by foreign armies. The *strangers* who *pass through it* are neither tourists, nor merchants, nor resident aliens. These are the soldiers who defiled Jerusalem by exiling its population (vv. 2–3) and spilling the innocent blood of its inhabitants (v. 19). Joel does not offer a vision of an isolated, 'ethnically pure' place, but of a city no longer subjected to the polluting violence of conquest.

The holy presence of God reaches beyond the confines of Jerusalem to bring supernatural fertility to the land. In this paradisal bliss three precious commodities associated with life, satiation and jubilation are so abundant that they flow freely through the land: *wine, milk* and *water.* The link between the holiness of the city and the fertility of the land is made explicit at the end of verse 18:

> *a fountain shall come forth from the house of the LORD*
> *and water the Wadi Shittim.*

The picture of a supernatural river flowing from the temple and bringing life to the surrounding country is developed in more detail in Ezekiel 47:1–12 (cf. Zech. 14:8). In Ugaritic mythology the dwelling of the high god El was located at the 'spring of the rivers' (Ahlström 1971: 87). The link of the holy habitation of God with a life-giving river and security from external danger was part of the theology and worship of the Jerusalem temple (Ps. 46:4–7). Revelation 21:27 – 22:2 places the ultimate fulfilment of this imagery in the new creation.

The identification of *Wadi Shittim* is uncertain. Since the river flows eastwards from Jerusalem, many commentators suggest that Wadi en-Nar, the continuation of the Kidron Valley towards the Dead Sea, is in view (Wolff 1977: 83–84; Allen 1976: 124). The overall context of Joel 3 (MT 4) makes it more likely that the name is symbolic (cf. the valley of Jehoshaphat). Shittim is a place name on the eastern side of the Jordan where Israel encamped before entering the land (Josh. 2:1; 3:1) and where they worshipped Baal and provoked the Lord's anger (Num. 25:1; cf. Mic. 6:5). In Hebrew Shittim means 'acacia trees' (hence 'valley of acacias' in NIV, NJPS, NJB, NKJV). These trees grow in very dry places, but also they provided the material for a number of cultic objects used in the temple. Based on these multiple associations, Shittim may symbolize (1) the start of a new era (Josh. 2:1; Nogalski 2011: 249); (2) the healing of Israel's sin (Num. 25:1; Seitz 2016: 221); (3) the healing of the dry wilderness of the Jordan Valley (Josh. 2:1) and the Dead Sea, symbolizing the renewal of the people (Sweeney 2000: 184); (4) the future paradise where God will provide constant supply of material for cultic objects required in temple worship (Ahlström 1971: 94–95); (5) the transformation of even the most dried-up and desolate valleys where acacia trees grow (Simkins 1991: 239–240; Jeremias 2007: 54). The last of these proposals fits best with the immediate literary context.

*The mountains shall drip sweet wine, / the hills shall flow with milk*: a variant of this appears in Amos 9:13b. In Amos the hills 'melt' (*mûg*) with sweet wine, while in Joel they *flow* (*hālak*) with milk (the NRSV obscures the difference by translating the two different Hebrew verbs in Amos and Joel with the same English verb 'flow'). The phrase is a traditional image of extravagant abundance used independently by both prophets. Ahlström (1971: 87) points out that a similar expression is found in Ugaritic texts: 'the heavens will rain with fatness, the wadis flow with honey'. More important than the link with Amos is the connection with the first part of the book of Joel. The *sweet wine* (*'āsîs*) which was cut off from the mouth of the wine-drinkers (1:5) is now found in abundance. The *watercourses* (*'ăpîqê māyim*) which were dried up (1:20) are now the *stream beds of Judah* (*'ăpîqê yĕhûdâ*) flowing with *water* (*māyim*). The Day of the Lord comes as a complete reversal of all previous calamities.

**19–21.** *Egypt* and *Edom* serve as symbols and representatives of the nations in chapter 3 (MT 4). The choice of these two particular peoples is determined by the traditions that stand in the background of Joel. The allusions to Egypt and the exodus narrative play an important role in the first part of the book (see above on 1:2–14, 15; 2:27). From 2:28 (MT 3:1) onwards Joel (2:32; 3:3, 4 [MT 3:5; 4:3, 4]) makes a few references to the book of Obadiah where Edom stands as a representative of all enemy nations, to be defeated on the Day of the Lord (Obad. 15). Therefore, the *violence done to the people of Judah* and the shedding of *innocent blood* in their *land* do not envisage specific historical incidents. They capture the endemic violence of the nations and the continuing oppression of Judah, of which the events in 3:1–8 (MT 4:1–8) serve as an example. Likewise, the *desolation* of Edom and Egypt is another symbol for the Lord's judgment on the nations. The permanent settlement of *Judah* and *Jerusalem* stands in contrast to the devastated and abandoned land of their enemies. The verse restates the thought of verse 17: the paradisal conditions will not be disturbed by foreign armies ever again. The first line of the last verse is difficult to translate;[5]

---

5. The MT literally says: 'and I will leave unpunished [*wĕniqqêtî*] their blood, I did not leave unpunished [*lō' niqqêtî*]'. NJPS attempts to render the Hebrew 'thus I will treat as innocent their blood which I have not treated as innocent'. As God takes up his residence in Zion, he will clear the former guilt of his people and will punish them no longer. However, Judah's guilt plays no role in the immediate literary context. For this reason Wolff (1977: 73, 84) regards the line as a gloss (cf. Jeremias 2007: 47 who links it to Exod. 34:7 and Nah. 1:3). The NIV renders the first clause as a question (cf. Jer. 25:29; Allen 1976: 117; Stuart 1987: 264–265). *DCH* (5.750) suggests the meaning 'pour out'

perhaps it affirms that God will *avenge* the innocent *blood* of Judah by punishing the *guilty* nations of Egypt and Edom. *The LORD dwells in Zion* reiterates the fact that the security and prosperity which from now on will mark the existence of God's people have their sole basis in the divine presence in their midst.

## Meaning

The book of Joel ends with the contrasting pictures of two lands: the desolate wilderness of Edom, and the fertile hills around Jerusalem flowing with wine, milk and water. Human beings are divided into two camps: those destroyed in the valley of judgment and those who inhabit a renewed creation, purified by the holy presence of God himself. In its original historical context, the prophecy sees the dividing line primarily along ethnic lines. The people of Judah are blessed, and their oppressors are punished. The New Testament, however, redefines this division by placing it in a different theological context. The book of Revelation looks forward to a time when God and the Lamb will be present in the midst of the new Jerusalem, coming down from heaven, and the river of life will flow through it, bringing healing to the nations (Rev. 22:1–2). Those cast outside, into a wilderness of judgment, are not foreigners or members of any particular ethnic group, but 'the cowardly, the faithless, the polluted, the murderers, the fornicators, the sorcerers, the idolaters, and all liars' (Rev. 21:8). As for those who bow the knee before the Lamb, God will 'wipe every tear from their eyes' (Rev. 21:4) as he ushers them into his holy presence and settles them in a land flowing with wine, milk and water.

for *nqh*: 'and I will pour out the blood of those I have not (hitherto) poured out'. Most EVV, following the lead of the LXX, emend the verb *nāqâ* ('to leave unpunished') to *nāqam* ('to avenge').

# AMOS

## INTRODUCTION

### 1. The book of Amos as a work of literature

The text of Amos is not a random collection of prophetic oracles but a complex literary work that exhibits considerable sophistication and skill. The material of which the book consists falls into three large blocks. At the start we find a series of eight oracles against various nations (OAN), culminating in an address to Judah and Israel (1:3 – 2:16). At the end, there is a series of five visions (7:1 – 9:6), together with two intervening blocks of material: a narrative (7:10–17) and a collection of oracles (8:4–14). The middle section (chs. 3–6) consists of numerous prophecies against the kingdom of Israel. The parallel superscriptions of 3:1 and 5:1 split this material into two large sections: a divine speech against the 'sons [*people*] of Israel' (chs. 3–4) and a prophetic speech against the *house of Israel* (chs. 5–6).

#### a. Literary patterns in the OAN (1:3 – 2:16)
The OAN are a carefully crafted composition held together by a variety of interconnected structural arrangements. All individual oracles in 1:3 – 2:5 follow a similar pattern:

1. Introductory messenger formula: *Thus says the LORD.*
2. Numerical formula: *For three transgressions of* [*name*]*, and for four, I will not revoke the punishment.*
3. Description of transgression beginning with *because* ('*al*).
4. Description of punishment: *I will send a fire on* [*X*] *and that shall devour the strongholds of* [*Y*].

There are two versions of this pattern. The first pair (Damascus and Gaza; 1:3–8) and the third pair (Ammonites and Moab; 1:13 – 2:3) have long descriptions of punishment (six lines), ending with the formula *says the LORD* (or *says the Lord GOD*). On the other hand, the second pair of oracles (Tyre and Edom; 1:9–12) and the oracle against Judah (2:4–5) have a short description of punishment consisting only of the stereotypical *I will send a fire* announcement. They all lack a concluding formula. The oracles of type A (long description of punishment) and type B (short description of punishment) alternate:

A: Damascus (1:3–5)
A': Gaza (1:6–8)
   B: Tyre (1:9–10)
   B': Edom (1:11–12)
A: Ammon (1:13–15)
A': Moab (2:1–3)
   B: Judah (2:4–5)

Between the four type A oracles there are several literary connections created by a network of repeated words and phrases (Fleischer 2001: 144–145), as shown in Table 3 on page 61.

The Israel oracle (2:6–16), which serves not only as the conclusion of the OAN but also as the introduction to the following material in chapters 3–6, differs considerably from the rest of the series. It has a complex structure that can be presented in several different ways, depending on what criteria the reader chooses to employ (for another example of multilayered structuring see 3:3–8). At the most basic level, the passage can be analysed as conforming to the pattern of the other OAN, even though its description of the punishment is very different.

Table 3 Literary connections in the type A oracles

| Damascus (1:3–5) | Gaza (1:6–8) | Ammon (1:13–15) | Moab (2:1–3) |
|---|---|---|---|
| threshed **Gilead** | handed over exiled communities to **Edom** | ripped open pregnant women in **Gilead** | burned . . . the bones of the king of **Edom** |
| *cut off the inhabitants from . . . and the one who holds the sceptre* | *cut off the inhabitants from . . . and the one who holds the sceptre* | with *shouting* on the day of battle, with a storm on the day of the whirlwind; then their *king* shall go into exile, he and his *officials* together | and Moab shall die amid uproar, amid *shouting* and the sound of the trumpet; I will cut off the *ruler* from its midst, and will kill all its *officials* with him |
| **exile** of the people | **death** of the people | **exile** of the leaders | **death** of the leaders |

1. Introductory messenger formula: *Thus says the* LORD.
2. Numerical formula: *For three transgressions of Israel, and for four, I will not revoke the punishment.*
3. Description of transgression beginning with *because* ('*al*):
   (a) Social injustice in the present (2:6–8).
   (b) Lack of appreciation of God's deeds in the past (2:9–12).
4. Description of punishment (2:13–16).

However, the middle section (2:9–12), narrating the acts of the Lord in his people's history, complicates things considerably. It allows the Israel oracle to be construed in other ways.

*Structure 1*
   1. Accusation (2:6–8)
   2. The Lord's actions in Israel's past (2:9–12)

(a)  First chiasm: exodus and conquest (2:9–10)
  Amorites
    Egypt
  Amorites
(b)  Second chiasm: prophets and nazirites (2:11–12)
  Prophets
    Nazirites
      Rhetorical question
    Nazirites
  Prophets
3. Punishment (2:13–16)

*Structure 2*
  1. The actions of Israel in the present: sin (2:6–8)
  2. The actions of the Lord in the past: salvation (2:9–11a)
    *Is it not indeed so, O people of Israel? / says the* LORD *(2:11b)*
  3. The actions of Israel in the past: sin (2:12)
  4. The actions of the Lord in the future: judgment (2:13–16)

*Structure 3*
  1. Israel is addressed in the third person (2:6–9)
  2. Israel is addressed in the second person (2:10–13)
  3. Israel is addressed in the third person (2:14–16)

*Structure 4*
  1. The sin of Israel (2:6–8)
  2. The first divine 'I': *I [*'ānōkî*] destroyed the Amorites* (2:9)
  3. The second divine 'I': *I [*'ānōkî*] brought you up out of . . . Egypt* (2:10–12)
  4. 4 The third divine 'I': *I [*'ānōkî*] will press you down in your place* (2:13–16)

The OAN introduce many of the key themes and motifs of the book. Judgment is portrayed as fire, military defeat, death and exile. Sin is the oppression of the weak. The climax of the series, the oracles against Judah and Israel, anticipates the overall structure of the book of Amos, particularly with regard to the accusation (see Table 4 on p. 63).

Table 4 The Judah–Israel oracle and the structure of the book

| Judah (2:4) | Israel (2:6–12) | Amos chs. 3–9 |
|---|---|---|
| *Rejected the law* | *Israel rejected the law (2:6–8)* | *Israel's lack of justice (chs. 3–6)* |
| | Social injustice (2:6b–7a[7b]) | 3:9–11; 4:1–3; 5:7–12, 24; 6:1–7, 12 |
| | Corrupt worship (2:[7b]8) | 3:13–15; 4:4–5; 5:4–6, 14–15, 21–23 |
| *Led astray by lies* | *Israel rejected the prophets (2:11–12)* | *Israel's rejection of Amos (chs. 7–9)* |
| | 'You shall not prophesy' (2:12b) | 7:10–17; 8:11–14; 9:7–10 |
| | Threefold divine *I* (*'ānōkî*) (2:9–13) | Threefold prophetic *I* (*'ānōkî*) (7:14) |

## b. The chiastic and linear structures of 3:1 – 6:14

The passage that stands at the heart of the book (5:1–17) has an elaborate chiastic structure that is now almost universally recognized. In fact, the chiasm extends further to the whole of 4:1 – 6:7 (Hadjiev 2009: 179–184):

Z:  Feasting on Mount Samaria (4:1–3)
   Y:  Criticism of Israel's worship (4:4–13)
      X:  Sin, repentance, judgment (5:1–17)
         A:  Death and mourning: the judgment of Israel (5:1–3)
            B:  Seek the Lord and live: call to repentance (5:4–6)
               C:  Lack of justice: the sin of Israel (5:7)
                  D:  The Lord is his name: praise to the Creator (5:8–9)
               C':  Lack of justice: the sin of Israel (5:10–12[13])
            B':  Seek good and live: call to repentance (5:14–15)
         A':  Death and mourning: the judgment of Israel (5:16–17)
   Y':  Criticism of Israel's worship (5:18–27)
Z':  Feasting on Mount Samaria (6:1–7)

In the final form of the text this chiastic composition is overridden by a linear arrangement that splits the oracles of chapters 3–6 into two speeches by means of the introductory calls in 3:1 and 5:1 (see the commentary below). The presence of such diverse, overlapping structures is the result of the process of the book's composition but it also impacts the ways in which the final form is read. Amos's prophecy is multidimensional and can be experienced in different ways. In the course of successive readings, the interpreter may focus on different literary arrangements that highlight with differing intensity various themes and concepts. For example, the main topic of the chiastic composition of 4:1 – 6:7 is the corrupt worship of Israel. The cavalier attitude of the people in 4:4–5 and 5:20–23 is emphasized and contrasted with the authentic encounter with God the Creator, who brings darkness (4:13; 5:8–9, 18–20) and death (5:1–3, 16–17). False worship is set in opposition to true seeking of God (5:4–6, 14–15) which entails renouncing injustice (5:7, 10–12) and, by implication, the luxury bought with it (4:1–3; 6:1–7). A reader who pays attention to the chiastic structure will likely focus on the topic of unacceptable worship and genuine seeking of God.

On the other hand, the linear structure organizes the relationship between the same units of text in a different way and brings to the fore a different set of motifs. For example, the prophetic speech in 5:1 – 6:14 revolves around the topic of the impending judgment of God and the reasons for it (see the commentary below). Wrong worship is one of those causes, but it plays a subordinate, supporting role in the passage. If a reader focuses on 5:1 – 6:14 as a discrete unit, he or she will probably give pride of place to the proclamation of judgment.

### c. The five visions (7:1–9; 8:1–3; 9:1–4)

The visions report at the end of the book also exhibits a high level of literary sophistication. It has a carefully crafted structure in which the first four visions are presented in pairs and the last one stands apart. Each pair follows an established pattern and is bound by the repetition of formulaic phrases and key terms (see Table 5 on p. 65).

Like the Israel oracle (2:6–16), the fifth vision (9:1–4) diverges from the established pattern of the preceding visions. It contains

Table 5 Structure of the first four visions in Amos

| First and second visions (7:1–6) | Third and fourth visions (7:7–9; 8:1–3) |
|---|---|
| 1 Introduction: *This is what the Lord God showed me* | 1 Introduction: *This is what [the Lord GOD] showed me* |
| 2 The vision: detailed description of an event – the coming of locusts/fire | 2 The vision: brief description of an object – plumb line/basket of summer fruit |
| 3 Amos intercedes: *O Lord GOD, forgive/cease, I beg you! How can Jacob stand? He is so small!* | 3 The Lord asks a question: *Amos, what do you see?* |
| 4 The Lord responds: *The LORD relented concerning this; 'This [also] shall not be,' said the LORD/Lord GOD.* | 4 Amos responds by naming the object in the vision |
|  | 5 The Lord proclaims that he *will never again pass them* [i.e. his people Israel] *by.* |

no dialogue, just a vision of God and an extended oracle. The use of the number five plays an important structuring role in the visions report and the surrounding material (also in 4:6–11). Apart from the obvious fact that there are five visions, the last vision lists five locations where the Israelites will not be able to escape (9:2–4), and Amos's oracle against Amaziah (7:17) consists of five lines.

### d. Style and rhetoric

Wolff (1977: 91–95) identifies three basic types of speech in the book of Amos. (1) The messenger speech is first-person divine discourse, marked by the use of formulas like *Thus says the LORD* (2:6; 5:16), *The LORD has sworn* (6:8) and the concluding *says the LORD* (3:15; 4:3, 5). (2) Free witness-speech refers to the Lord in the third person and can be found in the prophetic introductions to divine oracles (5:1–2) and in other types of prophetic discourse like didactic questions (3:3–8) and woe-oracles (5:18–20; 6:1–7). (3) Finally, there is the visions report in 7:1–8; 8:1–2; 9:1–4.

Houston (2017: 10–11) points out that the 'messenger' formula 'thus says [name]' can simply introduce a quotation (7:11) and does not necessarily require to be classified as 'message'. Most of the divine speech in Amos is in the form of proclamation of judgment, with (4:1–3) or without (3:13–15) a motivating accusation. In addition, one finds exhortations (5:4–6, 14–15), historical recital (4:6–11), ironic use of priestly instruction (4:4–5; 5:21–23), funeral lament (5:2) and doxologies (4:13; 5:8–9; 9:5–6). Most of the oracles are in poetry and that is how NRSV prints the text. Few passages, like 5:25–27; 6:9–10; 7:1–8; 8:1–2, are clearly in prose. The distinction between poetry and prose, however, is not straightforward. For example, NRSV prints as poetry 2:9–13 and 9:1–15 which Andersen and Freedman (1989: 144–149) regard as prose. It is worth remembering that the line between poetry and prose is not absolute and some of the prophetic poetry exhibits prosaic features.

Two features characterize Amos's style more than anything else: satire and formulaic repetition. Several passages are characterized by the recurrence of formulas and structural patterns: the OAN; 3:3–8; 4:6–12; and the visions. They all lead up to a final, climactic unit or statement (2:6–16; 3:8; 4:12; 9:1–4) so as to enhance its rhetorical impact and shape its interpretation. In addition, various words, phrases and images are repeated throughout the book drawing attention to key points of Amos's message: fire (1:4, 7, 10, 12, 14; 2:2, 5; 5:6; 7:4; cf. 4:11; 5:9); lion/roar (1:2; 3:4, 8; 5:19); and justice and righteousness (5:7, 24; 6:12).

Satire is evident in the ironic twist of established genres: the OAN (1:3 – 2:3) condemn Israel instead of their enemies, priestly instruction criticizes the cult (4:4–5; 5:21–23), a call to worship proclaims judgment (4:12) and a review of God's actions in the past condemns the listeners instead of extolling divine goodness (2:9–12; 4:6–11). The mocking reversal of the audience's expectations and beliefs about the exodus (3:2; 9:7), the Day of the Lord (5:18–20), God's presence (5:6, 14) and deliverance (3:12) carries similar ironic overtones. The extensive use of satire and the confrontational style of many oracles give the text an unmistakably polemical flavour. In addition, Amos often quotes the audience's words in order to indict them (2:12; 4:1; 5:14; 6:13; 7:16; 8:5–6, 14; 9:10). Möller (2003: 122–147) argues that the whole book of Amos is arranged in a way that seeks to present the prophet as having a debate with his audience. This proposal is unconvincing as an explanation of the final form of the text, because the objections of the audience rarely come to the surface; in fact they do so only towards the very end of the book (7:10–17; 9:10). On most occasions the objections need to be imagined by the reader and remain speculative. There are also certain sections, most notably the epilogue (9:11–15; see, however, Firth 1996 and the discussion below in footnote 4 of section 4b, 'The contexts and purposes of the book', p. 82) but also some of the accusations and announcements of judgment (4:1–3; 5:1–3, 7–12), which do not exhibit the same level of polemical intensity. It is important to recognize that aspect of Amos's style, but in my view its explanation lies on the historical rather than on the literary plane (see below).

## 2. Amos the prophet

### a. The quest for the historical Amos

Traditionally, scholars date Amos's ministry to around 760 BC and place it in the Northern Kingdom (Soggin 1987: 1–6; Hubbard 1989: 89–90; Fleischer 2001: 122 among many others). That would make him chronologically the first of the 'writing' prophets. Andersen and Freedman (1989: 5–9, 83–88, 590–608) envisage a longer period of activity stretching from 790 to 750 BC. They also attempt to reconstruct the different stages of the ministry of the prophet using the five visions as a guide. In their view, Amos began by calling the people to repent (5:14–15) and successfully interceding for them. During his first and second missions he preached chapters 5 and 6 respectively and experienced the first two visions (7:1–6). At that time the plagues described in 4:6–11 were also taking place. Since neither the plagues nor the prophetic exhortation had the desired effect on Israel, Amos's message began to shift to proclamation of doom. After receiving the third vision (7:7–8) he preached the oracles in chapters 3–4, and after the fourth vision (8:1–2) he preached the 'Great Set Speech' of chapters 1–2 at Bethel. Following his confrontation with Amaziah Amos was

arrested and taken to Samaria. The fifth vision and the material in
8:3 – 9:6, which condemns the leadership of the nation, come from
this time. In contrast, Hayes (1988: 38–39) suggests the book
consists of several speeches, written either by Amos or by someone
in the audience, that were delivered at Bethel on a single day just
before the autumn festival of 750 BC.

Many scholars, however, have grown increasingly sceptical
about the amount of material from the book that can be traced
to the historical prophet. Kratz (2015: 39–40) assigns only a few
isolated sayings to Amos (3:12; 4:1; 5:2, 3, 7, 18, 19) who, in his
opinion, was active during the last decade of the Northern
Kingdom. The book gradually grew around this central core of
original material over a long period of time. Radine (2010: 127) is
more radical, rejecting any link between the text of the book and
the prophetic ministry of a historical individual. Eidevall (2017: 7)
calls for abandoning the quest for the historical Amos altogether.
The enterprise, in his view, is too speculative and unproductive.
There is little to be gained and, given the paucity of evidence and
the absence of any external controls, there is no prospect of arriving
at a secure historical picture of Amos's ministry.

Those who disassociate the origins of the book of Amos from
eighth century BC Northern Israel have proposed two alternative
historical contexts for its production. The first is monarchic Judah
at the end of the eighth or during the seventh century BC (Eidevall
2017: 16–19, 24–25). This view is argued in detail by Radine (2010:
46–79) primarily on the basis that certain verses (5:26; 6:2; 8:14)
reflect post-722 BC conditions. These texts, however, are generally
regarded as later additions and it is a dubious procedure to use them
to date the whole first edition of the book. As for the social context
and purpose of this original composition, Wood (2002: 100–113)
thinks Amos's songs were originally performed at the symposium,
or *marzēaḥ*, in Jerusalem during Manasseh's reign. Möller (2003: 296)
envisages public readings of the scroll in the First Temple. Both
agree that the book served as a warning to Judah by seeking to draw
historical lessons from the demise of the Northern Kingdom.
Radine (2010: 77, 140) suggests that Amos functioned as a lament
for the fall of Samaria which legitimized the new position of Judah
as the only people of the Lord. Simultaneously, the lament would

have served to prevent the repetition of the disaster in the Southern Kingdom.

The second context proposed for the composition of the book is the Persian period (Coggins 2000: 76; Linville 2008: 20–26). Davies (2006: 126–131) speculates that a small collection of oracles from Amos was preserved in the archives of the Bethel temple. During the fifth century BC it was used as a basis for the current book whose main goal was the assertion of the priority of the Jerusalem temple over all other Yahwistic sanctuaries, and the polemical claim that Judah was the true heir of the identity of Jacob/Israel as the people of God.

I take the traditional view that Amos was a layman from Judah who prophesied for a brief period in the Northern Kingdom during the reign of Jeroboam II. Several considerations support this assumption (Hadjiev 2009: 12–17; Houston 2017: 71–73).

1. The general nature of the predicted punishment in Amos does not read like a post-factum description of the events of 722 BC (even less so of 587 BC). It uses traditional motifs (siege, fire, deportation, etc.) to depict the coming disaster and does not betray any specific knowledge of the circumstances of Samaria's demise. Unlike most other prophetic books, the empire which executes the Lord's judgment, Assyria or Babylon, is not identified in Amos (cf. 5:27; 6:14).

2. The geo-political perspective of the OAN as a whole is that of the eighth century BC. The prominence of Israel's traditional foe Damascus in the OAN (1:3–5; cf. 9:7) makes most sense before 732 BC when the Aramean kingdom was conquered by Assyria and incorporated into its provincial system.

3. The almost complete lack of emphasis on the hope for restoration (only in 9:11–15) is untypical for post-exilic literature.

4. The polemical tone of the oracles and the profile of the audience that can be reconstructed from them fit best with Israel during and after the time of Jeroboam II. The sense of security and power (6:1–7) based on recent military victories (6:13) and the conviction that a disaster cannot befall them (9:10; 3:3–8) do not fit well with a situation after 722, and even less with the conditions post 587 BC. It is true that a similarly arrogant attitude was common in eighth-century Judah (Mic. 3:11) and so Amos's words would have been applicable then as well. However, their specific

formulation, which does not engage with Zion and Davidic theology and talks about Samaria and Bethel, makes more sense as aimed originally at a Northern audience. Moreover, while many of the oracles exhibit an aggressive stance and a combative tone, the overall literary shape of the book is not polemical. Prophetic words, originally used in the context of debates in the North, were later reworked and reapplied to Judah in a calmer and more reflective atmosphere.

5. The dating of Amos's ministry to *two years before the earthquake* (1:1) suggests that a written collection of prophetic words existed not long after that ministry was over. The *earthquake* is not used as a symbol of the fall of Samaria in the book. Its mention in the superscription is most logically explicable by the hypothesis that Amos's earthquake predictions (3:14–15; 6:11; 9:1) were fulfilled two years after his ministry ended and this was seen as a validation of his message which had been a source of controversy and strife. The earthquake probably gave the original impetus for writing down the prophecies of Amos.

6. As Houston (2017: 9, 73) correctly observes, the genre of Amos is not that of 'literary-predictive texts' proposed by Radine and so cannot be explained primarily as a response to the events of 722 BC. The book must have had an important role to play in the life of monarchic Judah and was likely redacted and reinterpreted in that process. However, it did not originate there.

Finally, one might ask what, if any, historical information can be gleaned from the narrative about Amos's clash with Amaziah at Bethel (7:10–17). Admittedly, the historical value of this text is disputed. Many scholars think it is late and, therefore, contains no reliable data (Stökl 2012: 182–184; Eidevall 2017: 202–204). Schmidt (2007: 226–233), on the other hand, argues for the early dating (cf. Hadjiev 2009: 82–86). He suggests that Amos's denial of being a prophet (7:14) points to a pre-Deuteronomistic origin of the narrative, while the prediction of doom (7:11), which implies that a military catastrophe will befall Israel during the time of Jeroboam II, must be dated prior to the king's death. The narrative corroborates the information from the superscription that Amos was from Judah and prophesied doom to the Northern Kingdom during the time of Jeroboam II.

## b. The profile of Amos's prophetic activity

Biblical prophecy belonged to a wider religious phenomenon in the Ancient Near East which scholars describe with the technical term 'divination'. Diviners were people who received messages from the gods and relayed them to people. Depending on how such messages were obtained Ancient Near Eastern diviners fell into two distinct groups: those who used technical means (a biblical example would be obtaining answers from God via Urim and Thummim or the casting of lots) and intuitive diviners, like dreamers and prophets who received their messages spontaneously (Stökl 2012: 7–10). It is possible that in Israel there was no such clear-cut distinction and the term *nābî'* ('prophet') was initially used more broadly for various types of 'diviners' (Stökl 2012: 230). Many of them would have been part of the royal establishment and supportive of the monarchy and the cult. This is certainly true of the preserved Neo-Assyrian oracles and the two extrabiblical texts which reflect prophetic activity among Israel's neighbours in Syria and the Transjordan (*COS* 2.24, 35; Nissinen 2003: 202–207). The four hundred prophets of Ahab (1 Kgs 22:5–6) provide a biblical parallel to that phenomenon.[1] By revealing the will of the gods, prophecy and other forms of divination played an important role in Mesopotamian societies. They assisted decision-making and helped the king to maintain the divine order of creation. As part of that task they also warned and admonished the king when he failed to maintain the worship of the gods and to establish justice and righteousness, tasks directly linked to the harmony and well-being of society (Nissinen 2017: 257–263).

The prophecies of Amos, which criticize the leadership of Northern Israel for its lack of justice and threaten doom as a result, fit broadly within this pattern. Ancient Near Eastern prophets could on occasion be critical of the king, and two Mari letters report prophetic oracles in which the god Adad of Aleppo demands

---

1. Stökl (2012: 169–171) suggests that the Judean prophet mentioned in the Lachish correspondence was a member of the royal administration who was warning the king about a possible danger. The meaning of the letter, however, is disputed (*COS* 3.42B n. 14).

from King Zimri-Lim the promotion of justice (Nissinen 2017: 269–280; cf. 2003: 17–22). There are also threats and predictions of disaster (Nissinen 2003: 38–39, 66–69) whose main purpose was to mitigate the impending danger by appropriate action. Especially significant in this regard are the Deir Alla plaster inscriptions (*COS* 2.27; Nissinen 2003: 207–212) which contain 'the misfortunes/ warning of the book of Balaam, son of Beor, a divine seer' (cf. Amos 7:12). Balaam has a vision (cf. Amos 7:1–8; 8:1–2; 9:1–4) about an impending disaster planned by the gods. The disaster is described as the undoing of creation, and the return of chaos and darkness, with language ('the heavens with dense cloud, that darkness exists there, not brilliance') reminiscent of Amos 5:20 (Eidevall 2017: 23–24).

On the other hand, the radical and thoroughgoing criticism of Israel's life and institutions and the prediction of total and unavoidable disaster that will wipe out the entire nation (Amos 8:2; 9:1–4) have no counterpart in Ancient Near Eastern prophecy. There are three reasons for this. First, the information we have about Ancient Near Eastern prophets derives from royal archives which only preserved texts that were helpful to and supportive of the establishment. In contrast, Amos was an outsider who functioned at the periphery of society, not as part of its central structures. He was a foreigner from the Southern Kingdom, and a layman rather than a professional prophet (1:1; 7:12–15).[2] The fact that his preaching is dated to *two years before the earthquake* implies a relatively short duration of less than a year, probably because his activities ended abruptly with his expulsion from Northern Israel.

---

2. According to 1:1 Amos is one of the *shepherds* (*nōqĕdîm*) and in 7:14 he says he is a *herdsman* [*bôqēr*], *and a dresser of sycamore trees*. *Nōqēd* appears only once more in the OT, as a title of the Moabite king Mesha (2 Kgs 3:4). Therefore, some prefer to translate it as 'sheepbreeder' (NJPS, NKJV) and to take it as an indication of high social status (Wolff 1977: 314; Eidevall 2017: 94–95; differently, Andersen and Freedman 1989: 188). Paul (1991: 247–248) argues that *nōqēd* is an all-embracing term which implies Amos was both a breeder of cattle and a herdsman of sheep and goats.

It is reasonable to expect from him a more radical message of the type that would not have been preserved by royal officials.

Second, the categorical way in which Amos's prophecies of disaster are formulated needs to be read against the background of the resistance with which his message was met in the North and the debates that ensued. The commentary draws attention to the polemical flavour of many oracles, such as 3:1–8, 12; 5:18–20; 9:1–4, 7–10. The clash with Amaziah (7:10–17) and the prohibition to prophesy (2:12) are not isolated instances but capture the essence of Amos's experience as a prophet. In such a context the radical declaration of doom was a rhetorical tool for overcoming the scepticism of the audience and forcing a response. The calls to seek the Lord are not a constantly recurring feature of the text (5:4–6, 14–15) but they capture the implicit meaning of the proclamation of doom. It is worth bearing in mind that other, equally uncompromising, threats of disaster were perceived by their recipients as calls to repentance in disguise (Jon. 3:4–10; Dan. 4:25–27; Jer. 18:7–8). Thus, Amos may not have been all that different, at least initially, from his Ancient Near Eastern counterparts. He pointed out the evils that threatened the divinely created order and warned of the negative consequences if these evils were allowed to persist.

Third, the new situation after the fall of Samaria in 722 BC altered the way in which the prophetic warnings were read and heard. After the prophesied disaster became reality, the threats which had aimed to alter behaviour were naturally seen as explanations of the events of the recent past. The message of Amos was reapplied and reinterpreted in that new situation and this is the text we now have.

## 3. The political and social context of Amos's preaching

### a. The reign of Jeroboam II and the last years of the kingdom of Israel

The superscription of Amos dates the ministry of the prophet to the reign of *King Jeroboam son of Joash of Israel*. According to 2 Kings 14:23 Jeroboam II reigned for forty-one years. Scholars estimate that his reign began somewhere between 788 and 785 BC and finished around 748–745 BC. His military achievements are highlighted in

1 Kings 14:25: 'He restored the border of Israel from Lebo-hamath as far as the Sea of the Arabah.' Amos (6:13–14) refers polemically to some of these victories. However, the extent of Israel's territorial enlargement implied by this text is not entirely clear. Lebo-hamath ('the Pass of Hamath', NJB) could be the southern entrance of the Beka Valley, roughly at the level of the city of Dan (Hammershaimb 1970: 106; Hayes 1988: 192); the city of Lebweh, south of the headwaters of the Orontes River (Jeremias 1998: 119); or a reference to the region of Hamath in upper Syria (Sweeney 2000: 243). The additional claim that Jeroboam 'restored Damascus and Hamath to Judah in Israel' (2 Kgs 14:28, ESV) has been taken to mean that the powerful Northern Kingdom controlled as vassals both Judah in the south and Damascus and Hamath in the north, but the phrase is too unclear to carry the weight of such a historical reconstruction without any other supporting evidence. The often-repeated claim that Jeroboam's reign was a golden age of restoration and prosperity may only be partially true. It is not impossible that the latter part of his reign, at least, was marked by economic decline and civil strife (Houston 2017: 53–54). In any case, Jeroboam's son Zechariah was assassinated only six months after assuming the throne (2 Kgs 15:8). This ushered in a period of political instability and rapid dynastic change (2 Kgs 15:8–31; Hos. 7:3–7).

In 745 BC Tiglath-pileser III took the Assyrian throne and initiated a new era of Assyrian expansion. In 738 BC he made a show of force in Syria and received tribute from Menahem which was financed by a special tax levied on the population (2 Kgs 15:19–20). In 734–733 BC Damascus and Northern Israel formed an anti-Assyrian alliance and attacked Jerusalem with a view to replace the Judean king Ahaz who had apparently refused to join the alliance (2 Kgs 16:5–9; Isa. 7:1–9). They were unsuccessful. In 732 BC Tiglath-pileser III conquered Damascus and incorporated its territories into the empire. Israel survived as a rump state around Samaria, but most of its land was taken away and became part of the Assyrian provincial system (2 Kgs 15:29). The Northern Kingdom existed in this truncated condition for ten more years until the last Israelite king Hoshea conspired with Egypt and withheld tribute. In response, the Assyrians besieged and conquered Samaria in 722 BC, carried a large portion of the population into exile and put an end to Israel's existence as an independent state (2 Kgs 17:1–6).

## b. Samaria and Bethel

Two Northern sites are especially important in Amos – Samaria and Bethel. Samaria was the capital of the Northern Kingdom established by Omri in the ninth century BC (1 Kgs 16:24). Archaeological excavations have uncovered the remains of the royal acropolis built by Omri and Ahab with very fine ashlar masonry (Mazar 1990: 406–410, 503–504; *NEAEHL* 4.1304–1306). A wall, 1.5 m thick, encompassed an open paved area of 178 by 89 m, where the palace and the so-called 'ivory house' were located. Mazar suggests that the palace, of which only the southern wing has survived, followed the outline of Late Bronze Age Canaanite palaces with a large central courtyard surrounded by several wings. The 'ivory house' (1 Kgs 22:39; cf. Ps. 45:8) contains over two hundred pieces of ivory plaques carved in Phoenician style, probably used as decoration on palace furniture (cf. Amos 3:15; 6:4). At a later stage a stronger casemate wall to the north and west enlarged the overall area of the acropolis to about 200 by 100 m. There was an administrative building in the western part of the acropolis, known as the 'ostraca house'. A group of over sixty inscriptions on potsherds (known as the 'Samaria ostraca') were found there, recording deliveries of wine and oil to the capital. It is debated whether these were taxes paid in kind or products coming from royal estates (*ABD* 5.921–926). Taken together, all these discoveries illustrate the power and wealth of the Israelite monarchy, targeted by Amos.

Bethel, the 'House of God', was the royal and national sanctuary (Amos 7:13) where one of the two golden calves of Jeroboam I was located (1 Kgs 12:28 – 13:33). The bull image represented the Lord and symbolized his power (Koenen 2003: 99–132). In contrast to Hosea (8:5; 10:5), Amos never mentions the calf worship. His preaching, however, relates to theological concepts that were central to the Bethel cult (Koenen 2003: 169–175; Riede 2008: 202–208). The patriarchal traditions, especially the story about Jacob's dream at Bethel (Gen. 28:10–22; 35:1–8; Hos. 12:2–6), and the exodus tradition (1 Kgs 12:28) formed the basis of Bethel's theology.

The importance of the exodus for a North Israelite audience is shown by Hosea's frequent employment of that motif (11:1; 12:13; 13:4–5). Albertz (1994: 138–146) suggests that the exodus story provided theological motivation for Jeroboam's revolt against the Davidic dynasty and the secession of the North (1 Kgs 11 – 12). Solomon was presented as a new Pharaoh who sought to enslave the Israelites, while Jeroboam was a new Moses who stood up against oppression and led his people to freedom. The Jacob and the exodus traditions converged at one important point. They focused on the presence of God with his people, and his power to bless them, guide them and save them from their enemies (Koenen 2003: 141–169).

Several elements of Amos's oracles act polemically against Bethel theology. The vision report (7:7–8; 9:1–4) reverses the status of Bethel as a 'gate of heaven' and locus of the divine presence, central to Jacob's dream in Genesis 28. The motif of God's presence plays a key role in the prophecy. Amos denies that the Lord is present with Israel (5:15) and asserts that when his presence is finally manifested it will bring death and mourning (4:12; 5:17). The exodus tradition, and especially its theological implications for Israel's status and fate, also has an important function in the prophetic proclamation (3:2; 9:7).

### c. The society of Northern Israel in the eighth century BC
The population of ancient Israel existed in two different economic zones: rural and urban. Most people lived in villages and engaged in subsistence economy – that is, their agricultural production was primarily for self-consumption (Hopkins 1996: 124–125). The main socio-economic unit was the household, or extended family. Fewer people lived in towns but the monarchic period saw a steady increase in urban culture. The cities of ancient Israel differed in their nature and function. Some were residential centres while others, characterized by large public buildings and defence structures, served as administrative and military centres (McNutt 1999: 152–153). In urban contexts increased social stratification is evident over the course of the tenth to the eighth centuries BC. There, the members of the aristocracy lived in large, finely built houses (around 150 m$^2$), often in separate neighbourhoods. In contrast, the

people on the lowest end of the social ladder inhabited small houses (around 50 m²) with shared walls, built without any regular plan (Faust 2012: 46–68). In Hazor the governor's citadel at the western fringe of the city was over 500 m² with a wall that was 2 m thick (*NEAEHL* 2.602–603).

Houston (2008: 18–51) examines four possible models for the socio-economic system of Israel in the time of Amos and the mechanisms of oppression condemned in the book. (1) According to the *rent capitalism* model wealthy, city-based landlords exploited the peasant population who worked their lands as tenants, or even serfs. (2) In the *ancient class society* model the aristocracy exploited the economic hardship of independent farmers by providing high-interest loans in order to acquire their lands and reduce them to slavery. (3) The *tributary state* model postulates that the land in its entirety was owned by the crown which extracted the agricultural surplus of village communities in the form of taxes and then redistributed it to fund the state bureaucracy. (4) The abuse of the *patronage system* implies misuse of the informal, hierarchical relationship between a powerful patron and his client who expected to receive assistance and protection in return for gratitude, services and loyalty. Houston concludes that none of these models explains entirely the social and economic reality behind the text of Amos, and he prefers to adopt an eclectic approach. The formation of the Israelite state contributed to the creation of an urban elite class of royal officials, and perhaps some wealthy aristocrats who had a power base independent of the crown. These people took advantage of their economic and political muscle and exploited the vulnerable members of society.

Many scholars assume that the victims of oppression featured in Amos were the Israelite peasants who lost their land as a result of the predatory advances of the rich (Wolff 1977: 90). Boer (2015) provides a detailed analysis of the ways employed by the 'non-producers' to extract resources from the 'producers'. The Israelite ruling class appropriated the agricultural surplus of the village communes in the form of taxes. However, their chief economic basis was royal and temple estates patterned on earlier Mesopotamian and Egyptian models. Such estates required labour, and the aristocracy, through various means like corvée labour and debt servitude, pulled people from the villages to work on the estates, thus threatening the survival of those rural communities (Boer 2015: 131, 202–205).

On the other hand, Houston (2017: 58–65) argues that the exploitation which Amos condemns took place in the cities, not in the Israelite villages where kinship-based networks still remained intact and offered a measure of protection. The urban poor were people who for various reasons migrated from the villages to the cities and joined the ranks of small artisans, day labourers, beggars and criminals. As a substitute for the protective social network of the kinship group which they had left behind, such people developed patron–client relationships with the elite which could have provided them with work, and legal and financial help in times of need. This relationship was meant to be mutually benefi-cent but, since the power was always on the side of the patron, it was open to abuse.

## 4. Interpreting the book of Amos

### a. The genre of the prophetic book

In order to make sense of any book, the reader must first be able to answer the question: What am I reading? Amos is a 'prophetic book', that much is clear, but this statement is meaningless unless one can tell what constitutes a 'prophetic book' and what should be expected from it. While prophetic figures are known from many Ancient Near Eastern cultures, the phenomenon of the prophetic book is unique to ancient Israel and without exact parallels in the literary traditions of the surrounding peoples.

Recently, several attempts have been made to define more precisely the genre of Amos. One of the most radical and innovative belongs to Radine (2010: 80–109), who argues that Amos should not be regarded as prophetic literature at all because its contents and thematic focus differ significantly from comparable Ancient Near Eastern prophetic material. Instead, Amos bears a resem-blance to a group of Mesopotamian works called 'literary-predictive texts' (2010: 110–129). These scribal compositions narrate in the form of fictive predictions certain historical events in order to achieve a political purpose. That could be the legitimation of the reigning king, justification for an existing institution or polemic against an enemy. Others have turned to categories from ancient Greek literature to describe the nature of the book. Eidevall (2017: 13–14) suggests that Amos in its final form could be read 'as a drama of sorts' consisting primarily of divine monologues distributed across three acts. Wood (2002: 97–100) sees as the backbone of the book a cycle of seven interconnected tragic poems, forming a dramatic monologue that depicts the downfall of the nation.

Sweeney and Möller emphasize the persuasive nature of the text although they disagree on the identity of the primary addressees. For Sweeney (2000: 192–195, 199) Amos is an exhortation for the people of the Northern Kingdom to seek the Lord at the Jerusalem temple. It denounces Israel's oppression of Judah and calls for the destruction of Bethel and the re-establishment of the rule of the Davidic dynasty over the North. According to Möller (2003: 19, 104–107, 119), the book is a literary composition that paints the picture of a clash between the prophet and his Northern listeners. The rhetorical purpose of the unfolding debate is to convince the people of Judah, who are the real audience, to amend their ways in order to avoid the fate of their Northern neighbours.

A different strand of scholarship regards the prophetic book primarily as a work of scribal theological reflection inspired by the great tragedies of 722 and 587 BC (see Radine above). As scribes contemplated the fall of the Northern Kingdom, the destruction of Jerusalem and the exile of Israel and Judah they created literary works that explained God's actions in the history of his people, his demands on them and his purposes for their future (Kratz 2015: 30, 48–49). Linville (2008: 23–37) understands Amos as 'mythological literature'. It contributes to an overall mythical paradigm of creation–destruction–new creation that seeks to explain the world, define the identity of the exilic community and assert belief in the divine power that guides its history.

Most of these proposals are based on the conviction that the relationship between the historical prophet and the literary work that now bears his name is rather loose, or non-existent. Contrary to such trends, I think this link should not be severed so easily and quickly (see above). That, in turn, affects how we understand the nature of the text in its final form. In my opinion, the book of Amos, like the book of Zephaniah, is best defined as 'literary prophecy' (for details see Hadjiev 2020a: 89–92). That means the book is a collection of prophetic oracles which were proclaimed orally and subsequently written down, edited and reapplied to future generations of readers. In 'literary prophecy' we do not have a straightforward transcript of speeches, since in the very act of writing and copying the prophecies they were reinterpreted and transformed.[3] The purpose of the newly emergent literary composition is not archival. The prophet's words are preserved not as a monument to the work of a great individual from the past but because they are deemed to have relevance beyond the original historical circumstances of their delivery. The scribal act of collecting, editing and reinterpreting the prophetic word is in itself a prophetic activity (Nissinen 2017: 151–154). It wrests the proclamation from its original historical situation and places it in a new literary context, thereby transforming or augmenting its meaning.

The nature of the prophetic book is determined by the interaction between the original proclamation and its subsequent literary shaping. On the one hand, the book is the literary deposit of Amos's preaching, as it was reapplied by later generations of readers. On the other hand, it is a divine word addressing future audiences by drawing them into the literary world of the prophetic revelation. The book of Amos is revelatory literature, anchored in, but not confined to, the context of eighth century BC Northern Israel. From there it reaches into the indeterminate future to speak to the people of God whose history is still to unfold.

### b. The contexts and purposes of the book

If the above definition of genre is accepted, the book of Amos cannot have a single, overarching purpose. To define a purpose,

---

3. During the twentieth century the main point of contention was the 'authenticity' of the oracles. Some commentators argued that everything in the book went back to Amos himself (Hammershaimb 1970: 14; Paul 1991: 1–7). Others postulated a long process of redaction and supplementation by later editors (Wolff 1977: 106–113; Jeremias 1998: 2–9).

one must situate a text within a certain context, but the very nature of the prophetic book resists that. It involves several different contexts as the oracles are proclaimed, written down, collected and reapplied. For Amos at least three different primary historical contexts need to be taken into account: (1) Israel prior to 722 BC; (2) Judah during the monarchic period (722–587 BC); (3) exilic and post-exilic Judah.

The message of Amos to the Northern Kingdom was aimed at repentance and change. The prophet called his audience to seek the Lord by practising justice and looking after the poor and the needy. When this message was rejected, Amos or more likely the Israelite members of his support group engaged with the members of Israel's ruling class in polemic and debate. They tried, again unsuccessfully, to persuade their contemporaries of the truthfulness of the prophetic word and the dire consequences of disregarding it (Hadjiev 2009: 184–187, 193–198).

After the capture of Samaria and the end of the Northern Kingdom (722 BC) large numbers of refugees migrated to Judah. The scrolls of Amos also travelled south, not just geographically but also hermeneutically (cf. 1:1–2). In Judah they were applied for the first time to a community that was different from the original audience (Hadjiev 2009: 187–190, 198–200). Judah, of course, shared a bond with Northern Israel through their common worship of the Lord. On top, there were many parallels in the social, economic, political and religious conditions of the two kingdoms that facilitated the first reapplication of the prophecy (cf. 6:1–2). The scrolls of Amos now addressed two different situations and consequently had two different meanings. For the Israelite migrants to Judah they explained the events of 722 BC and asserted that God was still in control. What happened was no accident, but the fulfilment of Amos's predictions. For the people of Judah, they functioned, similarly as for pre-722 BC Israel, as a challenge and warning. At this stage Amos's proclamation of defeat and exile (2:13–16; 5:27; 6:7) both explained the meaning of events from the recent past (722 BC) and pointed forward to Judah's approaching doom (587 BC).

After the Babylonian sack of Jerusalem (587 BC) the book of Amos performed for the Judean community the same function it had performed for the refugees of Northern Israel at the end of the eighth century BC (Hadjiev 2009: 201–207). It explained the disaster (cf. 2:4–5) and offered direction. The message of hope at the end of the book (9:11–15) is often ascribed to this period and provides a helpful example of how the changing historical circumstances impact the focus and purpose of the prophetic word.[4] In the highly charged polemical atmosphere of pre-722 Israel (and presumably also pre-exilic Judah on the eve of the Babylonian invasion), when the main focus was to undermine the self-assurance of the opponents, a proclamation of hope would have been counterproductive. After the disaster had taken place the problem was no longer false sense of security but despair and confusion. The promise of hope in such a situation takes centre stage.

## 5. Theology and ethics in Amos

### a. Justice and righteousness: God on the side of the poor and the weak

The central accusation that Amos levies against Israel is related to the practice of justice. The audience are charged with violence

---

4. It is very difficult to postulate for this passage a convincing setting within the original ministry of Amos (for a survey of attempts see Hadjiev 2009: 119 n. 48). The best suggestion comes from Firth (1996) who argues that at the oral level 9:11–15 functioned as polemic against the monarchy of the Northern Kingdom. However, the tone of this section, in contrast to the preceding 9:7–10, is not polemical. There is no explicit reference to the Northern kings, their claims and their false sense of security, and *the booth of David* is depicted as a ruined city rather than a weak dynasty. Once the city is restored its main collective political and military action is directed to the south, towards Edom, not to the North (*all the nations*, which stands in parallel to Edom, is too general to be confined just to Northern Israel). Most importantly, the verbal and thematic links between 9:11–15 and the preceding material are best understood as deliberate literary allusions that seek to reverse the previously announced judgment. This suggests the passage did not have oral prehistory but was written with the current literary context in mind, most likely during the Babylonian exile (Hadjiev 2009: 119–122).

and oppression of the poor (2:6–8; 3:10; 4:1; 5:10–12; 8:4–6) and, more generally, with disregarding *justice* and *righteousness* (5:7, 24; 6:12). *Justice (mišpāṭ)* has decidedly legal connotations. It often refers to judicial decisions, and the laws and rules that were based on them. *Righteousness (ṣĕdāqâ)* describes the moral standards to which behaviour in the context of communal life and personal relationships needs to conform. These standards are held to be a self-evident part of the moral fabric of creation (*NIDOTTE* 3.743–769). When used together *mišpāṭ ûṣĕdāqâ* form a hendiadys the meaning of which goes well beyond the legal sphere. Weinfeld (1995: 7–44) has shown that the phrase points to the concept of social justice and includes in its domain of meaning not just fair judicial process and refraining from oppression, but also positive actions to support the poor and vulnerable members of society. According to Ezekiel, to do *mišpāṭ ûṣĕdāqâ* ('justice and righteousness'; cf. 18:5) involves giving bread to the hungry and clothing the naked (18:7).

Moreover, justice and righteousness have a cosmic dimension. They are the foundation of God's throne (Ps. 89:14) and a gift that God passes onto the king of Israel (Ps. 72:1). This gift to the king results not only in defence and deliverance of the poor but also in prosperity (*šālôm*), rains and abundant harvest (Ps. 72:1–7, 16). So justice and righteousness are not only the conduct which seeks the good of the community but also the blessings that result from it. More broadly, they are the principle of order and harmony established by God in creation which encompasses both the 'natural world' and the social, political and economic sphere of human existence (Houston 2010: 37–41; 2017: 35).

Israel's violation of the divinely established moral order of the universe takes different forms: physical violence, driving people into debt bondage and slavery, sexual abuse, corruption and bribery, and imposition of a heavy tax load. These actions were not all necessarily 'illegal' but they were definitely immoral. Amos does not appear as a champion of the law. He challenges the law and the actions of the elite on the basis of a higher moral standard to which people are accountable. The existence of such a standard can be seen most clearly in the OAN (Barton 2012: 57–61, 67–69). They condemn Israel's neighbours for inhumane acts and extreme cruelty.

The assumption is that a basic standard of human behaviour exists, which at the very least requires people not to abuse and exploit others for their own benefit. Amos expects everyone to be aware of this standard and to adhere to it.

### b. Rejection of worship: God against the royal establishment

The second major criticism in the book of Amos is directed at the worship of Israel (2:8; 3:14; 4:4–5; 5:5–6, 21–27; 7:9; 8:3; 9:1). Some commentators think this criticism is primarily religious. Worship at Bethel was wrong because it was idolatrous, or because it undermined the central position of the Jerusalem temple (Barstad 1984: 54–58; Eidevall 2017: 142–143). Others understand the condemnation in political terms – Amos rejects Israel's domination of Judah (Sweeney 2000: 228), or Israel's celebration of its recent military successes (Andersen and Freedman 1989: 434–435), or the civil strife in the country (Hayes 1988: 143–144). Such political realities would have been closely connected with religious ritual. These interpretations, however, are problematic because there is very little explicit textual detail in their support. On the other hand, the clear and unambiguous motivation of Amos's cultic criticism in the text is the social injustice practised by Israel (Hadjiev 2009: 17–19). To seek the Lord means to *establish justice in the gate* (5:4–6, 14–15). The lack of justice and righteousness makes all cultic actions odious to God (5:21–24).

The cultic criticism is directed at the elite. It is highly unlikely that the poor would have been able to afford the time or resources required to take part in the festivals to which Amos refers (Houston 2017: 27–28). Those who gathered to worship were the aristocracy (2:8; 4:1–5). As 7:10–17 makes clear, the cult and the monarchy were tightly connected at both a realistic and a symbolic level. We are not told explicitly why injustice made the cult unacceptable to God. It is possible that religion is seen as actively promoting oppression by legitimizing the power of the ruling class and justifying their actions. Alternatively, the fault may be one of omission. The cult was complicit in the crimes of the royal establishment because it turned a blind eye and did not 'speak truth to power'. In any case, it is clear that extensive involvement in worship activities contributed to the rejection of the prophetic word. The temple mediated a sense of divine presence which made the prediction of disaster appear nonsensical. In response to this Amos establishes a clear hierarchy between the 'social' and the 'spiritual' sphere. The practice of justice and righteousness is the primary way to seek God (5:4–6, 14–15), and in its absence all other worship activities are pointless.

### c. Doom, repentance and restoration: God as Judge and Saviour

The social and cultic abuses result in a series of divinely sent punishments. These include natural disasters like drought, famine, crop failure (4:6–9; 7:1–6) and, of course, the earthquake (1:1; 9:1; 3:14–15; 6:11). The primary means of judgment, however, is military defeat: the defeated, panic-stricken and decimated army (2:13–16; 4:10; 5:3); the enemy attacking the land (6:14), capturing and plundering the city (3:6; 3:11–12; 6:8) and leading people away in captivity (4:2–3; 5:5, 27; 6:7; 9:4). The picture of universal death and mourning (5:2, 16–17; 6:9–10; 8:3, 8, 13–14; 9:10) probably depicts the aftermath of military defeat, although a plague may also be in view. The judgment is a personal act of God (7:1–8; 9:1), the Creator of the world who wields unrivalled power over the destiny of the nations (1:3 – 2:16; 9:7) and the forces of nature (4:13; 5:8–9; 9:5–6). At times he is transcendent and exalted (9:5–6) but more often God is pictured as a roaring lion (1:2; 3:8; cf. 5:19), imminent, dangerous and violent. Amos never speaks of God's wrath, but the charged rejection of the cult in 5:21–23, given in first-person divine speech, implies some emotional involvement on God's part.

The judgment explicitly targets the upper class of Israel. Those who go into exile are the notables of the first of the nations (6:1, 7), the worshippers who do not practise justice (5:27), the cows of Bashan who oppress the poor (4:1–3). The owners of expensive houses, vineyards and luxury items will lose them (3:9–15; 5:11), and military leaders will experience defeat (6:13–14). According to Boer (2015: 195–200), in such circumstances the collapse of the state led to the re-emergence of subsistence economy and village-based communities that were able to keep their surpluses, free from the tribute demands of the local ruling class, at least for a while (for a different evaluation see Barton 2012: 105–106; Houston

2017: 47–48). The book of Amos may prefigure some of that with its promise about the raising of the *booth of David* (see below).

In two places Amos calls the people to repent (5:4–6, 14–15). How that call functions in the light of the announcement of punishment is not clear. One possible way of relating these two seemingly contradictory themes is to focus on the proclamation of doom and take *The end has come upon my people Israel* (8:2) as Amos's main message. The calls to repent never assumed that Israel would actually turn to God. Together with other accusations, they lay bare the guilt of the people and justify the coming disaster. In the final form of the text, repentance undoubtedly plays such a role. Both 2:12 and 7:10–17 convey the message that Israel's fate was sealed once they refused to heed the prophetic word. The implied hope was not of averting the inevitable but of a life with God beyond the disaster (Barton 2012: 92–103).

The alternative, which I favour, is to take the call to repentance as foundational and to subordinate the message of judgment to it (Hadjiev 2009: 191–193). Before the exile became a reality even the most categorically formulated announcement of disaster functioned as an implicit call to seek the Lord. It was only after the catastrophe had taken place that the prophetic message began to function as a theological explanation of what had happened. Repentance and judgment are not contradictory but exhibit a fluid dynamic which changes with the change of context. Before 722 BC judgment served to motivate the call to repent. After 722 BC the (unheeded) calls to repent explained the judgment and showed people how to respond to the judgment.

The book of Amos does not spend a lot of time talking about salvation and hope, but the last paragraph promises the survivors a future beyond the punishment (9:11–15). In this future, however, the *house of Jacob* will be remade into a new entity – the *booth of David*. The end of *my people Israel* (8:2), contrary to our initial impressions, is not a total extermination, but an opportunity for a new beginning. Israel continues in a new form. A flimsy, agricultural installation will replace the opulent dwellings of the ruling class. It is to a simple farmer's hut that the promise of prosperity, power and security is given. A new age of renewal dawns, and it rests solely on the divine initiative, on the mercy and grace of God, which have the final word.

### d. Israel's identity as the people of God

Amos's audience believed that they had a special relationship with God established in history (2:9–10; 9:7) and maintained in the cult (5:14). The Lord 'knew' Israel (3:2) and stood ready to save and bless them (5:18–20). In his preaching Amos systematically tried to subvert every single aspect of that belief system. In doing so he raises the broader question: What does it mean to be the people of God? The book provides two answers from two different perspectives.

First, Israel's identity is based on the past but is to be maintained in the present by an ethical lifestyle. It is not sufficient to celebrate that identity by historical commemoration and ritual assertions. Since the Lord is the Creator of the just cosmic order, the community that belongs to him needs to affirm and conform to that order by practising justice and righteousness. To be the people of God is to be part of creation and to practise justice. The primary function of the past is to determine the high ethical standards expected in the present (3:2). The opening series of OAN makes clear that through its conduct Israel has betrayed its divine calling and forfeited its special status. Identity, then, is a dynamic reality. Tradition constitutes it, but lifestyle either maintains or destroys it. Put simply, to be the people of God is to live justly.

Second, Israel's identity is constituted by the actions of the Lord. That process in Amos involves the *end . . . [of] my people Israel* (8:2), the destruction of the *house of Jacob* (9:8–10) and the raising up of the *booth of David* (9:11). In other words, the community which has rejected its calling (7:10–17) is not simply let go. Instead it is reconfigured and rebuilt. The booth of David in the epilogue has clear signs of continuity with the house of Jacob from the rest of the book. Both the booth and the house are called *my people Israel* (8:2; 9:14). Yet there are also marked differences: a booth is not a house. That process of reconstitution carries on beyond the book of Amos. In Acts 15 the booth of David continues its transformation, as it incorporates the nations that come to seek the Lord in the light of the resurrection of Christ.

Thus, being the people of God is simultaneously, and paradoxically, both a promise and a challenge. It is a free and creative act of divine love, but also a human achievement manifested in a lifestyle of justice.

ANALYSIS

# 1. INTRODUCTION (1:1–2)

# 2. ISRAEL HAS BECOME LIKE THE NATIONS (1:3 – 2:16)

   A.  Oracles against foreign nations (1:3 – 2:3)
        i.  Damascus (1:3–5)
       ii.  Gaza (1:6–8)
     iii.  Tyre (1:9–10)
     iv.  Edom (1:11–12)
      v.  Ammonites (1:13–15)
     vi.  Moab (2:1–3)
   B.  Oracles against Israel and Judah (2:4–16)
        i.  Judah (2:4–5)
       ii.  Israel (2:6–16)

# 3. A DIVINE WORD AGAINST THE PEOPLE OF ISRAEL (3:1 – 4:13)

   A.  The lion has roared: fear for your lives (3:1–8)
   B.  Israel's transgressions on Mount Samaria and at the Bethel altar (3:9 – 4:3)
   C.  Israel's transgressions in Bethel: lack of repentance (4:4–13)

## 4. A PROPHETIC WORD AGAINST THE HOUSE OF ISRAEL (5:1 – 6:14)

    A. Injustice, seeking the Lord, death (5:1–17)

    B. The Day of the Lord and Israel's corrupt worship (5:18–27)

    C. Israel's current prosperity and future failures (6:1–14)

## 5. THE INEVITABLE DESTRUCTION OF ISRAEL (7:1 – 9:6)

    A. The first two visions: the Lord relents (7:1–6)

    B. The third vision: the plumb line (7:7–17)

        i. The third vision (7:7–9)

        ii. Confrontation at Bethel (7:10–17)

    C. The fourth vision: the end has come (8:1–14)

        i. The fourth vision (8:1–3)

        ii. The oracles (8:4–14)

    D. The fifth vision: the destroyed temple (9:1–6)

## 6. THE RAISING OF THE FALLEN BOOTH OF DAVID (9:7–15)

# COMMENTARY

## 1. INTRODUCTION (1:1–2)

### Context

A superscription and a hymnic fragment introduce the book of Amos. The superscription provides information that is necessary for understanding the narrative in 7:10–17. Amos was a sheep-breeder, not a professional prophet, and came from Tekoa in the South but spoke concerning Northern Israel. Indirectly this is linked to the theme of the rejection of Amos's message that is central to the narrative in chapter 7 (see also 2:12; 3:1–15; 9:8–10). The mention of the earthquake anticipates another common motif in the book (2:13; 3:13–15; 6:11; 9:1). The reference to the reign of Uzziah (2 Kgs 15:1–7) and Jeroboam (2 Kgs 14:23–29) ties his ministry to the narrative of the book of Kings and places it somewhere in the middle of the eighth century BC. The king of Judah is mentioned first, as a reminder that the prophetic oracles were preserved, read and applied to Judah after the demise of the Northern Kingdom (Wolff 1977: 120–121). The hymnic fragment in verse 2 with its picture of God as a roaring lion causing devastation by the power of his word introduces the central message of the book – God's judgment (*Carmel*, cf. 9:3; *roars*, cf. 3:4, 8). The mention of Jerusalem anticipates the reference to David at the end (9:11).

## Comment

**1.** The opening formula *The words of Amos ... which he saw concerning Israel* is unusual on several counts. Other prophetic books open with the phrases 'The word of the LORD that came to Hosea/Joel/Micah/Zephaniah', 'The vision of Isaiah/Obadiah' or 'The oracle of Nahum/Habakkuk'. The exilic/post-exilic books of Ezekiel, Haggai and Zechariah begin with a dating formula followed by the phrase 'the word of the LORD came'. Only Jeremiah begins with the comparable 'The words of Jeremiah'. Amos is said to have 'seen' his words. Several prophetic books include the phrase *which he saw* (*ḥāzâ*) in their superscriptions, but what is seen is either a vision (Isa. 1:1), an oracle (Hab. 1:1) or the word of the Lord (Mic. 1:1), never a human word. It is not clear if the verb *he saw* here means more narrowly 'received in a vision' (Soggin 1987: 24), or more broadly 'received by divine revelation' (Stuart 1987: 298). In either case the verb implies that the words of Amos were not just his own words.

We are also given information about the profession and the place of origin of the prophet. He is *among the shepherds* [on the meaning of this term see Introduction section 2b, 'The profile of Amos's prophetic activity', footnote 2] *of Tekoa*, a town south of Bethlehem and north of Hebron at the edge of the wilderness of Judea which stretches to the east. *Uzziah* is called Azariah (perhaps his personal name) in 2 Kings 15:1–7. *Two years before the earthquake*: in Palestine earthquakes are a relatively frequent phenomenon. The fact that this earthquake was still remembered centuries later as 'the earthquake in the days of King Uzziah of Judah' (Zech. 14:5) means it must have been particularly devastating. Its mention in the superscription is also unusual and indicates it was perceived as a confirmation of Amos's proclamation of judgment.

**2.** The hymnic fragment appears in Joel 3:16 (MT 4:16), and a different version of it in Jeremiah 25:30. This is probably an independent adaptation of a hymnic tradition from the Jerusalem temple rather than a direct quote. The belief that the Lord lives in Zion from where he speaks and acts was a fundamental conviction of the theology of the Jerusalem temple (Pss 46:4–7; 48:1–3; 50:1–4). The verbs *roars* and *utters his voice* suggest two metaphors for God: a lion (3:8) and a thunderstorm (2 Sam. 22:14). The first image stresses his destructive capabilities (Hos. 5:14): lions kill people (1 Kgs 13:24; 20:36). The background to the second metaphor is the divine battle with the forces of chaos where the thunder of God's voice is one of the weapons he employs to subdue his enemies and display his royal power (Ps. 29). Here the Lord's enemy is not the sea and the waters which usually stand for the forces of chaos, but the Northern Kingdom represented by the *top of Carmel* and the *pastures of the shepherds*. The lion metaphor may suggest that Zion is not automatically excluded from the threat, since 'it only takes a slight change of perspective or position for the protective lion to become a destructive one' (Strawn 2016: 109). The verb *'ăbělû (wither)* can mean either 'to mourn' (ESV) or to 'dry up' (NIV) (*HALOT* 1.7). The ambiguity is probably intentional. By being dried up the earth mourns the coming punishment of the people.

*Meaning*

The introductory verses make clear the divine origin of the text we are about to read and summarize its message. This is a vision that Amos saw of the Lord's destructive roar against his land and its people. At the same time the opening of the book stresses more strongly than other prophetic books the human aspect of the message. These are the words of Amos, not just the roar of God. Prophetic preaching is a message fully incarnate in the words of the human herald. Therefore, it should come as no surprise that the prophetic book reflects the style, theology, concerns and thought-world of its author(s). The other important point is the northward march of the divine speech, implicit in the superscription and explicit in the hymn. Amos came to Israel from Jerusalem to speak a message of judgment against the Northern Kingdom. There is also an implicit southward movement. The message against the Northern Kingdom was preserved and read in the South.

# 2. ISRAEL HAS BECOME LIKE THE NATIONS (1:3 – 2:16)

## A. Oracles against foreign nations (1:3 – 2:3)

*Context*

OAN are found in most of the prophetic books of the Old Testament (Isa. 13 – 23; Jer. 46 – 51; Ezek. 25 – 32; Obad.; Nah.; Zeph. 2). What unites such oracles is not any fixed literary form but their content: they proclaim doom on a foreign people. In ancient Israel such oracles stemmed originally from the context of war. Prophets proclaimed divine help ahead of major battles, and military victories were celebrated in worship (Hadjiev 2020a: 49–50). Announcing the destruction of foreigners also served to reaffirm the identity of the community. God's judgment separates 'us', the people of God, from 'them', our enemies, and defines more clearly the dividing lines (Hagedorn 2007). Amos uses this genre in a novel and striking way. In a radical departure from the expectation of the audience, he completes the series with a denunciation of Israel itself (Wolff 1977: 148–149). The surprising turn in the final oracle is the main point of the series (Barton 1980: 36–38). The preceding OAN are a rhetorical ploy that lures the listeners into a false sense of security before they themselves become objects of criticism.

Even if the oracles functioned in this way during the oral proclamation of Amos, they do not perform the same role in the book. Surprise works only on a first reading, and in any case the book was preserved and read in Judah, after the threats against Northern Israel (2:13–16) had come to pass. In their current context the OAN introduce the main themes of the prophecy and address the issue of the identity of Israel. The oracles anticipate the portrayal of Israel not only in 2:6–16 but also in the rest of the book. The series is a carefully constructed literary composition (see the Introduction) which invites the reader to see it as a single unit and not to focus on the individual nations in isolation. The meaning of each oracle is found only in the way it contributes to the whole.

### Comment

The numerical formula *For three transgressions . . . and for four* is a well-established poetical device. Often it introduces a list of items which reaches the higher of the two sequential numbers: two/three (Sirach 26:28); three/four (Prov. 30:15–16, 18–19, 21–23, 29–31); six/seven (Prov. 6:16–19; Job 5:19–23). Sometimes the formula is used without a following list: two/three (Hos. 6:2); seven/eight (Mic. 5:5; Eccl. 11:2). Amos describes specific transgressions and thus creates an expectation that four sinful actions will be detailed, but then, surprisingly, mentions only one. The point of this rhetorical manoeuvre will become clear once we reach the final oracle in 2:6–8 (see below).

*I will not revoke the punishment.* The Hebrew is literally 'I will not return it', leaving the referent of the suffix 'it' tantalizingly nebulous. 'It' may point to the geographical name in the preceding line, meaning 'I will not restore him (the city or nation in view)/I will not let him return' (Barré 1986). Alternatively, the referent may be the voice of the Lord (1:2) which brings devastation (Hayes 1988: 70–71). Most commentators interpret the suffix as pointing to the impending divine punishment, or to the decision/decree/announcement of that punishment. The ambiguity is an intentional literary device that increases the suspense (Paul 1991: 47).

Every oracle begins its description of judgment with the promise
that the Lord will *send* [only in 1:14 *kindle*] *a fire*. Burning the
captured city was common in ancient warfare so there is a realistic
note in this, although fire here acts as a divine agent and assumes
a supernatural quality (Andersen and Freedman 1989: 239). *Strongholds* (*'armĕnôt*) could be the battle-towers situated on the city walls,
but more likely here the term refers to the royal citadel (1 Kgs 16:18;
2 Kgs 15:25).

### i. Damascus (1:3–5)

**3–4.** The transgression of Damascus is described metaphorically
as the threshing of *Gilead*, a contested boarder region in the Transjordan. The *threshing-sledges of iron* were wooden boards with iron
teeth underneath driven over the harvested grain in order to
separate the chaff. It is an apt metaphor of military violence (Isa.
41:15; Mic. 4:12–13). The parallel phrases *the house of Hazael* and *the
strongholds of Ben-hadad* refer to the Aramean royal dynasty in
Damascus, a major rival to Israel during the ninth and eighth
centuries (cf. 2 Kgs 13). Hazael, a contemporary of Jehu, was a 'son
of nobody', according to Assyrian records (*COS* 2.133G), who
assassinated his predecessor and usurped the throne (2 Kgs 8:7–15).
His son Ben-hadad (2 Kgs 13:3, 24–25) needs to be distinguished
from earlier Aramean kings bearing that name (1 Kgs 15:18–20;
20:1–43). Biblical tradition records Aramean military action in
Gilead from the time of Hazael onwards (2 Kgs 8:28–29; 10:32–33),
but Amos's language is too general to allow for precise dating, and
the reference could be to contemporaneous events of which we
have no record (Barton 1980: 26–31).

**5.** The judgment is described with traditional images of military
defeat. The breaking of the *gate-bars* signifies the moment when the
besieging army enters the city. This is followed by the slaughter
of the royal house. The *inhabitants* in Hebrew is singular, literally
'the one who sits [on a throne]' and is best rendered 'king' (NIV)
in parallel to the *one who holds the sceptre* (Andersen and Freedman
1989: 253–255). The *Valley of Aven* could be the el-Beqa' valley in
Syria (Jeremias 1998: 27), and *Beth-eden* is often taken as a reference to the Aramean state Bit-Adini which in the first half of the
eighth century was an Assyrian province ruled by the powerful,

semi-independent governor Shamshi-ilu (Malamat 2001). However, a word of judgment against the semi-independent Assyrian
province on the Euphrates does not make a lot of sense in an oracle
condemning the crimes of the royal house of Damascus in Gilead.
In Hebrew *'āwen* means 'wickedness' and *'eden* 'pleasure, luxury,
delight', so the twin expressions 'The Valley of Wickedness' and
'The House of Pleasure' are best taken as symbolic designations of
the kingdom of Damascus. Their rhetorical effect is to strengthen
further its negative presentation. Within the literary horizon of the
book they play an even more important role by introducing
the motif of sinful luxury that attracts divine displeasure. This, as
Amos will point out later, is one of Israel's major failings (3:9–15;
6:1–7; Fleischer 2001: 153–154).

After the capture of the city and the execution of its leaders, the
population will *go into exile [gālû] to Kir*, back to its place of origin,
according to Amos 9:7 (cf. 2 Kgs 16:9). This introduces the theme
of exile which is prominent in the OAN (1:6, 9, 15) and in the book
as a whole (5:5, 27; 6:7; 7:11, 17). The mention of exile (*glh*) and
Damascus in 5:27 and the reappearance of the themes of exile
and luxury in 6:1–7 strengthen the parallels between the Arameans
in this paragraph and Israel in the rest of the book.

Paul (1991: 54–55) notes that even though mass deportations
became a major policy tool of the Assyrians from the time of
Tiglath-pileser III, deportations of the elite, as well as entire
populations, are well attested before that time. The prediction of
exile as punishment for the Arameans, therefore, fits the historical
context of Amos, although this prediction would have acquired
new meaning for later generations of readers/listeners after 722
and 587 BC.

### *ii. Gaza (1:6–8)*

**6–8.** The Philistines, who occupied the southern coastal strip of
Canaan, were Israel's traditional enemies from the pre-monarchic
and early monarchic period. At the early stages they were organized
in a confederation of five major royal cities. By the time of Amos
one of those cities, Gath, had lost its prominence (cf. 6:2) and so
only the remaining four are mentioned in his oracle. These were
independent cities, ruled by their own lords, but extrabiblical and

biblical sources recognize the Philistines as a distinct ethnic group and so the four cities are often branded together (Jer. 25:20; Zeph. 2:4). *Gaza* at the beginning acts as a representative of all Philistines.

The sin of the Philistines is that *they carried into exile entire communities, / to hand them over to Edom*. NJB inaccurately renders *hagôlām gālût šĕlēmâ* 'deported entire nations'. Amos is talking about village communities whose members have been captured in border raids and sold as slaves (cf. 1 Sam. 30). The identity of the victims is not explicit, but it is fair to assume that they were Israelites or Judeans. The recipient of the slaves is *Edom*, a nation that will play an important role in the OAN and the book as a whole (see below). The structure and language of the oracle follows very closely that of the preceding section. While the Arameans are taken into exile, *the remnant of the Philistines shall perish*. This does not imply a different fate for the two nations: exile and death will befall both. The variation within the established pattern is for literary effect and reminds us that the oracles need to be read together as parts of a larger picture. The same parallelism appears in 1:13 – 2:3. The *remnant* anticipates 5:15 and 9:12.

### iii. *Tyre (1:9–10)*

**9–10.** This oracle repeats almost verbatim the accusation from 1:6. The main difference is that the Phoenicians only *delivered entire communities over to Edom*; they did not 'exile' or 'capture' them. The variation could suggest a joint venture in which the Philistines raided villages to acquire slaves and then passed them on to the Phoenicians who delivered them to Edom. Geographically this does not make a lot of sense because Tyre is to the north of Philistia while Edom is to the south-east. Moreover, the text does not say that Gaza and Tyre worked together. The verbal repetition may simply be a literary device to link the oracles in a sequence, not a reflection of the realities of the slave trade.

More significantly, the transgression of Tyre is 'disregarding a treaty of brotherhood' (NIV). It is now widely recognized that the term 'brother' belongs to the diplomatic language of the Ancient Near East and means something like a 'covenant partner' (1 Kgs 20:32–33). A treaty existed between Tyre and Israel in the days of Solomon (1 Kgs 5:1[15]; see the address 'my brother' by the Tyrian king Hiram in 1 Kgs 9:13). Some suggest that this treaty was renewed under Jeroboam II (Rudolph 1971: 134; Hayes 1988: 87–89), or that Tyre and Israel were in a covenant relationship by virtue of being co-vassals to Assyria (Soggin 1987: 39). It is unnecessary to identify the specifics of Tyre's transgression because the main focus of the oracle is not on the actions of the Phoenicians but on the way these actions prefigure Israel's behaviour. Betrayal of a brother and failure to live up to covenant obligations is a reprehensible thing. The mention of brotherhood anticipates the next oracle and the grand betrayal of Edom.

### iv. Edom (1:11–12)

**11.** The actions of Edom are general: *pursued his brother with the sword* and 'killed/raped his women' (NRSV: *cast off all pity*)[1] implies the cruelty was committed during a time of war. Scholars have tried to identify the context in which Edom might have done this: the pre-monarchic period (Num. 20:14–21), the time shortly after Jehu's revolt in 841 BC, Edom's war of independence from Judah (2 Kgs 8:20–22) or an Edomite reaction to Amaziah's campaign (2 Kgs 14:7) (Bartlett 1989: 126–127; Stuart 1987: 313; Paul 1991: 63). However, biblical tradition portrays Edom during the monarchic period as weaker than Judah and more likely the victim than the

---

1. The word *raḥămîm* is the plural of *raḥam/reḥem* ('womb') used in the abstract sense to denote a 'motherly feeling' towards someone who is weaker and in need of help, hence 'compassion, pity'. Rudolph (1971: 127) has 'brotherliness' and Barton (1980: 17, 21) 'treaty obligation'. The problem here is that the verb *šiḥēt* ('destroys') requires a person as its object, not an abstract feeling. This is why NIV, taking its cue from LXX, renders 'slaughtered the women of the land' (Hubbard 1989: 134; Paul 1991: 64–65). Andersen and Freedman (1989: 266–267) prefer 'destroyed his allies'. While *raḥămîm* has a well-established sense of 'compassion' the more concrete meaning 'women' is not impossible (Judg. 5:30; Mesha's inscription line 17) and makes better sense in the context of Amos. Possibly it is a vulgar term for women, used primarily in the context of rape and war (*HALOT* 3.1218), in which case the coarseness of the language contributes further to the horrendousness of the crime.

perpetrator of such violence (2 Sam. 8:13–14; 1 Kgs 11:15; 22:47; 2 Kgs 14:7). It was in the sixth century, when the Edomites allied themselves with the Babylonians to help the conquest of Judah (Ps. 137:7–8; Obad. 10–14), that they were powerful enough to inflict significant damage and provoke such an outrage. For this reason, many scholars believe that the oracle is part of an exilic updating of the book of Amos (Jeremias 1998: 30; Fleischer 2001: 155; Hadjiev 2009: 42–45). The last couple of lines, *maintained his anger perpetually* ['his anger tore perpetually', ESV][2] / *and kept his wrath for ever*, suggest a continued period of hostilities, although this could also refer to a prolonged and vicious campaign.

More important than the historical realities behind the prophecy is the literary and theological role that Edom plays in the book of Amos as a whole. In a series unified by the repeated formula *For three transgressions . . . and for four* Edom appears in fourth place and is mentioned four times as a collaborator (1:6, 9), a perpetrator (1:11) and a victim (2:1) of violence. The oracle stands out from the rest because the four lines of the indictment make it unusually long (cf. 2:4–5). This seems to be part of a deliberate design.

> A:  Damascus (one verb: *threshed*, 1:3)
>> B:  Gaza (two verbs: *carried into exile . . . to hand over*, 1:6)
>>> C:  Tyre (two verbs: *delivered . . . and did not remember*, 1:9)
>>>> D:  Edom (four verbs: *pursued/cast off/maintained/kept*, 1:11)
>> B':  Ammon (two verbs: *ripped open . . . to enlarge*, 1:13)
> A':  Moab (one verb: *burned*, 2:1)

At the end of the book Edom is the only nation mentioned by name in parallel to *all the nations* (9:12). In biblical literature Edom

---

2. The ESV translates MT while NRSV emends the verb *wayyiṭrōp* ('and he tore') to *wayyiṭṭōr* (from *nṭr* 'to keep, maintain'). NJPS accepts this emendation but postulates new meaning for the two verbs on the basis of Akkadian cognates, yielding 'his anger raged unceasing and his fury stormed unchecked'. Similarly, NIV 'anger raged/fury flamed' (see Paul 1991: 66).

sometimes functions as a symbol or representative of the nations of the world (Isa. 34:1–5), a role facilitated by the closeness of the name *'ĕdôm* with the Hebrew word *'ādām*, 'humanity'. Its prominence in Amos suggests that it performs a similar function here.

**12.** *Teman* (meaning 'south' in Hebrew) is the name of a region in Edom and also the name of one Edomite clan (Gen. 36:15) which inhabited the 'land of the Temanites' (Gen. 36:34). It is not certain whether the region was in the north, around Bozrah, or in the south of the country, perhaps the Timna Valley just a few kilometres from the port of Elat. *Bozrah* (modern-day Buseirah) is the capital of Edom, situated in the northern part to the west of the King's Highway and close to one of the significant sources of copper ore, Faynan. Excavations there have uncovered a city wall and the remains of a royal palace from the Assyrian period (Bartlett 1989: 40, 45–46; *ABD* 1.774–775). Both Teman (Obad. 9) and Bozrah (Isa. 34:6; 63:1; Jer. 49:22) are used in parallel with Edom in prophetic texts. Here the two geographical terms signify the whole country.

### v. Ammonites (1:13–15)

**13.** The kingdom of the Ammonites was situated in the Transjordan, south of Gilead. Biblical tradition records clashes between Israel and the Ammonites in that region from early times (Judg. 11; 1 Sam. 11). Amos accuses them of having *ripped open pregnant women in Gilead*. This type of atrocity is mentioned several times in the Old Testament, often in parallel with the killing of the children of the defeated foe (2 Kgs 8:12; 15:16; Hos. 13:16). It suggests a desire for total extermination of the conquered population so that its land may be appropriated by the victors. Amos confirms that the atrocities of the Ammonites were committed *in order to enlarge their territory*. Land is seen as more precious than human life. The reference to *Gilead* and to *exile* (v. 15) connects this passage to the Damascus oracle (1:3–5).

**14–15.** The punishment is described with the traditional imagery of ancient warfare. The fire is *kindle[d]*, not sent – a small change in the established formula for the sake of literary variation – in the walls of the Ammonite capital *Rabbah*. The *day of battle* is metaphorically described in the parallel line as a *day of the whirlwind*, and the *shouting* of the besieging army is compared to the thunderous sound of an approaching *storm*. *Storm* (*saʿar*), *whirlwind* (*sûpâ*) and *fire* are the Lord's weapons in Psalm 83:15 ('tempest/hurricane'). In Amos the anonymous army coming against Rabbah is a manifestation of the divine storm (Nah. 1:3) in which God himself confronts his enemies. Verse 15 takes us to the aftermath of the battle when the *king* and his *officials go into exile* (see above on 1:5).

### vi. Moab (2:1–3)

**1.** Moab occupied a territory in the Transjordan to the east of the Dead Sea, south of Ammon and north of Edom. It was a vassal of Israel during the time of the Omrides but rebelled and gained its independence after the death of Ahab (2 Kgs 3:4–27). In an inscription that commemorates the Moabite war of independence King Mesha boasts how he captured two Israelite towns, Ataroth and Nebo, and massacred the entire population as a 'sacrifice' (*ryt*) and a 'sacred ban' (*ḥerem*) to his god Kemosh (*COS* 2.23). He also appropriated some new territory in the course of the war. In later times the territory north of the river Arnon, up to the northern edge of the Dead Sea, was considered part of the Moabite realm (Isa 15:2, 4), even though Israel also laid claim to that region (Judg. 11:11–28). Amos, however, does not accuse the Moabites of any war crimes against Israel/Judah, or of stealing Israelite territory. Instead, Moab's transgression is that *he burned to lime / the bones of the king of Edom*. It is not entirely clear what the precise nature of the transgression is, since the expression *lāśśîd* can be translated either 'to ashes' (NIV; cf. NJB) or 'for lime' (Paul 1991: 72). The actual substance *śîd* appears in only two other places in the Old Testament: literally, as plaster used to create a smooth surface on a stone for writing (Deut. 27:2, 4) and metaphorically, of total annihilation (Isa. 33:12). The king of Moab may have burned the bones of the Edomite king to obtain lime so that he could plaster a building with it; 'a man had been treated as material', as Wolff aptly remarks (1977: 162–163). Alternatively, the bones were pulverized in order to eradicate completely the king's existence (Jeremias 1998: 29). Hayes (1988: 98–100) quotes several Assyrian inscriptions that describe Ashurbanipal's desecration of Elamite royal tombs. In order to humiliate his defeated enemy, Ashurbanipal removed and crushed the bones of former kings, laying 'restlessness upon their shades' and depriving them of food and drink offerings. It is likely that a similar sort of action stands in the background of Amos's indictment.

Why is such a deed condemned so strongly? Desecrating a grave and disturbing the dead was widely regarded as reprehensible in the ancient world (Barton 1980: 56; Soggin 1987: 45). Amos assumes that his audience would share such a view and see the action of the Moabite king as deplorable. There is, however, a deeper rhetorical purpose behind this choice. A dead victim cannot defend himself against violation. In that sense he makes a good parallel to the pregnant women in 1:13 and anticipates the weakness of the poor and the oppressed in 2:6–8.

The most significant aspect of the oracle is the fact that an Edomite king is the victim of the abuse. First, this strengthens the parallel between the first two oracles (1:3–8) and the oracles against Ammon and Moab (1:13 – 2:3). As the oracles against Damascus and the Ammonites mention Gilead in their indictment, so the oracles against Philistia and Moab mention Edom. Second, this mention brings the overall references of Edom in the OAN to four and so underlines the centrality of Edom to the series (see above on 1:11–12). Third, the fact that an Edomite king is the victim for the first time overtly shows that the Lord's interest is not motivated solely by nationalistic concerns. Up until this point, the reader could assume that the crimes of the foreign nations were against the people of Israel/Judah whom the Lord wants to protect. With the Moab oracle it becomes clear that the Lord's concerns extend beyond the borders of his chosen people. He protects the dignity of the Edomite king despite Edomite guilt (1:6–12).

**2–3.** The divine fire is directed against the *strongholds of Kerioth*. Its mention here gives the impression that it was the capital of Moab, or an important urban centre, but its attestation is surprisingly rare (Jer. 48:24, 41) and the LXX ('the foundations of her cities') does not even take it here as a proper name. Mesha's inscription mentions Kerioth as the location of the sanctuary of the god Kemosh. Its location is disputed, and some scholars suggest that Kerioth is another name for the Moabite city of *Ar* (Isa. 15:1), since both Kirya and Ar in Hebrew mean 'city'. It is possible that the reason for the choice of this particular city here is literary. Its name recalls *qîrâ* ('towards Kir') of 1:5, the place where the Arameans would be exiled, and thus creates an *inclusio* that envelops the OAN.

As in 1:14–15, the punishment is depicted with general imagery of a military attack: *uproar, shouting*, the *sound of the trumpet*. Note the wordplay between *šôpār* (*trumpet*) and *šôpēṭ* (*ruler*). The Moab and Ammon oracles focus on the fate of the *ruler/king* and his *officials* and need to be read together as a parallel to the Damascus and Gaza units at the start of the series (1:3–8). In both pairs the exile in the first oracle (1:5, 15) is followed by death in the second (1:8; 2:3). The four passages together create a comprehensive picture of military invasion followed by capture of besieged cities, executions and exile.

*Meaning*

The sins of Israel's neighbours are military atrocities (Aram, Edom, Ammon), slave trade (Gaza, Tyre) and defiling of graves (Moab). In essence, these are acts of violence and aggression motivated by greed and self-interest (Gaza, Ammon), by anger (Edom) or by desire to humiliate an enemy (Moab). Together they show Israel's neighbours to be brutal, self-centred and arrogant people. Their punishment, therefore, will be severe: exile (Aram, Ammon) and total extermination (Gaza, Moab).

The nations are not accused of idolatry, but of inhumane treatment of others. Initially the series hints that the victims might be Israelites and allows for the possibility of nationalistic outrage. With the Moab oracle this possibility is imploded. The Lord condemns the violence against Edom, itself a transgressor and a perpetrator of violence. Once we reach the final accusation (2:1) the anonymity of the earlier victims takes on a new meaning. God is not a partisan, concerned only about the well-being of his own people. He protects everyone, regardless of their ethnicity. The criticisms imply that the nations have violated moral norms which are universally applicable to all people and recognized through convention and custom (Barton 1980: 39–45; 2012: 57–60). Even though the nations do not have a special revelation of the divine will, they still have a responsibility to follow the general moral principles, available to them through the created order of which they are part (Rom. 2:14–15).

The foreign nations anticipate the portrayal of Israel in 2:6–16. The violence of Aram, Edom and Ammon prefigures the violence of Israel against the poor and the afflicted (2:7a). The delivering of whole communities of exiles by Gaza and Tyre mirrors the selling of the righteous and the needy into slavery (2:6b). The atrocities of Ammon, motivated by desire for territorial gain, echo the selling of people into slavery for financial gain (2:6b). The violence committed by Edom and Ammon against women links in with the sexual exploitation of female servants in Israelite households (2:7b). In their transgressions the nations are a mirror image of Israel. Thus, the OAN present the reader with a stark theological proposition: by acting unjustly towards the poor, Israel has lost its distinctive identity as a people of God and has become like the neighbours it hates and abhors.

## B. Oracles against Israel and Judah (2:4–16)

*Context*

The Judah oracle (2:4–5) follows closely the structure of the preceding OAN, and in particular 1:9–12. Like the Tyre and Edom oracles, it lacks an elaborate description of judgment and a concluding *says the LORD* formula (2:5). The connection between Edom and Judah is further strengthened by the elaborate four-line accusation. The link underlines the similarity between the people of God and the foreign nations, created by transgression. Conversely, the complex structure of the Israel oracle (2:6–16; see the Introduction) sets it apart from the rest of the series and underlines its climactic role. After the capture of Samaria in 722 BC Judah remained the sole heir of Israelite identity. A series of OAN, which was originally directed against a Northern audience and culminated with the denunciation of the kingdom of Israel, was reapplied to readers in the South. Thus, in the final form of the text the two concluding passages (2:4–5 and 2:6–16) are not to be regarded as prophecies against two discrete political entities but as a twofold word against the whole people of God.

The oracles introduce the major themes in Amos: justice, worship, rejection of prophecy, and judgment. They also anticipate the overall structure of the book. The history of Israel unfolds in three successive stages. First, the sin of oppression and corrupt worship compromises the people's standing with the Lord (2:6–8 = chs. 3–6). The Judah oracle interprets this as a rejection of the law (2:4). Second, the Lord and his servants seek to rectify this (2:11–12 = 7:1–17) but fail. The people prohibit prophecy (2:12) and walk after lies (2:4). The threefold divine *I* (*'ānōkî*) of 2:9–13 is echoed by the threefold prophetic *I* (*'ānōkî*) in 7:14. Third, once Amos is forbidden to prophesy (2:12 = 7:16), the only thing left is the coming punishment (2:13–16 = 8:1 – 9:6). (See Table 4 above, p. 63.)

## Comment
### i. Judah (2:4–5)

**4–5.** The numerical formula *For three transgressions . . . and for four* is followed, just as in the case of Edom (1:11), by a four-line accusation. The Judeans *have rejected* [*mā'as*] *the law* ['Teaching', NJPS; 'instruction', NAB] *of the LORD / and have not kept his statutes*. It is tempting to interpret these words in the light of a text like 2 Kings 17:15 which blames the exile of Northern Israel on the fact that it 'rejected [*mā'as*] [the] statutes and [the] covenant' (NKJV) of the Lord and 'went after false idols'. The transgression of Judah would then be rejecting the law of Moses and engaging in idolatry (Hubbard 1989: 138). However, the wording is ambiguous and could have a broader meaning. Andersen and Freedman (1989: 297–300) point out that the Hebrew term *tôrâ* could denote (1) prophetic instruction which was situationally bound; (2) priestly teaching on matters of liturgy and ritual; (3) more general instruction about the people's ethical and religious obligations; (4) the law of Moses. A good example of the more situational use of the term is the request 'for a ruling [*tôrâ*]' in Haggai 2:11–13. In Hosea 4:6 the 'instruction' (*tôrâ*) of God is synonymous with the knowledge of God which, as Hosea 4:1–2 makes clear, is manifested primarily in an ethical lifestyle. Similarly, in Isaiah 5:24 'reject[ing] the instruction of the LORD' (almost exactly the same phrase in Hebrew as Amos 2:4) means rejection of justice and righteousness (Isa. 5:7, 8, 16, 23).

Therefore, the rejection of the law of the Lord in Amos could involve the rejection of the prophetic message and the practice of injustice and oppression. The indictment prepares the way for the Israel oracle and gives the acts in 2:6–8 an explicitly theological meaning.

Their *lies* (*kizbêhem*) is often understood as a synonym of 'vanities' (*hăbālîm*), that is, the idols after which Israel walked (Wolff 1977: 163–164); see NIV: 'led astray by false gods'. However, 'lies' is never used in the Old Testament as a shorthand for false gods, with the possible exception of Psalm 40:4 ('false gods', NRSV, NIV). More often, it is employed in the sphere of political discourse (Hos. 7:13; 12:1; Isa. 28:15–17; Dan. 11:27) and more specifically to describe the deceptive revelations of false prophets (Ezek.13:6–9, 19; Mic. 2:11) which often had political implications. Therefore, Hayes (1988: 103–104) understands the term in connection to Judah's political sins, while Andersen and Freedman (1989: 301–304) think it refers to false prophets. Probably the text is deliberately ambiguous. The word could be understood as a condemnation of idolatry but equally could refer to deceptive leaders and political ideologies. Speaking lies came hand in hand with political fickleness, subversion of fair judicial process and the practice of violence and oppression (Ps. 58:1–3; Prov. 6:16–19; 14:5; Zeph. 3:13). This prepares the way for 2:6–8.

### ii. Israel (2:6–16)

There is some debate as to how many sins Amos lists in verses 6–8. Hubbard (1989: 141) counts four, treating the bicola in verses 6b and 7a as synonymous descriptions of the same transgression, but it is much better to recognize seven offences (Paul 1991: 76). The first five are expressed in a single line and centre around the victim (the righteous, the needy, the poor, the afflicted, the girl; vv. 6b–7), while the last two are formulated in two lines each, beginning with the mention of a cultic place (altar/temple) before going on to focus on an object that speaks of some unjust practice (garments/wine; v. 8). The line *so that my holy name is profaned* (v. 7b) provides a bridge between the two groups of transgressions, linking the social injustice with cultic practice. A similar pattern of 5+2 can be observed in 3:3–8. Counting seven sins in verses 6b–8 means that there is a certain balance between the opening of the Israel oracle and its conclusion in verses 14–16 where seven groups of military personnel are mentioned. The number seven functions symbolically to convey the idea of perfection. The fullness of Israel's sin at the start of the oracle is matched by the completeness of the Lord's judgment at the end.

**6.** Amos directs his first accusation at the practice of debt-slavery (Hamborg 2012: 202–207), a crime that recalls the actions of the Philistines and the Phoenicians (1:6–10). People working the land usually borrowed money in order to survive periods of poor harvests, caused by drought and crop disease, or to pay exorbitant taxes imposed by royal authority (Neh. 5:1–5). The interest on such loans could be 20–30% or higher (Soggin 1987: 47). If the debtor was unable to pay back the loan, he had to sell either himself or some of his children into slavery to meet his financial obligations (Lev. 25:39, 47; Neh. 5:5). Houston (2008: 62–63) suggests the debtors were the adult male heads of nuclear families living in the cities and working as servants, craftsmen or day labourers who relied (in vain) on their patrons for support. The creditors driven by greed forced such people to sell themselves. The debtor is described as *righteous* (*ṣaddîq*), better translated here as 'innocent' (NIV; cf. 'those whose cause was just', NJPS). The term could refer to the person who is 'in the right' in the context of a court case (Deut. 25:1), but in this case the meaning is more broadly a person who is innocent of his or her inability to repay the loan. The fact that the debtors bear no responsibility for the difficult situation in which they find themselves does not provoke compassion. In the parallel line, the *needy* person is sold into slavery *for a pair of sandals*, that is, for a trivial debt. These acts do not violate any law, but they are nevertheless deeply immoral (Houston 2008: 66–67). The legal right of the creditors to receive their money back is challenged by their moral obligation to the people who are in need.

**7.** It is common to understand the next two lines as metaphorical descriptions of corruption in the courts (Wolff 1977: 166; Eidevall 2017: 114–115). Wolff argues that to *push the afflicted out of the way* means 'to pervert the course of justice'; see NIV: 'deny justice to the oppressed'. However, Paul (1991: 80–81) demonstrates that the *way* here cannot mean 'the way of justice', and the language in

Amos does not have any specific legal connotations. In fact, an almost identical expression is used quite literally in Job 24:4 in the context of physical actions of violent oppression, like unjust appropriation of land and livestock. It is best, therefore, to interpret [*they*] *trample the head of the poor into the dust of the earth / and push the afflicted out of the way* as a literal description of violence inflicted upon the poor (Hamborg 2012: 207–209). Such bullying of the weaker members of society is designed to humiliate and frighten them into submission. The reference is not to a 'comparatively harmless gesture of jostling a person on the street' (contra Jeremias 1998: 36), but to unrestrained physical aggression which, by degrading other people, symbolically establishes and reinforces social hierarchy. The use of violence to advance personal interests was at the core of the actions of the Arameans and the Ammonites (1:3–5, 13–15). The transgression of Israel again echoes the transgressions of its neighbours.

*Father and son go in to the same girl.* The verb *go* means 'have sex with' (Paul 1991: 82)[3] but the precise nature of the problem is understood differently. (1) Incest and sexual immorality. The phrase *my holy name is profaned* comes up in Leviticus 20:3 (cf. Lev. 18:21; 19:12) and suggests that the offence should be interpreted in the light of the sexual laws of Leviticus 18 – 20 (Stuart 1987: 317; Hubbard 1989: 142; Eidevall 2017: 115). These prohibit sexual relationship with the wife of one's father (Lev. 18:8; 20:11) and the wife of one's son (Lev. 18:15; 20:12). However, the *girl* here is a sexual partner, not a wife, so the levitical laws are not relevant. (2) Religious apostasy. Verse 8 talks about worship, temples and altars, and opens up the possibility that the actions in verse 7b are also religious in nature. Andersen and Freedman (1989: 318–319, 829) suggest that 'the Girl' is either the goddess mentioned in 8:14 or a cultic prostitute representing her. However, the problem in

---

3. Not all commentators agree. Barstad (1984: 33–36) argues that the people in vv. 7b–8 'go to', i.e. visit a *marzēaḥ* feast (see below, 6:1–7) and the 'girl' is simply the *marzēaḥ* hostess. Moughtin-Mumby (2011) thinks that *Naarah* ('girl') is a proper noun: the name of the village north of Jericho (Josh. 16:7; 1 Chr. 7:28) where the feast was held.

verse 8 is not religious apostasy but injustice, and there is nothing in the text of verse 7 to support the idea of cultic prostitution. (3) Oppression and exploitation. It is best to take *hanna'ărâ* ('the girl') as a 'servant-girl' (Exod. 2:5; Esth. 4:4, 16; Prov. 9:3; 31:15; cf. 2 Kgs 5:2, 4) who belongs to the household, and to interpret the situation in the light of the stipulations of Exodus 21:7–11 (Rudolph 1971: 142–143). A young woman who is sold into slavery by her father in order to cover his debts is to be protected in the new household by being married either to the head of the house or to one of his sons. Instead, the woman is married to neither but exploited sexually by both. The transgressions of the Edomites and the Ammonites (1:11–15) involved violence against women. Israel is not all that different.

The phrase *my holy name is profaned* is characteristic of priestly language and is often used to describe actions that cause ritual impurity in the context of temple worship (Lev. 21:6; 22:2, 32; Ps. 74:7; Ezek. 20:39). Amos here deploys it to characterize the sexual abuse of a female servant as an offence whose gravity is equal to the profanation of the worship of God. The striking implication is that the Lord identifies himself with the victims of oppression (cf. Jer. 34:16). The use of cultic language in connection with social abuse also highlights the structural role of verse 7b in the oracle. It forms a bridge between the injustices condemned in verses 6b–7a and the criticism of worship in verse 8.

**8.** The picture painted in this verse is that of a cultic celebration. The unnamed perpetrators *lay themselves down beside every altar* and *in the house of their God*[4] *they drink wine*. This is not a description of an orgy taking place at a pagan shrine (contra Stuart 1987: 317; Soggin 1987: 48–49), but a reference to the participation in a sacrificial meal within the context of the worship of the Lord. The problem is that the people recline *on garments taken in pledge* and drink wine *bought with fines they imposed*. It is common to interpret the first phrase with a reference to the law of Exodus 22:26–27: instead of returning it by the evening, the creditors are preparing to spend the night lying

---

4. The translation 'the house of their gods' (Barstad 1984: 15) is grammatically possible but unlikely.

upon the cloak taken in pledge beside the altar. This, however, reads a little too much into a text which mentions neither evening nor sleeping (Hayes 1988: 113). It is more likely that the garment is not given as a pledge at the time when the loan is extended but seized by force in order to guarantee payment when the debtor has defaulted on his debt (Andersen and Freedman 1989: 320; Paul 1991: 83–86). Various objects, and even people, could be taken in distraint in such situations: a hand-mill (Deut. 24:6), clothing (Deut. 24:17; Job 22:6), animals (Job 24:3) and children (Job 24:9; 2 Kgs 4:1). An ostracon found at Yavneh Yam provides an illuminating parallel (*COS* 3.41). It is a letter by a poor person (it is not clear if he is a servant, a slave or a hired harvest worker) to a royal official, complaining that his garment had been seized by a certain Hoshayahu. The practice was often abused by creditors (Ezek. 18:12, 16). The legal traditions attempt to place some restrictions on it, in order to protect vulnerable people, but do not prohibit it entirely. In contrast, Amos issues a blank condemnation of distraint on property. The legality of the action is not the issue. Seizing the garments of poor people who cannot pay their debts is immoral and unjust, and that is all that matters.

Likewise, the legality of the imposed *fines* is not the focus of the parallel bicolon. We do not know why the fines were imposed in the first place, and it doesn't really matter. The worshippers have used their legal and economic power to extract resources from those who cannot protect themselves.

This last accusation does not correspond to anything in the preceding OAN which purposefully avoid the topic of worship. It introduces a theme which is going to play a key role in what follows: worship tainted by injustice.

**9–10.** The previous verse ended with the word *their God*, and verse 9 opens with an emphatic personal pronoun, the divine *I* (*'ānōkî*), repeated in verses 10 and 13. In verses 9–10 the pronoun is grammatically superfluous, but the threefold repetition connects with 7:14 and plays an important role in the overall structuring of the book (see the above *Context*). God now speaks directly to narrate his actions against foreign nations on behalf of his people Israel. *Amorite* comes from a cognate Akkadian word meaning 'west'. Ammuru was the name of a territory in Syria, and later the word was used as a general term to designate the population of Canaan prior to Israel's arrival (Josh. 10:5–6; 2 Sam. 21:2). Here its choice is probably dictated in part by a desire to create an elaborate wordplay across the Israel oracle: *Amorite* (*'ĕmōrî*) in Hebrew sounds very close to *'āmar* (*says*), verse 6; *'āmîr* ('sheaf'), verse 13; and *'ārôm* (*naked*), verse 16. Amos stresses the power of the Amorites in order to contrast that power with their ultimate fate. They were tall as *cedars* and strong as *oaks*, yet their destruction was complete. *His fruit above, and his roots beneath* is a merism for the whole tree.

The reference to the exodus from *Egypt* and to the *wilderness* wanderings prepares the ground for another important motif in the book (3:2; 5:25; 9:7). Egypt was the 'house of slavery' from which the Lord delivered Israel when it was weak and helpless. Taken together the two foreign nations stand for those who have power (Amorites) and use it to oppress others (Egypt). This is precisely the transgression of which Israel stands accused. The recital of divine acts in history serves as a bridge between the accusation and the punishment. On the one hand, it implicitly condemns Israel for imitating the practices of foreign nations. On the other, it raises the possibility that the Lord will act against his people in defence of the poor, just as he acted against their powerful enemies.

**11–12.** The second building block of the middle section has an integrity and a structure of its own (see Introduction). The mirror structure underlines the central concern of this subsection, which is the way Israel responds to the deeds of the Lord. The law in Numbers 6:1–21 specifies that nazirites must not drink wine, cut their hair or touch a corpse for the time period of their vow, but it treats this as a voluntary and temporary state. Samson (Judg. 13:3–5) who is designated a nazirite from birth may be representative of a different version of this institution which fits better the picture in Amos (see also Samuel in 1 Sam 1:11; esp. 4QSam[a]). The *nazirites* are singled out primarily for literary reasons. Forcing them to drink *wine* (*yayin*) echoes the drinking of wine (*yayin*) financed by oppression in the house of God (v. 8). There is an ironic connection between the current sins of Israel, committed hypocritically in the presence of God, and the people's rejection of God's actions in their history.

The more important group are the *prophets*, who begin and end this unit. The command *You shall not prophesy*, better translated

'Do not prophesy' (NAB; NJB; NKJV), is the last phrase before the announcement of punishment ensues. It forms the climax simultaneously of the rehearsal of Israel's history with God and of the indictment of Israel's sin. With this transgression the people cross to the point of no return. The phrase is repeated verbatim in 7:16 (cf. NKJV) in the narrative of Amos's clash with Amaziah. It echoes and anticipates the opposition to Amos's preaching and introduces the theme of the rejection of the prophetic word as Israel's final and decisive transgression. The rhetorical question *Is it not indeed so, O people of Israel? / says the* LORD intensifies the emotional atmosphere by underlining the shift from third- (vv. 6–8) to second-person address (vv. 10–12). At the same time, it increases the suspense by providing a pause before the climactic verse 12.

After the rhetorical question two lines sum up the two steps of Israel's descent to doom. First, the drinking of wine recalls Israel's sin of injustice and violence (vv. 6–8) which will be explored in chapters 3–6. Then, the rejection of the prophets points to Israel's refusal to listen to the word of the Lord, the theme of chapters 7–9. The Israel oracle anticipates the overall shape of the book and its major themes.

**13.** Unlike the preceding OAN, there is no mention of fire devouring the walls and palaces of Samaria, nor of the king being slaughtered or going into exile. These elements appear later (5:6; 6:7; 7:4, 9, 17), strengthening the connection between the Israel oracle and the following material. Instead, the Lord threatens to do something to Israel *just as a cart . . . full of sheaves* does it. The divine action is described with the verb *'ûq* or *'îq* which appears only here with an uncertain meaning (*HALOT* 2.802; *DCH* 6.314, 368). A quick survey of modern translations and commentaries demonstrates this:

1. *I will press you down in your place, just as a cart presses down* (NRSV);
2. 'I will slow your movements as a wagon is slowed' (NJPS);
3. 'I am groaning beneath you, as a wagon groans' (NAB);
4. 'I will split open (the ground) beneath you as the cart splits (it) open' (Jeremias 1998: 33, 43);
5. 'I will make it sway under you, just like a wagon sways' (Eidevall 2017: 112, 119).

Those who go for one of the last two options think that Amos is predicting an earthquake. However, a cart loaded with grain is not the most obvious object to evoke the image of an earthquake. Moreover, the description of an army in disarray in the following verses rather suggests that a military defeat is in view. Therefore, either option 1 (NRSV) or 2 (NJPS) is to be preferred.

**14–16.** Judgment is described as a complete paralysis of the army. If we are meant to imagine a battlefield, then the paralysis is the direct result of the Lord pressing, hindering or stopping the people (v. 13), ensuring their defeat and subsequent slaughter. Seven groups of soldiers are listed in quick succession, united by their common inability to cope with the disaster. Under divine pressure human skill loses its usefulness. Such a denial of human ability to evade the coming crisis is another characteristic theme of Amos's proclamation (3:12; 5:18–20; 9:2–4, 8–10). It stems from the polemical context of the prophet's ministry and challenges his listeners' conviction that somehow they will escape judgment.

The unit is carefully crafted. The first three groups, the *swift* (*qāl*), the *strong* (*ḥāzāq*) and the *mighty* (*gibbôr*), are single words in Hebrew. The second triplet, *those who handle the bow* (*tōpēś haqqešet*), *those who are swift of foot* (*qal běraglāw*) and *those who ride horses* (*rōkēb hassûs*), are phrases with two words each. The seventh category, *those who are stout of heart among the mighty* (*'ammîṣ libbô baggibbôrîm*), is a phrase with three words. The first and the second triplet end with identical, refrain-like expression [*shall not*] *save their lives* (*lō' yěmallēṭ napšô*). Symmetry, repetition and accumulation characterize this passage and create a comprehensive picture of utter failure.

*Meaning*

The Israel oracle needs to be read in the light of the OAN (1:3 – 2:3), on the one hand, and the Judah oracle (2:4–5), on the other. The series seeks to establish a parallel between Israel and the foreign nations, so that their transgressions can be regarded as essentially similar acts of violence and oppression. The comparison is deliberately shocking. It suggests that the brutality of mass killings during a time of war belongs to the same category as giving a socially inferior person a humiliating beating, or that the kidnapping and selling into slavery of an entire village is of the same order as the perfectly legal and widespread practice of selling a person into slavery to cover debts, or indeed of taking that person's garment in distraint. Amos is trying to force his audience to change their perspective on actions commonly regarded as normal. He does so by employing a rhetorical strategy which places such actions in the same category as war crimes.

The connection with the Judah oracle strengthens the religious dimension which is already present in 2:7b–8. The prophecy elevates humane treatment of others to the level of a religious duty. Social injustice constitutes rejection of the instruction of the Lord. It soils the cult and makes true worship impossible. To practise it means following a lie. The stark juxtaposition of cultic terminology and condemnation of social abuses in 2:7 implies that the Lord is not only on the side of the weak, but actively identifies with them, so much so that his name is profaned when the defenceless are humiliated and destroyed. The Judah–Israel oracle raises the question of the identity of God's people, usually defined over against foreign groups with their own history, customs and gods. Amos blurs such boundaries by ignoring the question about the idolatrous worship of the neighbouring nations and focusing on the essential ethical similarity between their behaviour and the lifestyle of Israel. Even the peculiar history of Israel, marked by the mighty acts of the Lord in deliverance and revelation, is not enough to set them apart. The present has negated the past. Israel is defined and constituted only by true worship of God manifested in acts of justice and compassion and marked by receptiveness to the prophetic word.

# 3. A DIVINE WORD AGAINST THE PEOPLE OF ISRAEL (3:1 – 4:13)

The middle section of the book (chs. 3–6) is divided into two roughly equal parts by the two parallel calls to attention (Jeremias 1998: 47–49):

| | | | |
|---|---|---|---|
| 3:1 | *Hear this word* | *that the LORD has spoken against you,* | *O people of Israel* |
| 5:1 | *Hear this word* | *that I take up over you in lamentation,* | *O house of Israel* |

The addressees in 3:1 are the *people* [lit. 'sons'] *of Israel* (*běnê yiśrā'ēl*), a phrase that appears in chapters 3–4 (3:12; 4:5) but not in chapters 5–6. Conversely, the addressees in 5:1 are the *house of Israel* (*bêt yiśrā'ēl*), a phrase that comes up exclusively in chapters 5–6 (5:3, 4, 25; 6:1, 14). Such a careful distribution of terms can hardly be a coincidence and betrays the desire of the final editors to structure the material in two big speeches.

The speech in chapters 3–4 picks up a number of motifs and themes from the first two chapters: Egypt and the exodus (3:1,

9 = 2:10); the *roar* of the lion (3:4, 8 = 1:2); disaster announced by a *trumpet* (3:6 = 2:2); prophesying (3:7–8 = 2:11–12); *strongholds* (*'armenôt*) (3:9–11 = seven times in the OAN); *transgressions* (*piš'ê*, 3:14 = eight times in the OAN); oppression of the poor (3:9–10 = 2:6–8); *poor* and *needy* (4:1 = 2:6b–7a); drinking (4:1 = 2:8, 12); *altar* (3:14 = 2:8). At the same time, the oracles in chapter 3 have a clearly recognizable polemical flavour. In the light of the links to chapters 1–2 the reader has to imagine that after Amos's speech the audience raised objections to his proclamation of disaster, and the oracles in chapter 3 are the prophet's response to these objections. This is not to suggest that the current text is an actual transcript of a real-life event. It is a literary presentation of the types of debates Amos must have been involved in throughout his ministry.

## A. The lion has roared: fear for your lives (3:1–8)

*Context*
Amos's listeners could not square the message of impending disaster with their understanding of divine election which meant, in their view, that they were entitled to God's help and protection. The prophet addresses this objection in 3:2. Relationship with the Lord does not make one immune to the consequences of one's own transgressions but, on the contrary, implies a higher level of moral responsibility. We must imagine an acrimonious exchange as a result of that argument, leading to the command, addressed to Amos: *Do not prophesy* (2:12; 7:16). The rhetorical questions respond to that prohibition. Amos asserts that he has no choice but to prophesy and his audience would be foolish not to be gripped by fear.

*Comment*
  **1–2.** Strictly speaking the word *family* (*mišpāḥâ*) means a 'clan', a subdivision of the tribe. It is used loosely to refer to the whole nation of Israel (v. 1) and then to all the other nations of the world (v. 2). The choice of term is probably deliberate and stresses the commonality between Israel and the other nations. The family of Israel is part of the *families of the earth*. Its election is to be understood against the background of that commonality.

The fact that the Lord has *brought up* Israel *out of the land of Egypt* means that he has *known* them ('singled out', NJPS), that is, chosen them in order to have a relationship with them. On a first reading Amos's words sound odd. God is going to punish Israel because he has chosen it?! Such a provocative statement makes sense only within the context of a debate. It implies that an objection to Amos's proclamation of disaster (2:6–16) has been raised: the Lord cannot punish Israel so severely because the exodus from Egypt implies that God is on Israel's side and is committed to helping and supporting it. Amos counters the objection by pointing out that divine election is not a licence to immoral behaviour. On the contrary, it requires a higher moral standard. For this reason, Israel's perfectly legal exploitation of the socially weak members of society is as horrendous in the eyes of the Lord as the military atrocities of its neighbours.

**3–6.** On purely formal grounds the nine rhetorical questions in verses 3–8 can be divided into three groups: five (vv. 3–5) begin in Hebrew with the interrogative particle *hă*; the next two (v. 6) with the particle *'im* ('if'); and the last two (v. 8) have a statement in the first line followed by the interrogative pronoun *who* (*mî*) in the second (the literary design is apparent in the NIV but not in most other EVV). In terms of content a slightly different pattern emerges. All questions, except the very first one (v. 3), come in pairs that revolve around a central motif: lions (v. 4); birds/snares (v. 5); a city (v. 6). This forces the reader to see the last two questions as a pair as well in which Lord/lion and fear/prophesy stand parallel to each other (see Table 6 on p. 119).

The rhetorical effect of these patterns is twofold. On the one hand, it highlights the role of verse 3 as an introduction and verse 6 as a conclusion to 3:3–6. On the other hand, the literary pattern presents verse 8, which differs both thematically and formally from the rest, as the climax of the whole. Verse 7, a statement not a question, clearly stands outside this arrangement. By delaying the arrival of the culmination in verse 8, it frustrates the expectations of the reader/listener, increases the suspense and in this way contributes to the climactic role of the last pair of questions.

The translation *Do two walk together / unless they have made an appointment?* is problematic. The context requires that all questions

Table 6 Literary structures in 3:3–8

|       | Content | Form (see NIV) |
|-------|---------|----------------|
| v. 3  | 1 Two people walking | Does (something happen) unless/when (something else happens/has happened)? |
| v. 4  | 2 Lion | |
| v. 5  | 3 Lion | |
|       | 4 Bird/snare | |
| v. 6  | 5 Snare/(bird) | When (something happens) will not/has not (something else happen/happened)? |
|       | 6 Trumpet in city/fear | |
|       | 7 Disaster in city/the Lord | |
| v. 8  | 8 Lion/fear | Something has happened |
|       | 9 Lord/prophesy | Who will not (do something)? |

must elicit a clear positive response, yet it is a fact of life that people can walk together without necessarily having made arrangements to do so – for example, when they meet by chance (Paul 1991: 109–110). For this reason, NJPS renders it: 'Can two walk together without having met?' However, what is the point of such a banal statement? Some commentators interpret it allegorically as an allusion to 3:2 which pictures the initial harmonious relationship between the Lord and Israel as two people walking together (Hayes 1988: 124; Eidevall 2017: 125). Others suggest that the verse deals not with people walking together but more generally with things that go together – in other words, it is a propositional statement about the link between cause and effect which governs the whole series (Andersen and Freedman 1989: 388; Jeremias 1998: 52; Sweeney 2000: 221). It is better to regard the opening rhetorical question not primarily as an introduction to a logical argument about cause and effect, but as painting the first brush of an impressionistic picture. Amos portrays a mundane, uneventful scene of two people who have met and now walk together.

The peacefulness of the scene is suddenly disturbed by the roar of a lion in a nearby forest. Lions roar when they are hungry or when eating, not while they hunt, so the threat is not imminent (Strawn 2016: 101). Still the roar creates a sense of danger, evokes fear and reminds the reader of the Lord's roar against the Northern Kingdom (1:2). The emotional intensity is alleviated by the picture of bird-hunting in the following verse (v. 5). The sense of danger is less acute, but the overall atmosphere of death and destruction still remains. The focus now moves from the terrifying awesomeness of the predator (lion) to the helplessness of the prey (birds). The *snare* which *spring[s] up from the ground* introduces the additional idea of disaster that is sudden and unexpected. The main point of the trap is that the victim is unsuspecting to the very last minute, just like the people of Israel who believe that no evil will befall them. The parallel between the bird which *fall [s]* (*npl*) as a snare springs from the ground (*'ădāmâ*) and the virgin Israel who has *fallen* (*npl*) on her *land*/ground (*'ădāmâ*) in 5:2 underlines even more strongly the point for the reader of the book (Fleischer 2001: 168). The 'falling' to the *earth* (*'ereṣ*) in 3:5a also anticipates the 'falling' of the horns of Bethel's altar to the *ground*/earth (*'ereṣ*) in 3:14.

With verse 6 we are moving away from the animal kingdom into the human realm and so closer to the main concern of the passage. The picture now is one of a besieged city. The two questions focus on two different temporal points and two different aspects of the event. The first takes us to the start of the siege when the blowing of the *trumpet* warns the inhabitants of the impending danger; it looks at the effect the alarm has on the people: mass panic. The second rhetorical question focuses on the aftermath of the *disaster* and explores its cause: the Lord.

**7.** The prosaic statement interprets verse 6a allegorically. Because the *Lord GOD does nothing, / without revealing his secret / to his servants the prophets*, Amos's preaching must be understood as equivalent to the trumpet sound. It warns people of what the Lord is going to do, namely, bring disaster on the city. The word *secret* (*sôd*) can mean 'a confidential discussion' (Gen. 49:6), the 'council' or 'gathering' (Job 19:19; Ps. 89:7; Jer. 6:11) where it takes place, and the 'plans' (Ps. 83:3) or 'secrets' (Prov. 20:19; 25:9) discussed there (*HALOT* 2.745). According to Jeremiah (23:18, 22), the true prophets stood in the 'council' of the Lord and were privy to its secret deliberations (1 Kgs 22:19–23). The claim of 3:7 is that Amos's words are a public proclamation of the hitherto secret decisions of the divine council as to how the Lord will deal with Israel.

**8.** The opening lines of the two questions, *The lion has roared* and *The Lord GOD has spoken*, are synonymous descriptions of the one same event. God's speech is like a lion's *roar* (1:2), and lions in Amos's day were closely associated with the divine (Strawn 2016: 95–98, 109). The following lines describe the necessary reactions of different groups to this event: Amos/the prophets and his audience. The roar of a hungry lion means that he will eventually start hunting and no-one will be safe. The only natural reaction to this is *fear*. On the other hand, the only possible reaction on the part of Amos is to prophesy what he has heard. The rhetorical questions defend his prophetic activity in the face of a challenge from the audience which believes that he should not preach disaster to them (Möller 2003: 232–233). The passage cannot be understood apart from 2:12, whose meaning is in turn illuminated by the narrative of 7:10–17. Amos's scandalous proclamation of judgment evoked a strong reaction of resentment: 'the land [was] not able to bear all his words' (7:10). This led to arguments and objections to the prophetic proclamation based on the theology of the exodus.

*Meaning*
The series of rhetorical questions is Amos's response to a prohibition against prophesying. They are not an argument designed logically to defend his authority but a forceful assertion in the face of rejection. Amos stubbornly declares that he will continue to speak because he must. In addition, he implies that his speech ought to inspire dread in the hearts of his audience. There is an unspoken accusation of ridiculous foolishness here. To ignore the prophetic threat is as absurd as being faced with a lion and calmly continuing your leisurely stroll.

Is this passage a call to repentance or a proclamation of judgment? In other words, is Amos like the trumpet of verse 6, which warns people to hide behind the city walls and escape the danger? Or is the disaster about to befall the city now inevitable and all the trumpet blast does is to underscore that bitter inevitability? The passage meant both of those things in different historical periods. It is likely that in the initial stages of Amos's proclamation the main goal was to persuade the audience and bring it to repentance. As the opposition hardened and especially after the disaster became a reality, the prophetic word served as a witness against Israel's unrepentant spirit and an explanation for its doom. God's mercy is manifest in the fact that through the prophetic ministry the 'secret' of divine judgment is out in the open, and people can do something about it if they have the good sense to respond appropriately.

## B. Israel's transgressions on Mount Samaria and at the Bethel altar (3:9 – 4:3)

*Context*

This passage consists of four originally separate oracles (3:9–11; 3:12; 3:13–15; 4:1–3) with their own structure and introductory and concluding formulas. In their present arrangement the oracles are placed together as the integral parts of a larger composition which revolves around the theme of judgment of Samaria, the capital of the Northern Kingdom, and Bethel, the main royal sanctuary. The phrase *Mount Samaria* (3:9; 4:1) appears at the beginning and the end, and frames the whole section, while Bethel comes up in the middle (3:14). The overall structure is determined by three calls to *Proclaim* (3:9) or *Hear* (3:13; 4:1) that all use the same verb *šāmaʿ* in the Hiphil (3:9) and Qal (3:13; 4:1) masculine imperative plural.

1   Proclaim (*šmʿ*) on Mount Samaria
   (a)  The sin of oppression (3:9–10)
   (b)  The punishment of military invasion (3:10–11)
    2  Hear (*šmʿ*) the impending punishment of Bethel –
      invasion/earthquake? (3:13–15)
3  Hear (*šmʿ*) on Mount Samaria
   (a)  The sin of oppression (4:1)
   (b)  The punishment of military invasion (4:2–3)

*Comment*

**9–10.** The proclamation is initially addressed to the *strongholds* of the *land of Egypt* and the Philistine city of *Ashdod* who are called to come and witness Samaria's transgressions. The idea is, on the one hand, to humiliate the people of God by exposing their shameful deeds to outsiders and, on the other, to suggest that their sins are so great that even sinful foreigners would be appalled if they learned of them. The specific sins mentioned are the *great tumults,* *oppressions*, not knowing *how to do right*, and *violence and robbery*. Egypt is chosen presumably because it was the prime oppressor from which Israel was delivered (2:10; 3:1–2) but which it now imitates. The choice of *Ashdod* is surprising. LXX translates here 'the regions among the Assyrians', but this is unlikely to reflect the original since Amos never mentions Assyria in his preaching and Ashdod is the harder reading. It is more probable that Ashdod represents all the Philistines who were a major foe in earlier times and continued to be a significant competitor to the kingdoms of Israel and Judah throughout their history.

**11–12.** The punishment is military conquest described in two phases, each introduced with the formula *thus says the Lord GOD/ LORD*. The description is general and even the *adversary* remains anonymous. Historically, this may reflect a time when it was not yet clear who that adversary might be. Rhetorically, the anonymity shifts the attention from the earthly power that executes judgment to the divine will which stands behind the event. Hermeneutically, it allows the verse to be applied to later circumstances (i.e. the events of 587 BC). The ironic recurrence of the *strongholds*, both as the storehouses of goods gained by oppression and as the target of enemy plunder, shows that the judgment of Israel is intrinsically linked to its sin.

In the wake of the invasion there will be no hope of rescue. Verse 12 is another polemical statement which addresses the scepticism of Amos's audience (Möller 2003: 243). More specifically, it tackles the conviction that even in the face of a disaster they will be rescued by God, a conviction that seems to stand in the background of several sayings (5:18–20; 9:1–4, 8–10). Amos counters such confidence by ridiculing it. He alludes to the custom requiring a shepherd to produce the remains of an animal placed in his care when that animal had been allegedly killed by a predator (Exod. 22:13). The point of the custom was to demonstrate to the owner that an attack had indeed occurred and the shepherd had not disposed fraudulently of the animal. So, at first, Amos agrees with his listeners' expectations; yes, there will be a rescue. He then ironically subverts those expectations and renders them meaningless. The rescue will be as painful and pointless as the survival of a few scraps from a sheep's body. The meagre deliverance from judgment will serve only as further proof and a reminder of the totality and finality of that judgment.

The second part of the verse is extremely difficult to translate. Two modern versions render it as follows:

| NRSV | *so shall the people of Israel who live in Samaria be rescued,* | *with the corner of a couch and part of a bed* |
| NJB | so will the children of Israel be salvaged who now **loll** in Samaria | **in** the corners of their beds, on their **divans of Damascus** |

The problems are caused by the fact that (1) the participle *hayyōšĕbîm* can mean both 'dwelling' and 'sitting' ('loll', NJB); (2) the preposition *beth* in the second part can mean 'with' (NRSV), 'in' (NJB) or 'like' (*beth essentiae*); (3) the meaning of the penultimate word *bidmešeq* is unclear. That word is usually either interpreted as a reference to some part of the furniture (NRSV) or as 'a piece of fabric [from a couch]' (NIV), or is emended to 'Damascus' (NJB). The best solution to this problem was proposed by Rabinowitz, who divided the consonants into *bd mšq* and translated 'piece of a leg [of a bed]' (Hadjiev 2008: 658–662). Ancient beds were often decorated with lion-shaped feet which were intended to ward off evil (Strawn 2016: 102–105). After the lion's attack (3:4–6) the inhabitants of Samaria escape only with, or like, a piece of a (lion-shaped) leg of a couch. There is bitter irony in this. The protective power of their lions is futile when the Lord roars (3:8).

The verse paints a pathetic picture of the future deliverance of Israel. They will be saved either *like* the pieces of broken furniture, or only *with* pieces of broken furniture – in other words, this is all they will be able to salvage from the wreckage. In the original context of Amos's disputation with his audience the reference to the pieces of the bed was likely intended as a metaphorical description of Israel. After the 'rescue' the people will be like the two legs of a sheep, or a part of the leg of a couch. In the present literary context, which talks about the plunder of the strongholds (3:11) and destruction of luxurious houses (3:15), the references to furniture can also be taken literally: this is all that is going to be left of Israel's vast wealth (Hadjiev 2008: 662–664).

**13–14.** The central section moves geographically from Samaria to *Bethel*, and so thematically from condemnation of oppression to criticism of the cult, symbolized by the *altar* desecrated in the cutting off of its *horns*. The close connection between these two themes continues the line of 2:6–8. The key to interpreting the verses lies in understanding the precise nuance of the opening imperatives *Hear, and testify*. The verb *hāʿîdû* can mean to (1) 'bear witness'; (2) 'call someone as a witness'; or (3) 'warn, admonish, exhort' (*DCH* 6.287–288). The ambiguity of its meaning allows it to be read differently in different historical circumstances. Originally, Amos called an unnamed group of people, perhaps the imaginary envoys of 3:9, to hear his message and *testify* (Deut. 8:19; 32:46; cf. 1 Kgs 21:10, 13) against the house of Jacob, justifying the impending destruction. The fictional call serves a polemical function within the context of the prophet's debate with his audience. Later Judean readers could perceive more clearly another layer of meaning. The prophet was also trying to 'warn' (NJPS; cf. Exod. 19:21, 23; 2 Kgs 17:13, 15) the *house of Jacob*, and by extension, later generations as well. Heeding the prophetic testimony and amending one's ways is the only alternative to judgment.

**15.** The cutting off of the altar's horns in verse 14 parallels the *tear[ing] down* of the houses of Israel's leaders. The fourfold occurrence of the word *house* (*bayit*) is a play on the name *bêt ʾēl*, designed to explain what is wrong with the altar of *Bethel*, the 'house of God'. The luxury of the nation's elite has tainted its worship. The words of Amos are often understood as a general criticism of the rich who had two residences, one in the cooler hill country of Samaria for the summer and another in the warmer and drier Jordan (or Jezreel) Valley for the winter (Sweeney 2000: 224). However, it is possible that a more specific target is in view here, namely, the royal house. As far as we can tell from our sources it was mainly kings (Jehoiakim, Jer. 36:22; Ahab, 1 Kgs 21:1, 18; Bar-rakib, *COS* 2.38; Cyrus, Xenophon, *Cyropaedia* VIII 6:22) who possessed a *winter house* and a *summer house*. On the link between the *houses of ivory* and the royal acropolis in Samaria, see the Introduction. And, of course, Bethel itself was a royal sanctuary (Amos 7:13). Amos does not refer directly to the king, probably because it was politically dangerous to do so (2 Chr. 24:20–22; Jer. 26:21–23), but the overall impression is that the spiritual problem of Bethel can be traced to its association with the royal power of Samaria.

**4:1.** The third call to listen is addressed to the *cows of Bashan*. Since both the noun *cows* and the following Hebrew participles *oppress, crush* and *say* are feminine plural, scholars are generally agreed that Amos here addresses the aristocratic women of Samaria.[1] The bovine metaphor should not be read through modern spectacles and seen as an insult. Just like the comparison of the beloved to a 'mare' in Song of Solomon 1:9, it is intended, at least initially, to be seen in a positive light (Eidevall 2017: 138). The suckling cow is a widespread motif in Ancient Near Eastern iconography, associated with blessing and prosperity. The region of Bashan was renowned for its fertility, its bulls were especially strong and frightening (Ps. 22:12) and its cows well fed. The phrase is an apt image for the rich and powerful women of Israel's capital, living in luxury and ease.

Since the Bethel cult included the worship of the calf image, condemned by Hosea (8:5–6; 10:5–6) and Kings ('the sin of Jeroboam'), some commentators see in the cow imagery of Amos similar religious significance: an allusion to, or perhaps even a criticism of, the bull worship practised by Israel (Barstad 1984: 41–44; McLaughlin 2001: 115–116). This, however, is to read too much into the text. There is little direct evidence to support the understanding of the phrase as a cultic title linked to bull worship. Rather, the problem is the same as in 2:6b–7a: oppression of the *poor* and the *needy*.

---

1. That the addressees are female is confirmed beyond any doubt by the announcement of judgment in v. 3 which uses two feminine verbs as well as the noun *'iššâ* ('[each] woman'; usually rendered *each one*). The picture is complicated by the presence of a masculine plural imperative in 4:1 and three masculine plural suffixes in vv. 1–2. Because of that some argue that not just the women but the entire population of Samaria is addressed (Barstad 1984: 37–40; Nwaoru 2009: 464–465, 469), or even that *cows* is a derogatory description of men (Nogalski 2011: 299–301). However, the mixture of masculine and feminine forms when referring to feminine nouns is not entirely anomalous in Hebrew and can be explained grammatically; cf. GKC 135o, 144a; Hadjiev 2009: 146–147.

The third injunction, *who say to their husbands, 'Bring something to drink!'*, is less clear. Most scholars understand the reference as a synecdoche for lavish parties or, more generally, for a lavish lifestyle whose demands fuel exploitation. In support it may be noted that the motif of drinking wine is linked elsewhere to unjust practices (2:8) and a life of extravagant luxury (6:6). However, the causal connection between drinking wine and exploitation seems tortuous. The use of the word *'ăḏōnêhem* ('their lords/masters') to designate the women's *husbands* is slightly unusual and holds the key to interpretation. In the patriarchal society of ancient Israel, the husband was considered to be the 'lord' of his wife. Thus, the women's command to their lords to perform an action appropriate for a servant breaks the established gender hierarchy (Irwin 2012). This subversion of social norms places the men in a humiliating position and is consequently unacceptable. Amos is saying that injustice is as scandalous as a woman disrespecting her male superior. The modern reader would find it difficult to appreciate the shocking nature of the connection, since in our culture men are no longer the 'masters of their women' and the picture of a woman giving orders to a man is not instinctively regarded as outrageous. This is a good example of how deeply the prophetic word is embedded in the culture of its day.

**2–3.** The practice of oppression (3:9–10) leads to judgment in the form of military defeat (3:11–12). The details of the picture are uncertain because the Hebrew is difficult to translate.[2] Consequently,

---

2. There are several textual problems here (Paul 1991: 130–133). First, the instruments with which the women will be taken away can be translated *ṣinnôt*, as (1) hooks, (2) shields, (3) ropes or (4) baskets (*DCH* 7.134–135); and *sîrôt dûḡâ* as (1) fish-pots, (2) fishhooks or (3) harpoons (*DCH* 6.149–150). Second, *you shall be flung out* in v. 3 is active in MT ('you will throw'), but since this makes little sense most follow the cue of the LXX and repoint to Hophal (*BHS*). Third, the identification of the place to which the women will be thrown is unclear. Many emend the MT to 'Hermon' (the highest peak of the Anti-Lebanon range to the north) or, more radically, to 'the refuse heap' (NJPS). Alternatively, one can preserve the MT and interpret *Harmon* as an unidentified destination which Amos deliberately uses to achieve a sense of mystery and uncertainty (Nwaoru 2009: 463–464).

it is unclear whether these verses continue the metaphor from verse 1 and depict the cows being dragged and/or mercilessly prodded on their way to exile (Rudolph 1971: 168), or we have an entirely different metaphor here of fishing (Nwaoru 2009: 467–468) or carrying away the already caught fish (Paul 1991: 134–135). The reality behind the metaphor is also disputed. Amos may be referring to the deportation of Samaria's women, led like cattle with rings and hooks through their noses (Soggin 1987: 68; Eidevall 2017: 139), or to the disposal of their corpses, flung onto the garbage heap outside the city once the siege is over (Hayes 1988: 140–142). The main point, however, is clear enough. The opulence paid for by exploiting the poor will end in devastation, exile and death. The contrast between the abundance of food and drink, implied by verse 1, and the gruesomeness of the picture in verses 2–3 could not be starker.

*Meaning*
This section is a detailed exposition of the main point established in the Israel oracle (2:6–16). The social injustice practised by the leading circles in the capital of Samaria will inevitably lead to a military defeat. The luxury of the ruling class financed by this injustice comes more sharply into focus (3:15). There is also a growing sense of confrontation and debate between the prophet and his audience (3:12), following on from 3:1–8. The brief mention of the altar of Bethel (3:14) at the very centre of a passage dealing predominantly with Samaria highlights another central concern of the book: the indissoluble link between the abuse of royal power and the tainted religious worship.

## C. Israel's transgressions in Bethel: lack of repentance (4:4–13)

*Context*
With 4:4 the theme changes from condemnation of royal oppression to criticism of Israel's worship. There is a corresponding change of location from Samaria (3:9; 4:1) to Bethel and Gilgal (4:4), anticipated already by the mention of the Bethel altar in 3:14 and more broadly by the critical remarks of 2:8. The unit consists of three different sections:

1. Call to worship at Bethel and Gilgal (4:4–5)
2. Rebuke of Israel's lack of repentance (4:6–12)
3. Praise of God the Creator (4:13)

The three sections are tightly interconnected. Verses 4–5a contain seven imperative verbs.[3] The section is organized into seven lines: six cola with three words each (vv. 4–5a) and a final longer colon in verse 5b. This is followed in verses 6–11 by a narrative of seven plagues: famine (v. 6), drought (vv. 7–8), crop diseases (v. 9a), locusts (v. 9b), pestilence (v. 10a), sword (v. 10b) and overthrow like that of Sodom and Gomorrah (v. 11). These plagues are organized into five strophes with the help of the fivefold recurring refrain *yet you did not return to me, / says the LORD*, culminating in the call to prepare to meet God in verse 12. A five-line hymn follows in verse 13, with five participles describing the actions of the Lord. It reaches a climax with the declaration *the LORD, the God of hosts, is his name!* The theme of meeting God is implicit in the references to sacrificial worship in verses 4–5 and becomes explicit in the call of verse 12. The ironic use of cultic language and motifs permeates the whole passage.

The movement from committing transgressions (vv. 4–5 = 2:6–8), to failure to respond appropriately to the Lord's actions (vv. 6–11 = 2:9–12), to manifestation of God's power in judgment (vv. 12–13 = 2:13–16) follows the patterns of the Israel oracle in 2:6–16. The direct address *for so you love to do, O people* [lit. 'sons'] *of Israel! / says the Lord GOD* echoes the language and style of the rhetorical question in 2:11b. The section is a satirical imitation of a liturgy in which a priestly call to worship (vv. 4–5) was followed by recitation of salvation history (vv. 6–11) culminating in invitation to meet God (v. 12) and praise his name (v. 13) (Paas 2003: 304).

## Comment

**4–5.** It is impossible to understand these verses without a proper appreciation of their literary form. Amos presents us here with a

---

3. Strictly speaking, one of those verbs, *qaṭṭēr* ('bring [thank-offering]'), is a Piel infinitive absolute functioning as imperative (cf. GKC 113*bb*).

parody of a priestly instruction (Lev. 19:5–8; Deut. 14:21a) or a
priestly call to pilgrimage (Pss 95:1–5; 100:1–5) in which an instruction to perform, or abstain from, a certain action is followed by a
motivation introduced by *kî* ('because') (Rudolph 1971: 175; Wolff
1977: 211; Jeremias 1998: 67–68). The irony is that Amos calls the
Israelites not to worship the Lord or follow his law, but to *Come . . .
and transgress . . . and multiply transgression*. And this is supported not
by a theological statement about the greatness of God but by a
proclamation of the idolatrous self-centredness of the people: *for so
you love to do*. The parody is designed to shock; it betrays a polemical
situation similar to 3:1–12.

The translation *bring your sacrifices every morning* and *tithes every three
days* ('three years', NIV) interprets the words of the prophet as an
ironically exaggerated demand designed to mock the religious zeal
of his audience. However, it is better to translate 'present your
sacrifices the next morning and your tithes on the third day' (NJPS)
and assume that Amos is simply referring to the structure of the
festival celebration. The worshippers arrive at the sanctuary on
the first day and present their sacrifices on the following morning
and the tithes on the third day of the festivities. Giving tithes
at Bethel must have been a popular custom based on the Jacob
tradition (Gen. 28:22). Two specific sacrifices are mentioned: the
*thank-offering* and the *freewill-offering*, both subtypes of the offering of
well-being (peace/fellowship offering) (Lev. 7:11–18). This sacrifice
was partly consumed by the worshippers at the sanctuary in
celebration and enactment of their communion with the Lord and
the blessings that flowed from it. *Leavened bread* was not to be burned
at the altar (Lev. 2:11) but cakes of unleavened bread accompanied
the offering of thanksgiving (Lev. 7:13). Amos does not mention sin
and guilt offerings but it is methodologically problematic to read
into this silence an implied criticism of Israel's lack of awareness of
their sins. The focus, rather, is on the people revelling in their relationship with the Lord, the source of their joy, prosperity and
assurance. It goes without saying that the poor and the oppressed
did not possess the resources to participate in these sacrificial
rituals.

**6–9.** Here Amos combines features of two different genres: the
treaty curse and the historical recital. Lists of curses serving as

punishments for transgressions and covenant violations were common in the Ancient Near East, but they were usually conditional and looked to the future. In contrast, Amos sees the curses as operative in Israel's past (Paul 1991: 142–143) and uses them as an interpretative tool to glean the spiritual significance of recent history. In doing so he creates another parody, this time of the historical recital of the saving actions of God common in cultic songs (Paas 2003: 260).

The first three strophes of the recital deal with economic disasters. The series opens with a general reference to famine, described with the memorable phrase *cleanness of teeth*. The word *niqqāyôn* and its derivatives are mainly associated with the ideas of purity in the sense of freedom from guilt, obligation and punishment (*NIDOTTE* 3.152–154). In this case, Israelite purity ironically consists of freedom from food, not from guilt. The contrast between the hunger of the people and the locust that *devoured* their *fig* and *olive trees* adds another ironic touch. The second and third strophes portray various calamities that could be responsible for the *lack of bread*: drought (vv. 7–8), crop diseases (v. 9a), locust infestations (v. 9b). The repetitive style of this section powerfully conveys the magnitude of the disasters: *city/town* ('*îr*; x5), *rain* (*mṭr*; x4; and *gešem*; x1), *one/another* ('*aḥat*; x4), *field* (x2); *all your cities/all your places*; *your gardens/your vineyards*; *your fig trees/your olive trees.*

**10.** The fourth strophe depicts an unspecified military defeat: the soldiers are *killed . . . with the sword* and the *horses* of the army are captured and *carried away*. The accompanying *pestilence* either preceded the battle and contributed to its outcome or followed in its wake. In any case the death toll was so high that the corpses were left unburied until the *stench* of the decaying bodies in the *camp* could be perceived everywhere. The key phrase here is *after the manner of Egypt* (Isa. 10:24, 26). If we translate *derek* with its most common meaning 'on the way [of Egypt]', the expression could refer to a disaster that overtook the Israelite army travelling on the road to Egypt (Andersen and Freedman 1989: 443). Alternatively, an Egyptian plague (Deut. 28:27, 60) may simply mean an especially severe plague; Egypt apparently had a reputation in this regard (Hayes 1988: 147). A more pregnant theological statement is assumed by the NIV's rendering:

> I sent plagues among you
> > as I did to Egypt.

In another shocking reversal of the exodus tradition, Amos suggests that Israel has now assumed the role of Egypt in the plague narrative as the object of the Lord's punitive actions (Sweeney 2000: 229; Eidevall 2017: 147). The reversal of tradition fits well with Amos's polemical situation (see 9:7–10 below).

**11.** The event in which God *overthrew some* of the Israelites could be a major military setback: a defeat at the hands of the Arameans, the Assyrian invasion of 733 BC, or even the end of the Northern Kingdom in 722 BC. However, the comparison with the overthrow of *Sodom and Gomorrah* suggests a natural disaster, most likely an earthquake. Its magnitude is conveyed by hyperbolically depicting the survivors as *a brand snatched from the fire*. There is no need to read this image too literally as implying a very small number of survivors. Rather the emphasis is on the partial devastation which nevertheless proved to be extremely painful (Hadjiev 2009: 152–155). The general proverbial expression, however, allows for reapplication to later events, like the destruction of Jerusalem (see *Meaning* below).

**12.** The conclusion of the historical recital shifts the focus to the future. The Lord threatens twice to *do* something to *Israel*, but what exactly he is going to do remains unclear. There are three possibilities. (1) *Thus* and *this* may point to something outside the text, either an object that illustrates destruction or a dramatic, threatening gesture (Wolff 1977: 222; Hubbard 1989: 161–162; Paul 1991: 150). The problem with this unfalsifiable interpretation is that it treats the text as an exclusively oral phenomenon which is incomprehensible outside the limited situation of its original delivery. (2) The demonstrative pronouns may refer backwards to verses 6–11 and imply that the Lord is going to repeat on a grander scale the curses, especially the last one in verse 11 (Andersen and Freedman 1989: 450; Jeremias 1998: 74–75). This is possible but it does not achieve the sense of climax towards which the section is moving. (3) It is best to take *thus* as pointing forward, to the future encounter with God mentioned at the end of verse 12 (Rudolph 1971: 181). In contrast to the preceding partial punishments, this is going to be a final and complete judgment.

The call *prepare to meet your God* has a double meaning. On the one hand, both verbs appear in the Sinai account where Israel 'prepares' (Exod. 19:11, 15) to 'meet God' (Exod. 19:17) and receive the law. The phrase could have had liturgical significance within the Bethel cult. The three-day festival celebration, implied by 4:4–5, may have been patterned on the three-day preparation in Exodus 19:11, 15. On the other hand, the two verbs can be used in an adversarial sense to mean 'prepare' (Ezek. 38:7) to 'meet' (1 Sam. 17:48) someone in battle. This is the primary sense here. In the polemical context of his clash with his audience Amos exploits the linguistic possibilities inherent in this phrase and converts an invitation to enter God's presence into a threat of judgment.

**13.** This is the first of the three 'hymnic fragments' in the book of Amos (5:8–9; 9:5–6) which are united by their common use of participles to describe God, the shared theme of creation and the recurring cultic formula *the Lord . . . is his name*. The hymn paints an awesome and terrifying picture of the God whom Israel is about to meet (v. 12). The five participles correspond to the five occurrences of the refrain *you did not return to me*. The power of the Lord is demonstrated first and foremost in acts of creation. He is *the one who forms* the solid, immovable *mountains*, as well as the fleeting *wind*. Both stability and dynamic motion emanate from him. He has complete control over Israel's universe. The third participial phrase, which occupies the centre, could be translated 'declares to mortals their thoughts' (NAB); in other words, he brings to the surface the hidden plans and desires of human beings. Most scholars, however, prefer *reveals his thoughts to mortals* – that is, God not only controls the created world but communicates with humanity (3:7). *Makes the morning darkness* is unsettling. Whether it refers to a solar eclipse (Paas 2003: 277) or to clouds and smoke hiding the morning sun (Hubbard 1989: 162) the phrase does not depict the normal rhythm of day and night and carries ominous overtones. *Treads on the heights of the earth* (Job 9:8; Mic. 1:3) depicts a divine march and the subjection of the earth to the authority of its creator. The hymnic conclusion evokes a sense of awe with its picture of unstoppable divine power.

## Meaning

The cult offered worshippers a sense of security and so prevented them from taking the prophet's message of judgment seriously enough. Amos's cultic criticism is designed to shake Israel out of their complacency and clear the way for his proclamation.

A situation of joyful celebration is implied as the background of verses 4–5. Amos challenges this jubilation in the present by looking first at the recent past (vv. 6–11) and then at the future (vv. 12–13). A series of natural disasters and military setbacks represent God's persistent attempts to bring his people to their senses. The fivefold recurrence of the refrain *yet you did not return to me* hammers the main point of the historical recital. Israel has experienced the consequences of divine displeasure but has failed to perceive the implicit call to repentance hidden within the string of catastrophes. Therefore, as a measure of last resort Israel is threatened with a final personal encounter with the maker of the world who has the capacity to plunge his creation into chaos. As the Lord appears on the horizon, the morning of Israel's thoughtless festivities will drown into darkness.

In listing a series of catastrophes from the recent past, Amos relies on what is sometimes called 'communicative memory', that is, living memories that span no more than three or four generations in the experience of his audience. The general way events are evoked allows subsequent generations of readers to substitute the original disasters with their own experiences and thus to reapply the prophetic words to themselves (Williamson 2016: 138–141). This became especially important to the people who survived the tragic events of 722 and 587 BC. For them the 'overthrow' like that of *Sodom and Gomorrah* (v. 11) probably evoked the capture of Samaria or the destruction of Jerusalem. Consequently, the threat of verse 12 would have felt like a past experience synonymous with the overthrow, not something still to come in the future. The Assyrian and Babylonian exile would have healed them from the unbelief of the original audience. In this situation the passage suddenly acquires a radically different meaning. The polemical and satirical dimensions of the text recede into the background. The call to *prepare to meet your God* can revert to its original sense. It can be heard as an invitation to redeem the mistakes of the past, return to the Lord and repeat the Sinai experience (Jeremias 1998: 75). The hymnic conclusion, rather than underlining a threat, now contains an implicit promise. The God who can revert creation to chaos can also defeat chaos and re-establish order and harmony in the lives of his people.

# 4. A PROPHETIC WORD AGAINST THE HOUSE OF ISRAEL (5:1 – 6:14)

The divine speech addressed to the 'sons of Israel' in the preceding chapters is now followed by a prophetic speech to the *house of Israel* (see the introduction to the commentary on 3:1 – 4:13 above). This speech consists of three separate building blocks: (1) injustice, seeking the Lord, death (5:1–17); (2) the Day of the Lord and Israel's corrupt worship (5:18–27); and (3) Israel's current prosperity and future failures (6:1–14). The opening passage (5:1–17) introduces three main themes: judgment (death, military defeat, exile), worship (seeking God) and sin (injustice). The theme of judgment, both as death and as military defeat/exile, permeates the whole composition. The other two themes are developed in more detail in the following two sections: the second (5:18–27) focuses primarily on worship, and the third (6:1–14), on the luxurious lifestyle funded by oppression. This last section also contains more detail on Israel's punishment. There are several key motifs running through the composition as a whole: *justice . . . and righteousness* (*mišpāṭ ûṣĕdāqâ*; 5:7, 24; 6:12); *hate* (*śāna'*; 5:10, 15, 21; 6:8); *go into exile* (*gālâ*; 5:5, 27; 6:7). Thus, the prophetic speech in 5:1 – 6:14 provides an in-depth overview of all the major themes of Amos's prophecy centred around the proclamation of the coming judgment.

## A. Injustice, seeking the Lord, death (5:1–17)

*Context*

It is nowadays commonly agreed that this passage is arranged in the following way (the original proposal comes from de Waard 1977):

A:  Death and mourning: the judgment of Israel (5:1–3)
    B:  Seek the Lord and live: call to repentance (5:4–6)
        C:  Lack of justice: the sin of Israel (5:7)
            D:  The Lord is his name: praise to the Creator (5:8–9)
        C':  Lack of justice: the sin of Israel (5:10–12[13])
    B':  Seek good and live: call to repentance (5:14–15)
A':  Death and mourning: the judgment of Israel (5:16–17)

The chiastic structure highlights the three central themes of this passage: repentance, sin and judgment. Its theological focus is revealed in the hymnic fragment placed at its very core. Appreciation of this concentric arrangement is key, for two reasons. First, in a chiasm every subsection needs to be understood in the light of its corresponding unit. Second, the ending does not carry the same weight as in a linear literary structure. In fact, the unique and most important element is to be found in the middle.

*Comment*

**1–3.** On the overall structuring role of verse 1 see the introduction to the commentary on 3:1 – 4:13 above. The first-person singular here is the prophet, not God. The *word* he utters is a *lamentation* (*qînâ*), that is, a funeral song performed as a part of the mourning ritual for a dead person (*NIDOTTE* 4.867–868; cf. 2 Sam. 1:17–27; 3:31–35). The poetry of verse 2 follows an uneven rhythm, with the second line shorter than the first, probably in imitation of the rhythm that was often employed in such elegies. The song is composed for the funeral of a young woman, *maiden*

*Israel*, who has been tragically cut down in the prime of her life and now lies *forsaken* by her God and friends *on her land*. The reality behind this metaphor is explained in verse 3 as a military defeat. The *thousand, hundred* and *ten* were conventional terms for the different military units in Israel's army (Exod. 18:21; 2 Sam. 18:1). The picture is one of utter decimation of the army but, interestingly, not yet of exile, since the few survivors are returning to the city from which they originally marched. NRSV unjustifiably omits the concluding phrase 'to the house of Israel' which plays an important structuring role in the speech.

**4–6.** This little passage is divided into two sections by the repetition of the command *Seek me/the LORD and live*, and is unified by the three occurrences of the key term *dāraš* (*seek*). In biblical Hebrew to 'seek God' often means to seek oracular instruction via a prophetic intermediary (i.e. 'inquire of the LORD'; 1 Sam. 9:9; 1 Kgs 22:8; 2 Kgs 22:13–14; cf. Gen. 25:22–23), but it can also be used of visiting a sanctuary to worship (Deut. 12:5; 2 Chr. 1:5). The first section (vv. 4b–5) explains what the command does not mean. Amos is not inviting people to go to the sanctuaries at *Bethel* and *Gilgal*, or to *cross over* the southern border and visit the pilgrimage site of *Beer-sheba*, home to traditions about Isaac (Gen. 26:23–25; 46:1) that must have played an important role (Amos 7:9, 16) in the cultural memory of Amos's Northern audience (Rudolph 1971: 190–191). The reason is that these worship centres will soon be destroyed. The implication is that the Lord has already abandoned them and cannot be found there. *Gilgal shall surely go into exile* contains a powerful wordplay in Hebrew: *hagilgāl gālōh yigleh*. The theme of exile which has so far played a subsidiary role in the book (1:5, 15; cf. 4:2–3?) begins to take centre stage from now on.

At this point Amos does not clarify what the command positively entails. This becomes clear only once we connect verses 4–6 with their mirror passage in verses 14–15 which redefines seeking the Lord as living ethically and justly. Instead, the rest of this passage (v. 6) deals with the consequences of not heeding the call. Those who seek the Lord will *live*. In less urgent circumstances this promise might carry the implications of long, full and happy life (Deut. 5:33; Prov. 4:4; 9:6); however, in this context it starkly contrasts with the images of death in verses 2–3 and primarily means 'to survive' the disaster. The only alternative to this survival is to be *devour[ed]* by the *fire* (see above on 2:13) that is going to descend upon *Bethel*. The NRSV assumes that *Bethel* and the *house of Joseph* stand in parallel as the objects of destruction by fire. However, in Hebrew Bethel is preceded by the preposition *lamed*. ESV translates 'with none to quench it *for* Bethel', but it is better to take the preposition as locative and follow the NJB: 'with no one *at* Bethel able to quench the flames' (my emphasis). The point is that Israelite religious ritual, represented by the royal sanctuary at Bethel, is powerless to stop the divine judgment directed against the kingdom (Hadjiev 2009: 162–163).

**7.** There is no syntactic connection between this verse and the preceding passage. The rough transition reminds us that we are faced with an artfully constructed literary mosaic, not with the transcript of a sermon.[1] On *justice* and *righteousness* see the Introduction. There is irony in the use of *hāpak* (*turn*) which also appears in 4:11 (translated *overthrew*). The contrast between God's 'overturning' of Israel and the people who *turn justice to wormwood* underlines the close link between actions and consequences. Justice and righteousness were a key royal responsibility (2 Sam. 8:15; 1 Kgs 10:9; Ps. 72). Amos's words here are an implicit criticism of the monarchy.

**8–9.** The second hymnic piece (cf. 4:13) is syntactically unconnected to its context and breaks the flow of verse 7 and verses 10–12. The surprising nature of its abrupt appearance contributes to its climactic function as the centre of the chiasm. Like the first doxology, it underlines God's power both to create and to destroy. The *Pleiades and Orion* were thought to control the change of the winter and summer seasons. They were associated with fire and heat, and the release of heavenly waters for both beneficial (rain) and destructive (flood) purposes (cf. Job 38:25–35). The two star clusters also played a role in the maintenance of the order of human society (Koch 1974: 517–525). The harmony of God's creation

---

1. The Hebrew at the start reads: 'The ones who turn justice into wormwood'. NIV has 'There are those who'. Stuart (1987: 343) argues that the definite article is vocative; cf. NRSV: *Ah, you that*. Many insert *hôy* (*BHS*): 'Woe to those who' (NAB).

encompasses both the natural and the moral sphere. Therefore, an assault on justice and righteousness is an attack on creation itself that unleashes the destructive forces of chaos (Gillingham 1992: 174–177).

This interplay between order and chaos is central to the hymn. *Turns deep darkness into the morning, / and darkens the day into night* is primarily a description of creation harmony – the regular oscillation of morning and evening. However, while *ṣalmāwet (deep darkness)* could be simply 'midnight' (NIV) it also evokes the ominous darkness of death and the netherworld (Job 10:21–22; 38:17), as well as the 'terrors of deep darkness' of the deeds of the wicked (Job 24:17). It is a reminder that the rhythm of light and darkness is grounded in the initial act of creation when God subdued the forces of chaos. By turning (*hāpak*) justice into wormwood Israel is directly opposing the divine act of turning (*hāpak*) darkness into day and seeks to unleash that force of darkness upon the world. *Who calls for the waters of the sea, / and pours them out* may be a reference to God sending rain *on the surface of the earth*, but is more naturally understood as a picture of the flood and possibly even the reversal of creation. This is not a description of seawater evaporating to form clouds and then coming back to irrigate the soil, but an image of God summoning the chaotic waters of the primal sea and sending them on a mission of devastation. The doxology articulates a threat that the forces of chaos, released by Israel's practice of injustice, will be directed by the Lord against his own people (Paas 2003: 284–288, 322). This becomes even clearer with the transition in verse 9 from the realm of nature to the arena of history. The Lord who sends the waters of the sea against the earth will make *destruction flash out* against the *fortress* of the *strong* – in this case, the house of Israel.[2]

---

2. The meaning of *mablîg (flash)* is uncertain (Paul 1991: 169). It is used elsewhere in the OT in the sense of 'to be cheerful', which does not fit here. *The strong ('az)* is sometimes repointed to *'ōz* ('stronghold', NIV, NJPS) to provide a better parallel to *fortress* in the second line (cf. 3:11). Attempts to read astronomical allusions into this verse have not met with wide acceptance (Hubbard 1989: 170; Coggins 2000: 125–126; Paas 2003: 288–290).

**10–12.** The general accusation of verse 7 is given specific contours. The passage begins and ends with invectives against the corrupt judicial process and is framed by the mention of the *gate* (*ša'ar*). The city *gate* was a large structure with several chambers leading to an open space before it. In Old Testament times it served as a place where justice was administered and trade was conducted. Faust (2012: 100–109) argues that the term does not just refer to the gate building and square but also included the long, pillared public buildings adjacent to it. In his view, a lot of the activities of 'the gate' took place in these multipurpose buildings, but in addition they served to provide shelter for poor, homeless people and a place where more well-to-do citizens could bring them food.

In Amos, at least initially, the legal function of the gate is in view. It is not clear if the *one who reproves* is an 'arbiter' (NJPS) chosen from among the city elders to adjudicate a case brought before them (Wolff 1977: 246) or a defender of the one who was in the right (Rudolph 1971: 198). Likewise, the *one who speaks the truth* could be an honest judge, a plaintiff whose 'plea is just' (NJPS), or a truthful witness. The point is that any participant in the judicial process who acts with integrity and in the defence of the truth is *hate[d]* and *abhor[red]*. It is possible that there is also a veiled reference to the opposition Amos himself encountered when he tried to speak the truth publicly. Verse 12 picks up the language of 2:6–7 (*transgressions, righteous, needy, push aside*) but now places it in an explicitly legal framework. The *righteous* are those who are innocent or in the right but cannot prevail in court because the judges *take a bribe*. If Faust is correct, the accusation *push [them] aside* could refer to denying such people access to the 'social security system' of the 'gate'.

Wrapped in this attack on judicial corruption is a denouncement of the unjust practice of economic exploitation. It is best to read the *hapax legomenon bôšaskem* not as *you trample* but as 'levy a straw tax' (NIV; cf. NJPS) or 'exact corn tax' (*HALOT* 1.165) on the basis of an Akkadian cognate (Paul 1991: 172–173). It thus stands in parallel with the following *levies of grain*. This could be criticism of landlords who demand rent that is not due or charge tenant farmers exorbitant rates (Soggin 1987: 92; contrast Houston 2008: 26–30), or of the royal bureaucracy imposing crippling taxes (Jeremias 1998: 93) on village communities. These were not, strictly speaking, illegal but they were certainly immoral, as they financed a life of luxury (*houses of hewn stone*; *pleasant vineyards*) for the king and his entourage at the expense of people who were driven deeper into poverty. Both tax and tribute are 'the politer and slightly more regulated faces of plunder', reliant as they are on institutionalized violence behind which lurks the ever-present threat of military power (Boer 2015: 146, 149–156). To proclaim judgment on these extractive practices Amos uses a 'futility curse'. The link between an action and its intended beneficial consequence will be broken: they have *built* but *shall not live*; *planted* but *shall not drink*. *Hewn stone* was expensive to build with and was used mainly in the construction of royal palaces and other public buildings (Mazar 1990: 472–474) so this may be another criticism directed at the Israelite monarchy.

**13.** The opening *lākēn* (*Therefore*) leads one to expect that an announcement of punishment is about to follow. This suggests that the *evil time* is the time when the judgment, announced in verse 11, will become a reality (Goff 2008: 642). It is not entirely clear what is the point of the remark that *the prudent will keep silent*. *HALOT* 1.226 distinguishes three different roots of the verb *dmm*: (1) keep quiet; (2) wail; (3) perish, each of which is a possibility here. The silence may be an expression of horror or of patient waiting for God's salvation (Fleischer 2001: 203). Alternatively, Stuart (1987: 342, 344) translates 'the thoughtful person will wail'. The main problem with all these interpretations is that *maśkîl* (*prudent*), a Hiphil participle of the verb 'to understand, have insight, achieve success', fits awkwardly in the context of Amos 5. After the indictments of the preceding verses, one expects not a wise person but a rich and powerful oppressor to wail and mourn as the evil time comes.[3]

It is better to translate: 'Therefore the song will become at that time mourning' (i.e. the *maśkîl* song is personified as a mourner). *Maśkîl* appears as a technical term for a type of song in the titles of

---

3. The proposal of Smith (1988) to translate the participle as 'the prosperous' circumvents this difficulty. However, *maśkîl* usually means someone who is successful, i.e. whose actions achieve the desired result (most often in the context of war). It is never used to describe the rich and powerful in contrast to the poor (Goff 2008: 639).

thirteen psalms, meaning (1) a psalm of success; (2) a responsive song; or (3) an instructive or skilful song (*DCH* 5.503–504). The choice of this particular term in Amos may be dictated by the desire to achieve a wordplay with *kĕsîl* (*Orion*) in 5:8 and the threefold repetition of *kōl* (*all*) in verses 16–17. Thus verse 13 echoes the thought of 8:10 where God will turn the songs of the Israelites into lamentation (*lĕqînâ*), and of 8:3 where the 'songs of the palace' will 'wail'. In 6:5–6 singing and drinking of wine are part of the lifestyle enjoyed by the leaders of Israel and condemned by the prophet. In 5:11, 13 judgment reverses both of those. The whole subunit is finely balanced as sin (vv. 10–11a), punishment (v. 11b), sin (v. 12) and punishment (v. 13) alternate.

**14–15.** This section provides the key for understanding the whole of verses 1–17. It brings together many of the important terms of the preceding units: *seek . . . live* (vv. 4, 6), *evil* (v. 13), *hate* (v. 10), *justice* (v. 7), *gate* (vv. 10, 12), *Joseph* (v. 6); *remnant* (*šĕ'ērît*) is cognate with *left* (*taš'îr*) in verse 3. To seek the Lord means to *seek* and *love good*. The general word *good* is defined as the practice of social justice *in the gate*. Instead of hating *the one who reproves in the gate* (v. 10) the Israelites are called to *Hate evil*, that is, all the practices of judicial corruption and economic exploitation denounced in verses 10–12 that result in the arrival of the *evil time* of judgment (v. 13). The repetition of the lengthy title *LORD, the God of hosts* adds solemnity to the call. For a similar connection between a call to justice and a promise of life see Deuteronomy 16:20.

In the conditional promise *so the LORD, the God of hosts, will be with you, / just as you have said*, Amos for the first time refers explicitly to one of the key convictions of his audience. The belief in God's saving presence was based on the exodus faith (2:9–10; 3:2) or on the divine promise to Jacob at Bethel 'Know that I am with you and will keep you' (Gen. 28:15). The sacrificial worship at Bethel and other holy places actualized this saving and protective presence (4:4–5; 5:4–6). The prophet's argument is that injustice has polluted the sanctuaries and severed the link with God. The only way to recover what they falsely believe to possess is a wholehearted return to a life of justice.

*Joseph*, the ancestor of the tribes of Ephraim and Manasseh, is used here as a term for the Northern Kingdom. The fact that only a *remnant of Joseph* is addressed suggests that the oracle dates from the period 733–722 BC when Tiglath-pileser subdued Israel and incorporated large swathes of its territory into the Assyrian Empire, leaving only a rump state around the capital of Samaria (Hadjiev 2009: 185–187).

The concluding promise is very tentative. It opens with *'ûlay* ('Perhaps', NIV) which shows that Amos is not certain what the divine response to Israel's change of heart so late in the game will be. While the Lord is *gracious*, he is also free. Yet the uncertainty of the outcome does not diminish the value of repentance. Israel must do the right thing regardless of the potential benefits.

**16–17.** The concluding section of the chiasm corresponds to verses 1–3. It paints an extraordinary picture of universal mourning caused by death on a very large scale. The crisis is so huge that it interrupts the normal work of *farmers* and engulfs all public spaces: *squares, streets, vineyards*. The threefold recurrence of *all* and *wailing* further strengthens the sense of completeness. The wordplay between *mispēd* (*wailing*) and *mišpāṭ* (*justice*; 5:7, 15) emphasizes the link between actions and consequences. The same effect is achieved by the ironic contrast between the *pleasant vineyards* financed by exploitation (5:11) and *all the vineyards* that now become the scene of mourning. The cause of the devastation is left unexplained. It could be the decimation of the army (5:2–3) or a plague. The focus is on its theological meaning. In the flood of death and grief the Israelites will in fact experience God himself who will *pass though* their *midst*. The solemn reiteration of *the LORD, the God of hosts, the Lord* at the start of verse 16 drives that point home.

*Meaning*
The leaders of Israel overturn justice by subverting fair legal process at the gate, demanding high taxes and exploiting their weaker neighbours. In doing so they go against the just order of creation established by the Lord and unwittingly unleash the forces of chaos. God now becomes their enemy. The darkness, subdued at creation within the peaceful rhythm of day and night, will break free and engulf Israel, bringing with it defeat, death and mourning. In those circumstances the prophet calls the people to seek the Lord, to recommit themselves to justice, righteousness and good.

Amos is not sure what the outcome of that action will be. He speculates that *perhaps* the Lord will be gracious to the remnant of Joseph, but there are no guarantees. We may surmise that when the prophet originally proclaimed these words to Israel there was still hope of national regeneration. In later years, as the day of judgment was drawing closer and his disciples were preaching the oracles to their contemporaries, the hope of salvation was narrowed down from the nation as a whole to a remnant of faithful people who were ready to heed the prophetic word. Once the disaster had become a past reality the call to seek the Lord provided guidance to the remnant as to how to reorient their lives in the post-judgment situation. During the seventh and sixth centuries BC the people of Judah were going to travel down the same road.

## B. The Day of the Lord and Israel's corrupt worship (5:18–27)

*Context*
The opening *Alas* (v. 18) signals the beginning of a new section brought to a close by the solemn *says the LORD, whose name is the God of hosts* in verse 27. It is composed of two originally independent units: a disputation saying focused on the theme of the Day of the Lord (vv. 18–20) and an oracle criticizing the cult (vv. 21–27). The two units are built together into a single speech that picks up and develops the themes of 4:4–13 and 5:4–6. Thematically both the Day of the Lord (vv. 18–20) and sacrificial worship (vv. 21–25) were linked to the cult. In 4:4–13 Amos begins with current cultic practice (4:4–5), spends the bulk of the section on the past (4:6–11) and finishes with a fleeting glimpse of the future (4:12). In 5:18–27 the primary focus is on the future and how that future is determined by the worship practised in the present.

A. The future is darkness, not light (5:18–20)
    B. The present cult contrasted to what the cult should be (5:21–24)
    B'. The present cult contrasted to what the cult used to be in the past (5:25–26)
A'. The future is exile (5:27)

The section as a whole plays an important role within the prophetic speech of chapters 5–6 by developing in detail the topic of worship, while keeping alive in the reader's mind the motifs of justice and exile. Several of its details, therefore, connect with the wider literary context. The opening *hôy* (*Alas/*'woe') echoes the exclamation *hô hô* (*Alas! alas!*) from 5:16 and the general theme of mourning and lament (5:1, 13, 16–17). The threefold repetition which governs the structure of verses 18–20 and 21–23 fits with the threefold repetition of *all* and *wailing* in verses 16–17. The light and darkness hark back to 5:8. The opening of the second part (5:21) contains the third recurrence of the verb *hate* (5:10, 15). Justice and righteousness (5:7, 24), exile (5:5, 27) and the name of the Lord (5:8, 27) provide further links.

## Comment

**18–20.** These verses have a concentric structure: A (Day of the Lord; v. 18) – B (animal story; v. 19) – A (Day of the Lord; v. 20). Its organizing principle is the threefold repetition of all key phrases (*day of the LORD*) and motifs (light/darkness in vv. 18, 20; three animals in v. 19). The exclamation *Alas* belongs to the funeral setting (1 Kgs 13:30; Jer. 22:18) and is used here polemically. This is the earliest historical reference to the *day of the LORD* in Old Testament literature. The text assumes that both the expression and the underlying concept were familiar to Amos's audience. They *desire the day of the LORD* and anticipate that it will bring them *light*, most likely a metaphor for abundant blessings. A 'popular eschatology' is presupposed here, an expectation that the Lord will soon intervene in the world's affairs and grant Israel prosperity and power (Barton 2012: 61–66). Possibly the Day of the Lord was a festival, a ritual celebration of the move from darkness to light which signalled God's power over the forces of chaos and simultaneously contained within it the expectation that he would renew the life of his people and give them safety (Müller 2010: 582–591; Fleming 2010: 24, 30–38). Amos reverses the expectations of his listeners and announces instead the arrival of *darkness* and *gloom*. Similar imagery is used in Balaam's prophecy from Deir Alla to depict a cosmic catastrophe and the reversal of creation (*COS* 2.27; cf. Introduction).

A mini narrative at the centre of the pericope illustrates the metaphor. The story traces the fortunes of a person who manages to escape twice from dangerous animals. Unlike the swift soldier from 2:14 who is unsuccessful in his flight (*mānôs*), this person can flee (*yānûs*) not only from the *lion*, who has already appeared as a threat in 3:4, 8, but also, presumably, from the *bear*. Once the person arrives in the deceptive safety of the *house*, thinking the worst has passed, a poisonous *snake* hidden in the cracks of the *wall* bites the person's *hand*. The narrative seeks to unsettle the prophet's audience by undermining their illusions of security. Its message is that the calm of the present is deceptive, and past deliverance is no guarantee of future safety.[4]

**21–23.** The number three plays a role at the start of this passage: three aspects of the cult are mentioned – festivals (v. 21), sacrifices (v. 22), music (v. 23); and three types of sacrifices appear in verse 22. The first-person divine speech is designed to shock the reader with its categoric assertions. The Lord *hate*[*s*] the *festivals* just as Israel hates the arbiter at the gate (5:10), and *despises* (*mā'as*) them just as Judah despises/rejects (*mā'as*) the law (2:4). As in 4:4–5, Amos utilizes and ironically subverts another cultic genre, the priestly announcement that the Lord has accepted the offerings of the worshipper (Wolff 1977: 261; Eidevall 2017: 167–168). *I take no delight* (*lō' 'ārîaḥ*) means literally 'I will not smell', hence NIV: 'your assemblies are a stench to me'. The verb is used metaphorically of the Lord smelling the pleasing aroma of the sacrifice and accepting it (Gen. 8:21; 1 Sam 26:19). *I will not accept them* (*lō' 'erṣeh*) is a term used when determining if an offering meets the ritual requirements (Lev. 7:18; 22:23; cf. 1:4; 22:27). *I will not look upon* and *I will not listen*: in a strongly anthropomorphic statement the passage covers the senses of smell, sight and hearing to express the utter aversion of God.

There is nothing in the first half of the passage to suggest that the worship denounced is irregular in any way. The *festivals* (*ḥagēkem*)

---

4. There might be a subtle wordplay in Hebrew. The word 'to bite' (*nāšak*) reminds the reader of the word 'interest' (*nešek*) which was one of the means by which the ruling class drove people into economic dependence.

are the annual pilgrim festivals Passover/Unleavened Bread, Weeks and Tabernacles (Exod. 23:14–16). The *solemn assemblies* could have been held as part of the festivals (Deut. 16:8) or on separate occasions (2 Kgs 10:20; Joel 1:14 2:15). Three different types of sacrifices are mentioned: *burnt-offerings* (Lev. 1),[5] *grain-offerings* (Lev. 2) and the *offerings of well-being* ('peace offerings', ESV; 'fellowship offerings', NIV; 'communion sacrifices', NJB). On the last see 4:4–5. Music was an integral part of liturgical worship, but here the joyful *songs* of Israel are branded as mere *noise* and rejected. The *harp* (*nebel*) was a stringed instrument with a resonator box made of wood. The word also means 'jug', probably because of the similar shape of the two objects.

**24.** This verse explains the reasons for the Lord's disgust. The explanation is indirect, implying that *justice* and *righteousness* are not present in Israel's midst and it is precisely their absence that makes the cult odious to God. The comparison to an *ever-flowing stream* – that is, a river that does not dry up during the hot summer months – emphasizes the purifying and life-giving quality of social justice. Conversely, the absence of justice is like a deadly drought (see further, Introduction). The verb *roll down* (*yiggal*) comes from a root *gll* which sounds similar to the verb 'to go into exile' (*gālâ*; 5:5, 27) and the name Gilgal, where the oracle might first have been uttered. The same verb ('roll away [from you the disgrace of Egypt]') is used in the aetiology of Gilgal's name in Joshua 5:9. The analogy with the *ever-flowing stream* would have been particularly apt in view of the fact that Gilgal was close to the river Jordan (Fleischer 2001: 211–212).

---

5. V. 22a is syntactically rough. Literally it says: 'Even if/unless you offer me burnt offerings and your grain offerings I will not accept.' Wolff (1977: 259) takes the first line as a gloss. Rudolph (1971: 206) conjectures that a clause like 'they will displease me' was originally present after 'burnt offerings' and accidentally fell out (cf. Soggin 1987: 96–97). The solution of the NRSV is to take the second-person suffix of *minḥōtêkem* ('your grain offerings') as performing double duty for both nouns and then treat the resultant *your burnt-offerings and grain-offerings* as object of both the preceding and the following verb (cf. Paul 1991: 190).

**25–27.** There are three possible interpretations of these verses, depending on how the verb *nāśā'* at the start of verse 26 is translated (past tense continuing v. 25, or future tense preparing for v. 27) and how it is linked to its context. (1) The LXX renders *nāśā'* as aorist ('you even took up the tent of Moloch', *NETS*; cf. 'You also carried Sikkuth', NKJV) and thus makes verse 26 a continuation of the description of the wilderness period begun in verse 25 (Glenny 2013: 108–109). The emphasis of the rhetorical question in verse 25 falls on the preposition *to me*. During the forty years in the wilderness the Israelites did not offer sacrifices to the Lord. Instead, they practised idolatry, carrying around the images of their gods. This understanding of the passage is taken up in Stephen's speech (Acts 7:41–43) which connects it to the golden calf incident. Its main weakness is that, understood in this way, the verses do not fit very well with the argument of the passage as a whole. It is not clear how a reference to Israelite idolatry in the remote past supports the accusation of practising injustice in the present.

It is much better to see the idolatry of verse 26 as pointing to a present reality, and the reference to the wilderness period as the description of an ideal period, from a time long ago, which serves as a counterpoint to the corrupt present of verses 21–24 and verse 26. Admittedly, in Pentateuchal traditions the wilderness period is portrayed as a time of disobedience. However, in the cultural memory of Amos's audience the wilderness was an idealized time of faithfulness and devotion to the Lord (Jer. 2:2–3; Hos. 2:14–15) and a period when the lavish sacrificial cult practised after the settlement was not yet operative (Jer. 7:22–23). Thus, the impressive cultic practices of monarchic Israel, corrupted by injustice, are contrasted with the pure devotion of earlier times when Israel did not offer sacrifices but lived righteously. The usefulness and value of sacrifice is undercut by this historical argument: the past shows it is not necessary for a close relationship with the Lord.

This leaves us with two other possible interpretations of verse 26. (2) NRSV translates *nāśā'* as future (*You shall take up*), connects it with verse 27 and integrates it into the prediction of the coming exile (ESV, NJB). When the people of Israel are deported beyond Damascus, they will carry with them the astral deities which they even now have begun to worship (Andersen and Freedman 1989:

535–537). Alternatively, the verse may be saying that the Israelites will be forced to take part in cultic processions of Mesopotamian gods once they are in Assyria. The humiliation of defeat will be compounded by the humiliation of forced idolatry (Rudolph 1971: 207, 213). Radine (2010: 62–63) thinks of Assyrian religious emblems used in loyalty oaths that Israel will have to make after its subjugation. (3) Others take verse 26 as a continuation of the rhetorical question of verse 25 (Wolff 1977: 265–266; Hubbard 1989: 185; Eidevall 2017: 171). The sense then would be: 'Did you offer me sacrifices in the wilderness? No, you practised justice. And did you carry around your gods? No, there was no idolatry amongst you then, as there is now.' The two rhetorical questions, expecting negative answers, present the wilderness as the ideal counterpoint to the present with its twin problems of injustice and worship of other gods. The implication is that there is an intrinsic link between these two transgressions: idolatry leads to oppression. A similar meaning is achieved by NIV ('You have lifted up') which does not treat the verse as a question.

The objects carried by the Israelites are also unclear (see Table 7 on p. 151). It is widely agreed that the MT vocalization *sikkût* and *kîyûn* is polemically modelled on the Hebrew word *šiqûṣ* ('detestable thing') because the Masoretes understood the two words to be the names of foreign gods. These are identified with the Mesopotamian astral deities Sakkuth, which in a list of gods from Ugarit is identified with Ninurta, and Kaiwan, a name of the planet Saturn in Akkadian from where it was adopted into Syriac, Persian and Arabic (Paul 1991: 194–197; Barstad 1984: 123–126). A worship of a god Succoth-benoth is attested in Northern Israel (2 Kgs 17:30) but only after 722 BC. It is, however, not clear why Amos would single out such an obscure Babylonian deity as Israel's 'king'. Sakkuth was a cupbearer of the gods, associated with the city of Der bordering Elam (*DDD* 722). In view of the difficulties of the text[6] it is better

---

6. The problems in the Hebrew text can be clearly seen in the NKJV which follows closely the word order and meaning of the MT. Sikkuth is described as 'your king' (singular), but Chiun is surprisingly 'your images/idols' (plural). NRSV solves this by moving *your images* after *your*

Table 7 The objects carried in 5:26

| LXX (Acts 7:43) | 'the tent of Moloch' | 'and the star of your god Raiphan, their images' |
|---|---|---|
| NRSV | *Sakkuth your king* | *and Kaiwan your star-god, your images* |
| NIV | 'the shrine of your king' | 'the pedestal of your idols, the star of your god' |
| NKJV | 'Sikkuth your king' | 'And Chiun, your idols, the star of your gods' |

to consider an alternative approach to the translation of this verse, provided by NIV. It keeps the word order of MT but interprets the proper names as nouns: *sikkût* is *sukkat* (tent/booth = 'shrine') and *kîyûn* ('pedestal') is understood as derived from *kûn* ('to be firm'), perhaps synonymous with *kēn* (*HALOT* 2.472, 483; *DDD* 478; cf. Hayes 1988: 176 'palanquin'). Thus verse 26 denounces ritual processions during which the Israelites carried the tent and pedestal of a divine king and an astral god whose names are not given. This makes more sense within the book of Amos whose ending (9:11) envisages the restoration of another *sukkat* ('tent'/*booth*) in the context of true worship.[7]

Instead of blessing and prosperity, Israel's unacceptable worship will lead to exile. The verb *I will take you into exile* (*higlêtî*) plays on the exhortation [*let justice*] *roll* (5:24) and the name of the sanctuary Gilgal (5:5). It also brings to the fore the theme of exile which has

---

*star-god*, which then explicitly defines Kaiwan as an astral god and allows 'your idols'/*images* to refer to both deities. The LXX *tēn skēnēn tou Moloch* interprets *malkĕkem* ('your king') as the name of the god Molech (2 Kgs 23:10; cf. Jer. 39:35 LXX = 32:35 MT) and *sikkût* as the noun *sukkat* ('tent, tabernacle'). It takes the name of the second god as Raiphan, which is probably an inner-Greek mistake for Kaiphan (Gelston 2010: 84).

7. The connection between these two verses was already made by the Qumran community which interpreted the 'tabernacle of your king' here as 'the Books of the Law' by linking it with 9:11. The 'bases of your statues' are the 'Books of the Prophets' (CD 7:14–21).

already appeared in connection with Damascus and Ammon (1:5, 15). The place of exile *beyond Damascus* may be an oblique reference to the rising power of Assyria but it may also be a vague reference to the north without an attempt to identify precisely the nation which will accomplish the divine call. The title *God of hosts* and the mention of the Lord's *name* underline God's power to make his threat a reality by alluding to the hymn in 5:8–9.

### Meaning

The rhetorical questions and shocking reversal of expectations that permeate the whole of this passage point to its polemical setting (see 3:1–15 and 9:1–10). Amos is attempting to combat an attitude of overconfidence and optimism, the belief that the Lord is with his people when they come to worship (5:14) and therefore nothing really bad can happen to them (9:10). To cure them of such false optimism Amos pronounces on God's behalf an unequivocal rejection of the cult. The enumeration of the various aspects of temple worship and the piling up of first-person singular verbs expressing the Lord's disgust achieve an effect even more gut-wrenching than the sarcastic parody in 4:4–5. If Israel is serious about its relationship with God a return to the time of the wilderness, when sacrifices were not offered and instead justice and righteousness flowed like rivers, is the only possible course of action. Israel's present, however, is a complete contrast to that earlier period of simplicity and faithfulness. It is marred by injustice, lavish ritual and veneration of astral deities. Therefore, the Day of the Lord will be darkness, a snake bite and exile.

## C. Israel's current prosperity and future failures (6:1–14)

### Context

This passage ends the prophetic speech in chapters 5–6. In its general flow, as Jeremias (1998: 98–99) notes, it parallels to a point the structure of the preceding passage: a woe-oracle denouncing self-confidence (5:18–20/6:1–7) is followed by a statement that the Lord hates the festivals/strongholds of Israel (5:21–23/6:8) (because?) there is no justice and righteousness (5:24–25/6:12), and finally culminates in the announcement of judgment (5:27/6:14). On the other hand, the description of the *marzēaḥ* festival (6:1–7) exhibits links with 3:9 – 4:3 and needs to be read in the light of that passage (see *Mount Samaria* 4:1 = 6:1; *ivory* 3:15 = 6:4; *drink* [*wine*] 4:1 = 6:6; *couch/bed* 3:12 = 6:4). The connection is important because it shows that the problem with the festival in 6:1–7 is ultimately to be sought in the oppression of the poor practised by the same people who are featured in 3:9 – 4:3.

The second half of the chapter (6:8–14) consists of a collection of oracles that develop in more detail the announcement of judgment from 6:7. They contain a concentration of terms from the preceding material: *sworn* (v. 8 = 4:2); *hate* (v. 8 = 5:10, 15, 21); *strongholds* (v. 8 = 3:9–11); *the name of the* LORD (v. 10 = 5:27; cf. 4:13; 5:8); *house/great house/little house* (vv. 10–11 = 3:15); *turned* (v. 12 = 4:11; 5:7); *justice/righteousness* (v. 12 = 5:7, 24); *wormwood* (v. 12 = 5:7). The verb *abhor* (v. 8) alludes back to both *abhor* (5:10) and *desire* (5:18).[8] The density of allusions to earlier material and the almost exclusive focus on the coming judgment (although see vv. 12–13) makes 6:8–14 a fitting conclusion to both the prophetic speech of chapters 5–6 and the whole composition in chapters 3–6.

## Comment

**1–2.** The opening *Alas* parallels 5:18 and identifies the passage as the second woe-oracle in Amos. The audience of the prophet feel *at ease* and *secure*, and consequently do not believe that the prophesied disaster will strike them (5:18–20). *Mount Samaria* has already appeared as a target of prophetic criticism (3:9; 4:1), but the mention of *Zion* is surprising. The reference to the *ruin of Joseph* in 6:6 implies that the attention of this passage, as in the rest of the book, is primarily directed at the Northern Kingdom. Placing Zion

---

8. It is debated whether *metā'ēb* (from *t'b* II 'to make repulsive') in 6:8 is a byform of *t'b* 'to abhor' or a deliberate change of the original *t'b* to *t'b* I 'to long for' (*HALOT* 4.1672–1673). Whichever of the two is correct the resultant form reminds the reader not only of 5:10 where *hate* and *abhor* (*t'b*) stand in parallel, but also of 5:18 which talks about the people 'longing for' (*mit'awwîm* from *'āwâ*, 'to desire') the Day of the Lord.

in first position and in parallel to Samaria betrays the concern to apply the prophetic word to the Southern Kingdom, similar to the concerns in the superscription (1:1). For later Judean readers the tragic mistakes of the North were a warning to examine their own attitudes and lifestyle.

The feeling of security is coupled with the conviction that they are *the first of the nations*, either a ridiculously exaggerated view of the importance and power of Israel or a sense of spiritual superiority derived from their special relationship to the Lord. 'To whom the house of Israel comes' (ESV) is cryptic. This can mean that the people of Israel come to their leaders to honour them, or to receive guidance, protection and justice. If the clause is part of a Judean application of Amos's oracle, it may refer to a literal coming to Zion: the mass southward migration of Israelites seeking protection in Judah after the demise of the Northern Kingdom. The fact the ordinary people resort to the nobility for protection adds to the latter's feeling of self-importance.

This feeling is challenged in verse 2 with three commands followed by two rhetorical questions. The commands draw attention to three cities, *Calneh*, *Hamath* and *Gath*, whose demise was still part of the living memory of the Jerusalem elite. Gath was reduced to an insignificant town after its destruction by Hazael at the end of the ninth century BC, while Calneh and Hamath were conquered and incorporated into the Assyrian Empire between 738 and 720 BC (Hadjiev 2009: 170–172; Radine 2010: 56–60). The audience are asked to tour the cities, observe their devastation and apply this historical experience to their own situation. In the last question, *is your territory greater than their territory . . . ?* NRSV changes the MT and makes the comparison one-sided. Israel is not better or larger than these kingdoms and therefore cannot hope to escape a similar fate. However, it is possible to keep the Hebrew and translate:

> Are you better than these kingdoms?
>     Or is their territory greater than your territory?
> (ESV; NJPS)

The questions assert that there is no difference between Israel and the other nations: none of them is better or stronger (cf. 9:7).

**3–7.** The feast described in these verses is an outward expression of the inner disposition and attitudes criticized in verse 1. Its most striking feature is the extravagant luxury. The *beds of ivory* were beds decorated with ivory plaques like the ones found in the palace in Samaria (see above on 3:15). These were expensive luxury items that only the richest members of society could afford. Eating *lambs from the flock* and *calves from the stall* was an indication of affluence in a culture where most people ate meat very rarely and only on special occasions. Drinking *wine* from large *bowls*, rather than ordinary cups, and anointing *themselves with the finest oils* point in the same direction. The parties of the rich had culture and sophistication: singing *songs to the sound of the harp* (*nebel*) and improvising *on instruments of music* (lit. 'vessels of song'; *kĕlê šîr*). The parallelism *harp* (*nebel*)/'song' (*šîr*) connects with 5:23. The fact that both *bowl* (*mizrāq*) and *anoint* (*māšaḥ*) are used in cultic contexts further strengthens the link with the cultic criticism of 5:21–27.

The banquet is described in verse 7 as a *marzēaḥ* (revelry, NRSV, ESV; 'carousing', NAB; 'festive meal', NJPS; 'feasting', NIV; 'banquets', NKJV). This word appears only once more in the Old Testament (Jer. 16:5: 'house of mourning' [NIV 'funeral meal']) but is attested in many extrabiblical texts. It describes an institution that was widespread in the Ancient Near East over a long period of time. McLaughlin (2001: 9–79) provides a useful overview of the extrabiblical evidence. He concludes that the *marzēaḥ* was an exclusive upper-class institution, something like a club for rich men, which organized banquets characterized by excessive consumption of alcohol. There was a religious aspect to these clubs insofar as they were dedicated to one or more patron deities. Many scholars also postulate that the *marzēaḥ* was typically a funerary association but McLaughlin rejects this as a constitutive feature of the institution, and there is certainly nothing in Amos 6 to suggest that we are dealing with a funerary feast.

Even though the *marzēaḥ* had a religious aspect, the text of Amos does not suggest that the reason for its rejection is religious. No foreign gods are mentioned, and for all we know the Samarian *marzēaḥ* could have had the Lord as its patron. The grounds for denunciation are hinted at in verses 3 and 6b which frame the description of the festivities. The nobility *put far away* from their minds *the evil day*. The *evil day* is the day of disaster (5:13; 3:6) but in their overconfidence the leaders of Israel refuse to think about it as a possibility. They also *bring near a reign of violence*. If this *reign* is a reference to the impending rise of the Assyrians who established their authority by instilling terror in the conquered population, this could be an ironic depiction of the coming judgment. Alternatively, the *reign of violence* may characterize the rule of Israel's aristocracy, the way in which these people financed their luxurious parties (3:10). Finally, Amos objects that the Israelite ruling class is *not grieved over the ruin of Joseph*. This phrase refers to the breaking of social bonds in Israelite society or to the political disasters of 733 BC when large parts of Israelite territory were torn away and incorporated into the Assyrian Empire. After 722 BC the expression would become an apt description of the glee of the Jerusalem aristocracy at the fate of their Northern neighbour. The point is that the *notables of the first of the nations* (v. 1) act irresponsibly. They cannot foresee, or do not care about, the social and political consequences of their lifestyle and choices.

For that reason, *they shall now be the first to go into exile* (cf. 5:27). There is bitter irony in the triple use of the root *r'š* ('first'): the notables of the *first* (*r'š*) of the nations who anoint themselves with the 'first'/*finest* (*r'š*) of oils will be the *first* (*r'š*) to go into exile. The elaborate alliteration in the last clause (*s/ẓ-r-ḥ*), *and the revelry of the loungers shall pass away* (*wĕsār miẓraḥ sĕrûḥîm*), makes for a memorable conclusion which picks up the description of the nobles as people who *lounge [sĕrûḥîm] on their couches* from verse 4. *Sĕrûḥîm* elsewhere describes hanging curtains (Exod. 26:13), flowing turbans (Ezek. 23:15) and a spreading vine (Ezek. 17:6). Its use here underlines the excess and lack of propriety of the people, sprawled half drunk on the couches.

**8–11.** For a second time in the book (see 4:2) a solemn oath by God assures the audience that military defeat is inevitable. The Lord personally is going to *deliver up the city* and all its inhabitants to an unspecified conqueror. Originally the city of Samaria was probably in view, although later Judean readers would naturally think of Jerusalem as well. The aftermath of the divine action is described in the cryptic narrative of verses 9–10. It provides the depressing conclusion of a thread weaved through 5:2–3 and

5:16–17. The thousand soldiers have been reduced to a hundred and then to ten as they return from the battlefield to the city. Now in the city the *ten people*, who are concentrated in a single *house, shall die*, perhaps due to plague. The surviving relatives[9] must *take up the body* of each of the deceased and *bring it out of the house* in order to bury it. The loud wailing of 5:16–17 is replaced by ominous silence. Those who are left behind after the catastrophe do not dare to speak, for fear of inadvertently pronouncing *the name of the LORD*. They are scared of drawing divine attention to themselves and dying as a result.

After the dead bodies are brought out the *house* collapses. This is the implication of verse 11. The merism of *the great house* and *the little house* conveys the totality of the disaster. After the city is emptied of human life all its buildings disintegrate. Originally, the brief oracle may have been part of Amos's earthquake prediction (see 1:1). Its placement here contributes to the creation of an impressionistic picture of complete devastation, resulting from the oath (v. 8) and the *command* (v. 11) of the Lord himself.

**12–14.** Before the picture of Israel's punishment is complete there is a brief recapitulation of the nation's sins. The mention of the lack of *justice* and *righteousness* (v. 12) brings this recurring motif (5:7, 24) to a climax and highlights its central role in the book. Even more important is Israel's over-reliance on its military power, appearing at the start (see *secure* in v. 1), in the middle (v. 8, where *the pride of Jacob* is linked to *his strongholds*) and at the end of 6:1–14. The rejoicing over *Lo-debar* (Josh. 13:26 [Lidbar]; 2 Sam. 9:4–5; 17:27) and *Karnaim* (Gen. 14:5), two cities in the Transjordan, implies recent Israelite military victories there, probably recapturing some of the territories in the Transjordan from their perennial enemies, the Arameans.

As in the other parts of the book, the polemical setting of the original delivery of these oracles is not difficult to discern. The two

----

9. The meaning of the word *mĕsorpô* is unclear. The translation *one who burns the dead* is suspected because cremation was not normally practised in ancient Israel. The two main alternatives are 'the one who anoints him for burial' (ESV) and 'who is to burn incense for him' (NJPS).

rhetorical questions in verse 12a show the absurdity of Israel's transgressions. *Horses* do not *run on rocks* because their hooves will be damaged, and quite plainly nobody *plough*[s] *the sea with oxen.*[10] In perverting *justice* and *righteousness* Israel has acted in contravention of the divine order established in creation. The absurdity of its actions is also exposed by the pun Amos makes on the names of the two captured cities. *Karnaim* means 'two horns', a symbol of strength. *Lo-debar*, on the other hand, sounds like the Hebrew expression 'for nothing'. In other words, the recent displays of the people's strength amount to nothing. Their emptiness will soon be laid bare when an unnamed *nation* is raised up by the Lord to *oppress* Israel and nullify its victories.

Verses 13–14 form an effective conclusion to the passage by returning to the theme of the audience's arrogance (vv. 1, 8). *Nation* (*gôy*) serves as an *inclusio* (cf. v. 1), and the first-person divine speech expressed with 'behold' (ESV) followed by a participle harks back to verses 8 and 11 respectively. The nation is going to oppress Israel *from Lebo-hamath* [on the meaning of this term see the Introduction] *to the Wadi Arabah*. This is strikingly similar to 2 Kings 14:25 which states that Jeroboam II 'restored the border of Israel from Lebo-hamath as far as the Sea of the Arabah'. It is likely that Amos's polemic is directed at the uncritical exuberance produced by these military and political successes.

*Meaning*
The rulers of Israel and Judah are arrogant. They regard themselves as the *notables of the first of the nations* and feel secure in the capital city

---

10. The MT literally says, 'Does one plough with oxen?' to which the response is obviously 'Yes'. However, the context requires a negative answer. ESV and NKJV add the word 'there' as a reference to the rocks from the preceding question. The solution of the NRSV and NIV is based on the conjecture that the consonants of the original text *bqr* (oxen) and *ym* (sea) were brought together by mistake to form *bqrym* in which *ym* was incorrectly seen as the masculine plural ending. The word *bqr* (oxen), however, is a collective noun which does not appear anywhere else with a plural ending.

of a country which has recently flexed its military muscles and regained some of its lost territories. Amos takes us on a tour of one of their lavish parties and focuses our attention on its luxury and excess. Tragically, this display of affluence is coupled with politically irresponsible behaviour, inexorably leading the nation towards ruin. The leaders do not care. Their optimism knows no bounds. But their carefree attitude will not save them from the impending catastrophe. In fact they are no different from other nations and cities and their coming exile will prove just that. The personal involvement of God in the future disaster is meticulously stressed. He is the one who abhors the pride of Jacob and hates his strongholds, commands the destruction of the houses and raises up a nation to oppress his people. In the future the mention of his name will no longer be an occasion of jubilation but a source of dread. The passage is addressed simultaneously to the elites of Samaria and of Jerusalem. Originally Amos spoke primarily to the leaders of the Northern Kingdom, but his denunciations were just as applicable to the leaders of the South. When the Babylonians burned the houses of Jerusalem and led its citizens into exile, the people of Judah could see that their own oppression, affluence and injustice were just as odious to the Lord as those of their Northern neighbours from a century and a half before.

# 5. THE INEVITABLE DESTRUCTION OF ISRAEL (7:1 – 9:6)

*Context*

The backbone of the last major section of the book consists of a first-person report in which Amos narrates five visions he has received from the Lord. All the visions begin in the same way but diverge in the ensuing dialogue (see the Introduction). In the first pair (7:1–6) Amos takes the initiative to intercede for the people, and the Lord responds positively to that intercession. In the second pair (7:7–9; 8:1–3) the Lord takes the initiative to ask Amos a question about the object he sees, and once the prophet responds the Lord proclaims an oracle of judgment. Thus, while the first two visions depict averted judgment, the third and the fourth proclaim inescapable punishment. The role of the prophet changes. At the start he is active and bold. From the third vision onwards, he is passive and barely speaks. That change is due to the nature of the visions. The locusts and fire at the start are self-explanatory and allow for immediate intervention on the part of Amos. The plumb line and the basket of fruit are more ambiguous and require explanation. By the time that explanation is given the divine decision not to relent is proclaimed. The final, fifth vision (9:1–4) is the high point of this development. Its structure is different, and it is almost entirely dominated by divine speech. In it the prophet is neither asked a question nor given an opportunity to pray, and the inexorable doom is announced in terrifying detail.

The vision cycle, then, is more than the sum of its parts. Together the visions trace a development from a time when the Lord was willing to cancel the planned disaster to a point when this was no longer possible. It shows that at a certain point during Amos's lifetime (and ministry?) Israel crossed to the point of no return. After that, the Lord's determination to punish was firm and the people's fate was sealed.

Two passages are inserted into the visions report and break its flow. The narrative of the clash between Amos and Amaziah (7:10–17) comes after the third vision. It is closely related to it and aims to explain exactly why and how Israel reached the point when the Lord was no longer willing to forgive them. At the same time, it provides colour and substance to the implied polemical situation of the earlier and later oracles (3:1–15; 5:18–27; 9:1–10). The command *You shall not prophesy* (2:12) and the response *The Lord God has spoken; / who can but prophesy?* (3:8) prepare the ground for the narrative and find their resolution in it. The collection of oracles in 8:4–14 offers a provisional summary of Amos's message. It alludes to some of the main themes and motifs from the book in relation to Israel's sin and judgment.

## A. The first two visions: the Lord relents (7:1–6)

*Comment*

**1–6.** The first vision opens with a mysterious figure: 'one forming locusts'.[1] This is presumably God himself, the 'one forming mountains' (4:13). Attention, however, quickly shifts from the Creator to the creature. The word for *locusts* (*gōbay*) may refer

---

1. The EVV render this 'he [i.e. the Lord] was forming locusts' but in Hebrew the subject of the participle is not made explicit in 7:1 (contrast 7:4).

more specifically to the larva stage immediately after hatching (Hammershaimb 1970: 108). Locusts destroyed the crops and were a natural disaster of terrifying proportions (see above on Joel 1:4). The *latter growth* (*leqeš*) appears only here in the Old Testament and its precise meaning is unclear. It is attested in the Gezer calendar where two months of *leqeš* come after two months of ingathering in the autumn and two months of sowing. The root of the word means 'to be late' (cf. *malqôš*, the 'latter rains' in March–April) and the term may refer either to the later grass that sprouts after haymaking or to the 'late-sown crops' (NJPS)/'second crop' (NJB) made possible by the later spring rains. The explanatory note at the end of verse 1 dates the *leqeš after the king's mowings*, presumably a harvest of early vegetation (a mowing of grass to be used for fodder?) collected as a royal tax in kind.

In the second vision Amos sees a *shower of fire*[2] which came down from heaven and *devoured the great deep*. The NIV's 'dried up the great deep' conveys the fact that a severe drought is in view. The first vision takes place in the spring; the second, during the hot summer. The earthly reality of drought is conveyed with the help of mythological imagery. The *great deep* is the primal water beneath the earth (Gen. 1:2; 7:11), a source of fertility and blessing (Gen. 49:25; Deut. 33:13). Once this is consumed the fire crawls up and begins to devour *the land*. In both visions the actions of the Lord's agents are reported with the verb *'ākal* ('eat, devour, consume'; vv. 2, 4). The eating locusts and fire mean no eating for the people of Israel.

Amos's prayer for the Lord to *forgive* (v. 3) assumes an awareness that the planned destruction is a punishment for the people's sins. The verb *sālaḥ* (meaning originally 'to sprinkle') derives from the cult and describes divine forgiveness resulting in purification and removal of sin and of its consequences. In Psalm 103:3 'forgives all

---

2. The MT *lārib bā'ēš* means 'to contend by fire' (NJPS), hence 'judgement by fire' (ESV, NIV), 'fire in punishment' (NJB), 'conflict by fire' (NKJV). The translation *shower*/'rain' *of fire* (NRSV, NAB), which fits the context much better, is based on the recognition that the Hebrew consonants *lrb b'š* were incorrectly divided (see 6:12) and originally read *lrbb 'š* (Wolff 1977: 298–299).

your iniquity' stands in parallel to 'heals all your diseases' and in 1 Kings 8:34, 36 forgiveness comes with reversal of the adverse effects of human rebellion. Amos prays that the Lord will *forgive* Israel and consequently (in the second vision) 'refrain' (v. 5; NJPS; *cease*, NRSV) from translating the plans depicted in the visions into reality. The subtle change of verbs in Amos's prayers, from *forgive* (v. 3) to *cease* (v. 5), introduces a variation in the established pattern of the visions which will become more pronounced as the series progresses.

Moses' prayer for divine forgiveness in Numbers 14:13–19 is based on a concern for God's name and on recognition of God's gracious character. Amos focuses on the second of those with his rhetorical question *How can Jacob stand? / He is so small!* (vv. 2, 5). He accepts that the punishment is deserved but appeals to the Lord's pity by pointing out the vulnerability of the people. His strategy proves successful. God's declaration *It shall not be* announces a change in the divine plan, made in response to the prophetic request. Such an alteration in God's intentions is not unique to this passage (Andersen and Freedman 1989: 638–679). The Old Testament portrays the Lord on numerous occasions changing his prior resolve to punish or bless someone in response to intercession (Exod. 32:12–14), repentance (Jer. 18:8) or sin (1 Sam. 15:35; Jer. 18:10). The statements to the contrary (Num. 23:19; 1 Sam 15:29) must mean that he does not change his mind in an arbitrary and capricious manner. The verb *relented* (*niḥam*), describing the divine reaction, carries strong emotional overtones. It can describe feelings of compassion and pity (Judg. 2:18; 21:15) as well as regret (Gen. 6:6–7; 1 Sam 15:11).

*Meaning*
Taken in isolation the first two visions extol the power of prayer and the merciful nature of God who is willing to forgive. The Lord plans to punish Israel, but Amos dissuades him from doing so, not because the people do not deserve it but because they are small and weak. Some interpreters have postulated that this passage reflects the earliest period of Amos's ministry (cf. 5:4–6), when he was still hoping for a positive response to his message (see Introduction). Whether this is true is impossible to say. In the present shape of the

text the passage serves as an introduction to the rest of the visions with their message of irrevocable punishment. Its primary function within the book is to stress the tragic nature of the missed opportunities of the past.

## B. The third vision: the plumb line (7:7–17)

*Context*

The third vision (7:7–9) is at the heart of the visions report both in terms of place (positioned at the very centre) and in terms of literary form and function. On the one hand, it is clearly meant to be read together with the fourth vision (8:1–3). In contrast to the first pair of event-visions (forming of locusts/raining down of fire), the third and the fourth are symbolic visions centred around a particular object whose meaning is key to their message (plumb line/basket of fruit). They have a similar structure which deviates from that of the preceding two reports (see Introduction) and are connected by means of verbal repetition: *Amos, what do you see?*; *my people Israel* (contrast *Jacob* in 7:2, 5); *I will never again pass them by* (7:8 = 8:2). On the other hand, the third vision has a special connection with the fifth (9:1–4). They are the only two that begin with a vision of God himself, formulated in exactly the same way: *the Lord [was] standing beside* ('*ădōnāy niṣṣāb 'al*). Thus, the third vision, which marks the transition between the first pair (7:1–6) and the following fourth and fifth visions, binds the whole together.

The narrative in 7:10–17 interrupts the tight connection between 7:7–9 and 8:1–3. The switch from first- (7:7–8) to third- (7:14) and back to first-person speech (8:1–2) and the difference in genre, vision report/narrative, contributes to the sense of discontinuity. Yet the literary disjunction is counterbalanced by thematic continuity. The narrative which features the priest of Bethel and his royal patron develops the motif of 7:9 which focuses on God's action against the sanctuaries and the royal house. Its language reflects many of the words and phrases found in the vision: *in the midst of* (vv. 8, 10); *my people Israel* (vv. 8, 15); *I will never again* (vv. 8, 13); *Isaac* (vv. 9, 16); *sanctuaries* (vv. 9, 13); *with the sword* (vv. 9, 17); a wordplay between *plumb-line* (×4, vv. 7–8; '*ănāk*) and $I$ (×3, v. 14; *'ānōkî*). The narrative explains why the Lord is no longer willing to forgive Israel, provides the rationale for the change in the Lord's attitude after 7:6 and identifies the mysterious plumb line in 7:7–8.

At the macro level the narrative and the vision contribute to the overall shape of the book. The statement *Do not prophesy* in verse 16 sends the reader back to 2:12 and the threefold repetition of *I* (*'ānōkî*) in 7:14 alludes back to the threefold divine *I* (*'ānōkî*) of 2:9–13. The Israel oracle has introduced Israel's two-step descent into sin and judgment: oppression of the poor corrupting Israel's worship (2:6–8) and rejection of the prophetic word (2:11–12). The preceding speeches (chs. 3–6) with their focus on justice and worship have developed the first point in detail. Now we come to the second and final stage of the drama in which the people of God turn their backs on him by rejecting his prophet. With this the theme of exile looms large. The narrative picks up the wordplay *Gilgal shall surely go into exile* from 5:5 and converts it into a frame that holds the story together (vv. 11, 17). Thus, a theme which has been gradually gaining prominence (1:5, 15; 5:27; 6:7) now reaches a climax.

## Comment
### i. The third vision (7:7–9)

**7–8.** The interpretation of this vision depends entirely on what one understands the object at its centre to be. The difficulty comes from the fact that the Hebrew word *'ănāk*, used four times here, is a loanword from Akkadian and does not occur anywhere else in the Old Testament. Its meaning has to be determined on the basis of the Akkadian term. The traditional translation *plumb-line* is based on the view that the Akkadian cognate means 'lead' and *'ănāk* refers to the lead weight of a plumb line. However, in 1965 the eminent Assyriologist Benno Landsberger argued that the Akkadian term meant 'tin' not 'lead'. Since tin is too light to be used as a weight, *'ănāk* in Hebrew could not mean plumb line. Amos, therefore, saw the Lord standing on a wall of tin, holding a lump of tin in his hand and threatening to put tin in the midst of his people Israel. The problem with this picture is that it is largely meaningless. None of the attempts to explain the symbolism of tin in the vision have been convincing enough.[3] Moreover, subsequent studies have disproven the assertion that *'ănāk* here cannot mean plumb line (Williamson 1990; Noonan 2013).

Therefore, it is best to go with the traditional translation 'plumb line' (cf. *DCH* 1.342; *HALOT* 1.71–72) and see the vision as announcing the transition from forgiveness to punishment. The Lord stands *beside a wall* that was originally straight because it was *built with a plumb-line*. The *plumb-line* he now holds in his hand signals his intention to inspect the wall and see if it has not begun to bend. If that is the case, the wall will have become dangerous and will need to be pulled down. It is not clear at this stage who or what the plumb line actually represents. The following narrative will make clear that it is the preaching of Amos himself (see below). The statement *I will never again pass them by*, which means 'I will never again overlook their offences' (NJB), signals a change in disposition from the preceding two visions. The Lord is not inclined to turn a blind eye any more. Jacob's only chance to remain standing now is in being found to be straight and in good condition. The time of prophetic intercession has passed. The language alludes to the picture of universal mourning in 5:17 when the Lord *pass[ed] through the midst* of his people.

**9.** The proclamation in verse 9 assumes that the outcome of the test was negative. The wall needs to be pulled down. *My people Israel* are defined more narrowly as the *high places of Isaac*, the *sanctuaries of Israel* and *the house of Jeroboam*, that is, the religious and political hierarchy of the nation. All these will be dismantled by the direct military action of the Lord.

---

3. Such attempts include the following: (1) tin is an alloy of bronze and hence symbolizes bronze weapons to be used against Israel (Jeremias 1998: 130–132); (2) the tin wall symbolizes Amos in his clash with Israel (Campos 2011: 17–21); (3) tin is a soft metal so the wall of tin is symbolic of Israel's weakness and vulnerability (Paul 1991: 234–235); (4) tin bears no significance in and of itself; the point is to create a play on words like *'ănaḥă*, 'groaning' (Nogalski 2011: 339). Sweeney (2000: 254–255) argues for the meaning 'plaster' instead of 'tin'. Andersen and Freedman (1989: 759) suggest that three different roots are used: plastered (wall), (lump of) tin, grief (in the midst of Israel).

## *ii. Confrontation at Bethel (7:10–17)*

The narrative gives us more information about Amos than any other section of the book, but its intention is not biographical. Many commentators assume that the reported incident marked the end of Amos's ministry in the North; after the confrontation he was extradited to Judah or executed. However, this is all based on conjecture. The text is not interested in the person of the prophet or his fate. In some sense the character of Amaziah is actually more important. The story is told to introduce and explain the oracle in verse 17 and it is placed here in the vision report to explain the thematic development within it from forgiveness to punishment.

The narrative is almost entirely dominated by direct speech. In the first half Amaziah, the priest, speaks (vv. 10–13); in the second part Amos, the prophet, replies (vv. 14–17). Each of them quotes the other (v. 11, 16) and at the end Amos also quotes the Lord who has the final word (v. 17). There are four characters altogether. Amaziah and Amos, who appear on stage, represent respectively Jeroboam and the Lord. The narrative revolves around the clash between the priest and the prophet which mirrors the confrontation 'off stage' between the king of Israel and the Lord. The statement *Israel shall surely go into exile away from its land* frames the passage (vv. 11, 17).

**10–13.** The mention of *Amaziah, the priest,* and *King Jeroboam of Israel* follows on from the dual focus of verse 9 on the *house of Jeroboam* and the *sanctuaries of Israel.* The priest, who is a royal servant, fulfils his duties by reporting Amos's activities, as they have definite political implications. The charge that *Amos has conspired against* Jeroboam II is not as far-fetched as it might sound to the modern reader. Prophets played an active role in political life and were often involved in conspiracies against the crown (1 Kgs 11:29–39; 19:16–17; 2 Kgs 9:1–14; see Isa. 8:12). Prophetic support legitimized and emboldened potential claimants to the throne and could prove crucial in a rebellion or coup (2 Kgs 8:7–15). There is some irony in the fact that Amos has conspired 'in the midst of the house of Israel' (ESV); the phrase alludes back to 7:8 and 5:17. The claim that *the land is not able to bear all his words* implies that there is widespread dissatisfaction with Amos's preaching. This may be a self-serving exaggeration, but it could very well reflect accurately the situation. The oracles in the rest of the book indicate that the prophet's provocative statements met with scepticism and unbelief.

Amaziah summarizes Amos's message in this way:

> *Jeroboam shall die by the sword,*
>     *and Israel must go into exile*
>     *away from his land.*

This is not a verbatim quotation of anything that can be found in the preceding oracles. The only time King Jeroboam is mentioned by name, apart from the superscription, is in 7:9 where, however, the whole *house of Jeroboam* is in view. How are we to understand this discrepancy? One way would be to attribute a wealth of meaning to the minor differences between verse 9 and verse 11. Amaziah omits the threat against the sanctuaries in verse 9, perhaps so that he can present himself as a disinterested and objective reporter, and narrows the threat against the whole dynasty to the person of the king, in order to make Amos's words sound more subversive. In doing so he reveals himself to be a dubious character who plays a political game and tries to set the king against the prophet (Linville 2008: 143).

Alternatively, Amaziah's report could be taken either as a quotation of an oracle which did not find its way into the book (Soggin 1987: 131), or as an accurate and fair representation of the gist of Amos's preaching (Sweeney 2000: 258). This is by far the better reading. Criticism of the cult cannot be divorced from criticism of the king who was its patron. If Amos ever spoke of God rising against the royal dynasty with the sword (7:9), understanding this as a personal threat to the king was a fair assumption. Prediction of exile is clearly a part of the prophetic proclamation so far (5:5, 27; 6:7), and that prediction in itself carries a threat to the king and his dynasty.

Amaziah, then, understands correctly the challenge the prophet presents to the royal and religious hierarchy of Israel. His response is to order Amos to leave the Northern Kingdom and *flee away to the land of Judah*. The connotations of the title *seer* (*ḥōzeh*) are not entirely clear. Perhaps the term was used to denote Judean court and temple officials (Stökl 2012: 192–200). Amaziah's thinking is that Amos's negative message about the kingdom of Israel will more likely *earn* financial rewards (cf. 1 Sam. 9:7–9) in Judah than in the North. This must be understood as a slur, not friendly advice. Amaziah disparagingly brushes aside Amos's accusations as politically motivated drivel. The prohibition to prophesy at Bethel is explained by pointing out its status as *the king's sanctuary* and *a temple of the kingdom*. If there was any doubt about the close link between cult and monarchy, this final remark removes it completely. It also demonstrates why cultic and social criticism are so closely tied in Amos's preaching. Israel's worship is governed and administered by the royal court and serves to legitimize royal power.

**14–15.** Amos first deals with the priest's suggestion that he is motivated by money. The statement *lō' nābî' 'ānōkî* can be translated either 'I am no prophet' (NRSV; NJPS; NJB) or 'I was no prophet' (ESV; NIV). The correct interpretation is impossible to decide on purely grammatical grounds, since the Hebrew allows both. The context suggests that the present tense is more likely (Schmidt 2007: 226–228). Amos responds to Amaziah's insinuation that he is preaching for money by pointing out that he is not a professional prophet.[4] Saying that he used not to be a prophet (but now is) would not really address Amaziah's allegations. The following clause confirms this interpretation. Amos is not a *prophet's son*, that is, a member of a prophetic guild ('nor do I belong to a prophetic brotherhood', NJB). The 'sons of the prophets' were not necessarily

---

4. Petersen (1981: 51–88) argues that the terms 'seer' and 'prophet' refer to central morality prophets but *ḥōzeh* ('seer') was the Judean term while *nābî'* ('prophet') was employed in Northern Israel. There were some differences between these two institutions stemming from the different social realities of the two kingdoms. On this basis he suggests that both Amos and Amaziah agree that Amos is a *ḥōzeh* ('seer'), i.e. a Judean prophet, and the bone of contention is whether such a prophet from the South has the authority to prophesy in the North (Petersen 1981: 57–58). The text, however, does not allow such a neat distinction between the two terms. It is more natural to see the terms 'seer' and 'prophet' in this passage as synonymous, in which case Amos rejects both titles.

biological descendants of prophets but members of prophetic schools, circles or guilds (1 Kgs 20:35; 2 Kgs 2:3; 4:1, 38; 5:22; 6:1; 9:1). Instead, Amos is a *herdsman, and a dresser of sycamore trees*. He has an independent source of income and therefore does not need to earn his living by prophesying. He is at Bethel only because the Lord *took* him from *following the flock* and said to him *Go, prophesy to my people Israel*. The argument is essentially the same as in 3:8. Amos is driven by divine compulsion originating from hearing the Lord's voice.

Amos's opening response 'I [*ʾānōkî*] am not a prophet, and I [*ʾānōkî*] am not a prophet's disciple, I [*ʾānōkî*] am a cattle breeder' (NJPS) contains a threefold recurrence of the first-person singular pronoun *ʾānōkî* (on which see 2:9–13 above) which in Hebrew sounds very much like the *ʾănāk* object seen in the third vision (7:7–8). Scholars have long suspected that the choice of this exotic word in the vision has, in part at least, been dictated by desire to convey some meaning via wordplay. The similarity between *ʾănāk* and *ʾănaḥâ* 'groaning' is often noted, and it is possible it played a role, especially in the original formulation of the visions.[5] The link between the narrative and the third vision identifies the prophet Amos with the plumb line. He is the final test of the nation's spiritual condition. Israel's response to Amos's ministry will demonstrate whether the wall is salvageable or bent beyond repair.

**16–17.** We now come to the main point of the narrative. Amaziah has rejected Amos's prophecy and ordered him to flee to Judah. In this he has set himself up in direct confrontation with God, as the contrast between his command to Amos to *go* (*lēk*) south and *prophesy* in Judah (v. 12) and the Lord's command to *go* (*lēk*) north and *prophesy* in Israel (v. 15) shows. His prohibition *Do not prophesy against Israel* corresponds to Israel's actions in 2:12. The figure of Amaziah, therefore, achieves a symbolic significance. He

---

5. Another possibility is that originally the *ʾănāk* pointed to the divine *ʾānōkî* whose presence in the midst of Israel has already been seen to bring disastrous consequences (5:17). Koenen (2003: 173 n. 112) sees this as the original meaning of the oracle and a reflection of Bethel's 'divine presence theology' (see Introduction).

represents Israel in its response to the prophets. The confrontation between him and Amos is paradigmatic for the clash between Israel and the Lord.

As the priest represents Israel in its rejection of the Lord, so his fate embodies the doom of the nation. The five-line oracle deals with the judgment on the priest whose exile in an *unclean land* prefigures the *exile* of *Israel* from *its land*. He will lose everything when his *sons* and *daughters . . . fall by the sword*, and when his land is *parcelled out by line*. His present possessions and the future of his line will come to nothing. Wrapped in this description of total loss is a dual statement of his utter humiliation and defilement. The fact that his *wife* will become a *prostitute* is the source of unimaginable disgrace and defilement that will result in the loss of his priestly status (Lev. 21:7). Dying in an *unclean land* also implies defilement and contradiction of his priestly calling. The oracle ends with the explicit statement of the reality symbolized by the priest's dire fate: *Israel shall surely go into exile away from its land*. This line, which frames the narrative (v. 11), highlights the unstoppable nature of the word of God. Amaziah's efforts to ban Amos from Bethel do not prevent the disaster from happening, but only ensure the ultimate fulfilment of his oracles.

*Meaning*

With the third vision a major change comes in the cycle. The Lord's willingness to allow Amos to intercede evaporates. There is also a genre change – from event-visions to symbolic visions. We no longer have a picture of disaster that can be simply prayed about, but an everyday object which has some, as yet unclear, symbolic significance. That object is a plumb line, an instrument for checking the straightness of walls. It does not carry threatening overtones unless the wall is found to be beyond repair. Initially we do not know what the Lord's test consists of. The oracle in verse 9 tells us only that its conclusions are negative and the Lord has to pull down the wall – the sanctuaries and the royal house of Israel – with a sword (a change from a building to a military metaphor).

With the following narrative we get a glimpse into the mechanics of the actual test. The plumb line (*'ănāk*) is the prophetic *I* (*'ānōkî*), that is, Amos himself. His ministry is Israel's last chance to come to its senses and escape judgment. In the narrative Amaziah stands for the ruling elite of the nation. His response to Amos encapsulates Israel's rejection of the prophetic message. This last straw breaks the camel's back. If Israel will not listen to the Lord and repent of its ways, nothing more can be done for it. As in 2:12, where the prohibition to prophesy is immediately followed by the announcement of punishment, the only thing left to proclaim is Amaziah's, and Israel's, humiliation and death/exile.

## C. The fourth vision: the end has come (8:1–14)

### Context

The fourth vision follows closely the pattern of the third (7:7–9) and should be read together with it (see *Context* on 7:7–17 above). Its agricultural character points back to the first vision (7:1–3) which took place in the spring, at the 'beginning [*tĕḥillat*] of the sprouting of the latter growth' (7:1; literal translation). In contrast, 8:1–2 talks about *summer fruit* (gathered in August–September) and *the end* (*qēṣ*) of Israel (Riede 2008: 140, 145). Just as the third vision is followed by a narrative (7:10–17), the fourth is followed by a collection of oracles (8:4–14), summarizing the guilt (8:4–6) and punishment (8:7–14) of Israel. It provides an extended justification for and description of the 'end' announced in the fourth vision. The motif of the withdrawn word of the Lord (8:11–14) develops the theme of the rejection of the prophetic word in 7:10–17. More broadly, verses 4–14, with their numerous literary allusions to the preceding material (vv. 4–6 = 2:6–7; v. 7 = 6:8; v. 10 = 5:1, 8, 16, 21, 23; v. 11 = 4:2; vv. 11–12 = 4:6–8; v. 14 = 5:2), function as a preliminary summary of Amos's message of judgment.

### Comment

### i. The fourth vision (8:1–3)

**1–2.** The *basket of summer fruit* ('figs', NJPS) is an innocent enough object, associated with harvest, fruitfulness and festivities. Therefore, the proclamation *The end has come upon my people Israel* based on it seems surprising and unjustified to the modern reader. Yet the link between object and proclamation is closer than it appears. First, Amos has already used the harvest as an image of judgment in the picture of the cart loaded with sheaves of grain (2:13). The aptness of the metaphor is confirmed by later literature (Jer. 51: 33; Joel 3:13; Matt. 13:39) where the harvest is often used symbolically in that way (Jeremias 1998: 134). Second, the connection between *summer fruit* (*qayiṣ*) and *end* (*qēṣ*) is achieved via wordplay, which the NIV tries to convey with its translation 'basket of ripe fruit/The time is ripe'. The two words are derived from different roots but sound similar, and in the dialect of Northern Israel may even have been pronounced the same. A similar technique is employed in Jeremiah's vision of the almond tree (Jer. 1:11–12).

**3.** The *songs of the temple*, or the 'palace songs' (NJB): *hêkāl* can mean both palace and temple. The ambiguity is probably intentional. As in 7:9, both the cult and the royal court are objects of judgment. The joyful songs of worship (5:23) and of aristocratic parties (6:5) are here transformed into their very opposite and strikingly personified as women who wail (MT lit. 'the songs shall wail').[6] The many *dead bodies* that are *cast out in every place* (see 6:9–10; 5:16–17; 4:3) explain the reasons for the wailing and show that *the end* of which the vision speaks means death. The interjection *Be silent* (*hās*; cf. 6:10) creates a harsh contrast with the beginning of the verse as it brings the loud wailing to a sudden stop. The magnitude of the disaster is conveyed through both noise and silence. That silence stands in ironic contrast to the attempts of Amaziah to silence Amos in the preceding passage.

## *ii. The oracles (8:4–14)*

**4–6.** This version of the oracle in 2:6–7 does not condemn the audience for selling the *needy* and the *poor* but for *buying* them. Despite the considerable overlap in language, the scenario is different. The guilt of the Israelites is established by means of a direct quotation (4:1; 6:13; 8:14; 9:10) which gives insight into their innermost thoughts and motivations. These people want to trade. They want to offer for sale *grain* and *wheat*, presumably to the poor urban dwellers at the city market. However, their trading practices

---

6. NJPS 'the singing women of the palace' and NAB 'the temple singers' unnecessarily emend the MT to *šārôt* 'singing women' (*BHS*).

are fraudulent. The *ephah* is a unit of dry measure, roughly equivalent to 40 litres, used to calculate the amount of grain given to the customer. The *shekel*, a unit of weight of about 11 grams, is used to estimate how much silver the buyer owes for the purchased grain. By making *the ephah small* and the *shekel great* the merchants make sure they receive a greater amount of silver than agreed and part with a smaller amount of grain (Wolff 1977: 327; Paul 1991: 258). A third way of cheating the customers is by using *false balances*. The extent to which the economic and legal power is on the side of the sellers in these transactions is evident from the fact that they are even *selling the sweepings of the wheat*, that is, corn which had fallen to the ground, been trampled upon and mixed with straw and dirt.

We can deduce from the current passage that trading activities ceased (Jer. 17:19–27; Neh. 13:15–22) during the celebration of the *new moon* and *sabbath* (2 Kgs 4:23; Isa 1:13; Hos. 2:11; cf. 1 Sam. 20:5). In contrast to the rest of the book, religious practice here is not justification for oppression but an unwelcome hindrance. The greed of the merchants is so great that even a day of rest and celebration is seen as a tragic loss of opportunity to cheat and make profit. *Buying the poor for silver*: the cheated customers are converted into a commodity, like the wheat that is bought and sold. Whether this is a literal reference to debt-slavery or a metaphorical description of economic dependence is difficult to say. Alliteration (the repetition of the sound *š*) and wordplay contribute to the literary impact of the oracle. *Bring to ruin* (*lašbît*; 'annihilate', NJPS) sounds like *the sabbath* (*šabbāt*); *grain* (*šeber*) is a homonym of the *ruin* [*šeber*] [*of Joseph*] in 6:6.

**7–10.** A solemn oath marks the transition between accusation and announcement of judgment. Previously the Lord *has sworn* either *by his holiness* (4:2) or *by himself* (6:8). This time he swears *by the pride of Jacob*, an expression used negatively in 6:8 to denote the people's arrogance which God hates, and positively in Psalm 47:4 as a description of Israel's land. The parallel to the other oaths in the book suggests a third possibility, that the *pride of Jacob* is God himself (see Mic. 5:4). There is ambiguity and profound irony in the oath. The Lord, in swearing by himself (Soggin 1987: 135) or by Israel's land (Jeremias 1998: 148–149), is simultaneously swearing by the arrogance of Israel (Wolff 1977: 328). The sin of the people is so great that it has corrupted everything and has managed to defile even the most sacred realities of Israel's life.

Just as God's knowledge of Israel's sins is tantamount to their punishment in 5:12, so here God's refusing to *forget any of their deeds* means the same. The description of punishment combines two discrete motifs from the earlier chapters: mourning and the return of chaos. Turning *feasts into mourning* and *songs into lamentation* connects 5:16–17 with 5:21–23; 6:5 and builds on 5:13 and 8:3. On *sackcloth* and *baldness* as elements of mourning rituals see Ezekiel 7:18; 27:30–32 and also Genesis 37:34; 2 Samuel 3:31; Micah 1:16. *Mourning* the death of *an only* child was an especially bitter experience (Jer. 6:26; Zech. 12:10) because it signified the end of the family line (cf. Judg. 11:34).

The grieving is caused by a massive cosmic disturbance. *Shall not the land tremble on this account . . . ?* refers to an earthquake. But the comparison *and all of it rise like the Nile, / and be tossed about and sink again, like the Nile of Egypt* is puzzling, since the inundation of the Nile is gradual and takes place over an extended period of time (Hammershaimb 1970: 125). If a realistic parallel to the violent rising and sinking of the earth during an earthquake was the goal, a sea storm would have supplied a much better analogy. The Nile is mentioned here because of its symbolic overtones, and it also prepares the reader for the final hymnic piece in 9:5–6. In Israel's tradition Egypt is a place of oppression and chaos. The river is intimately linked to the pharaoh, the king of Egypt, who is the great dragon monster of the Nile (Ezek. 29:3). The Nile, together with the 'sea of distress', is an enemy of the people of God (Zech. 10:11). It symbolizes chaos and brings destruction to the world (Jer. 46:7–8).[7] *I will make the sun go down at noon, / and darken the earth in broad daylight*: even if a reference to a solar eclipse stands in the background the main issue is not any physical devastation caused by natural phenomena. The darkness of the sky and the rising of the waters of chaos signal a reversal of creation. The point is

---

7. Hayes (1988: 209) points out that Egyptian texts liken the destructions sometimes caused by the inundation of the Nile to the chaotic disorder at creation.

underlined by means of wordplay. *Like the Nile* (*kī'ōr*) points to *bĕyôm 'ôr* (*broad daylight*; lit. 'in a day of light'), which is in turn contrasted with the *kĕyôm mār* ('like a day of bitterness'; my translation). The mentions of the 'day' in the context of light turning to darkness allude to the Day of the Lord in 5:18–20.

Fraud in trade and exploitation of the poor undermine the just order of creation. The outcome is the undoing of creation harmony and the disintegration of the world into an abyss of darkness and grief. The point is similar to that of 5:7–9; note the repetition of *turn* in both places.

**11–14.** The description of punishment is divided into two sections. The first (vv. 7–10) deals with the people's relationship to creation; the second (vv. 11–14), with their relationship with the Creator. In the wilderness the Lord taught Israel through hunger that human beings do 'not live by bread alone, but by every word that comes from the mouth of the LORD' (Deut. 8:3). However, since the hunger experienced by the generation of Amos's day has not taught them that lesson (4:6–8) God will withdraw his word. The resulting spiritual hunger will be more devastating than the physical disasters inflicted earlier (4:6–11). Since the word of the Lord is the source of human life, its withdrawal has devastating consequences. First, there is frantic *seeking* of the *word of the LORD*. The people *wander* ('stagger', NIV, NJB) and *run to and fro*, but in vain. The word has been withdrawn and can no longer be found. Then, at the end of that pointless search, the people *shall faint for thirst*, and finally they *shall fall, and never rise again*. The fall/rise motif is an allusion to the death of Israel in 5:2. It is not the old and weary but the *beautiful young women* (*bĕtûlōt*; cf. *maiden* [*bĕtûlat*] *Israel*; 5:2) and the *young men* (*baḥûrîm*; cf. 4:10) who fall. Even the strongest and fittest will not survive. *Hearing the words of the LORD* establishes a connection with 7:16 and invites the reader to see 7:10–17 and 8:4–14 together. The withdrawal of the word of the Lord is not an arbitrary act of divine petulance, but a necessary response to Israel's rejection of that same word.

Wrapped within this picture of judgment is one final mention of the sin of Israel. The people *swear by Ashimah of Samaria*, by the life of the god of *Dan* and by the *way of Beer-sheba*. Oaths played an important role in the social life of Ancient Near Eastern peoples.

They were used to seal contracts, undertake obligations and confirm the veracity of statements. Swearing by the name of a particular god meant invoking that god's power to oversee the established relationships and enforce required norms of behaviour. People swore by the gods they worshipped, and the expression 'by the life of X' (or 'as X lives') was a common oath formula (Jer. 38:16). Israel was expected to swear only by the Lord (Deut. 6:13; 10:20), so swearing by the name of Baal (Jer. 12:16) or Milcom (Zeph. 1:5) was tantamount to idolatry. The indictment is the worship of other gods.

It is not clear which gods are mentioned here. NRSV and NAB repoint the MT to obtain the proper name of a goddess: *Ashimah of Samaria* (Barstad 1984: 157–181; cf. 2 Kgs 17:30), originally a North Syrian Aramaic deity worshipped at a later stage also by Arab tribes at Teima (*DDD* 105–106). Others prefer to preserve the pointing of the Hebrew and render 'the Guilt' (ESV; NJPS) or 'the Sin' (NJB; NIV) of Samaria, a polemical reference to the worship of (1) the Lord outside Jerusalem (Sweeney 2000: 268); (2) the calf at Bethel (Paul 1991: 270; cf. Hos. 8:5); (3) the Baal–Asherah idols (Stuart 1987: 386); or (4) a fertility goddess in Samaria (Andersen and Freedman 1989: 828–829). It is possible that 'the Guilt' is an ironic rendering of the name 'Ashimah'. The *god* of *Dan* could be the Lord himself (Eidevall 2017: 222), the second calf image erected by Jeroboam I (Hammershaimb 1970: 128) or a local, Baal-type city god (Barstad 1984: 187). Jeremias (1998: 153) notes the discovery of an inscription from Hellenistic times which reads 'to the god in Dan', and conjectures that a god without a name, identified only by its link to the Dan sanctuary, continued to be worshipped there. *As the way of Beer-sheba lives* is the most puzzling of all. Rudolph (1971: 270–271) assumes an oath by the pilgrimage to the sanctuary there and points out the parallel with the Islamic oath to the pilgrimage to Mecca ('Hurrah for the pilgrimage to Beersheba!', NJB). However, the oath formula and the parallel previous line presuppose a reference to a god, as the translators of the LXX recognized (followed by NIV 'as the god of Beersheba'). The solution of NAB 'By the life of the Power of Beersheba!' (Soggin 1987: 140–141; Stuart 1987: 382; Jeremias 1998: 152) assumes, on the basis of Ugaritic parallels, that the Hebrew word *derek*, 'way', had also the meaning 'power'

(*HALOT* 1.232), used here as a divine appellation. More important than the identities of the foreign gods, however, are the places where they are worshipped. The expression 'from Dan [in the very north] to Beersheba [in the extreme south]' is often used as a shorthand for the whole land of Israel (Judg. 20:1; 1 Sam. 3:20; 2 Sam. 3:10; etc.). Samaria, the capital of the kingdom, is a natural designation of the centre. The geographical locations indicate the pervasiveness of the sin of Israel which is matched by the totality of the cosmic judgment in the preceding verses.

Verse 14 performs an important literary function. First, the use of direct quotation to establish the guilt of the audience parallels verses 4–6 and creates a frame for verses 4–14. The passage begins and ends with two sets of accusations, one about injustice (vv. 4–6) and the other about worship (v. 14). This reflects the dual focus of Amos's social and cultic criticism, but also differs from it in important respects, because neither fraudulent trading practices nor idolatry have featured prominently so far. The connection suggests that those who fall never to rise in verse 14 are not just the young men and women of verse 13 but also the dishonest merchants of verses 4–6. Second, the reference to swearing (*nišba'*) links back to verse 7 and provides another frame, this time for the description of punishment in verses 7–14. It also invites the reader to place the ironic and ambiguous *pride of Jacob* in contrast to the 'guilt of Samaria' (Andersen and Freedman 1989: 829–830). The final verse, therefore, brings the whole of verses 4–14 to an effective, if devastating, conclusion.

### Meaning

This passage serves as a preliminary conclusion to the book, summing up, and perhaps even reapplying to a new situation, some of its previous main themes. The end of Israel is announced in the fourth vision. The following oracles describe it in detail and explain again the reasons for its arrival. They are framed by two complementary glimpses into Israel's depravity: unjust commercial practices at the start and worship of foreign gods at the end. They build on the prophet's earlier social and cultic criticism, but the focus is different. Idolatry and oppression combine to strike at the very heart of the just order of creation established by God.

Therefore, the people will experience the Lord's withdrawal, followed by a reversal of creation and the onslaught of the forces of chaos. These forces will bring darkness, undermine security, and sap all strength until even the young men and women fall into the bitter embrace of death. A frantic and pointless search for God's word, loud wailing and stunned silence at the descending horrors is in store. The silence is the most salient detail of the picture. As Israel tried to silence the prophet (7:10–17), so God now withdraws in silence as a response.

## D. The fifth vision: the destroyed temple (9:1–6)

*Context*

The final vision stands apart as the conclusion and climax of the visions report (7:1–9; 8:1–3; 9:1–4). Its opening, *the Lord standing beside*, connects it to the third vision (7:7), but there is little else that relates to the preceding material. The structure is different: no dialogue with the prophet ensues; an extended divine oracle occupies all the space. What Amos sees is neither an event (7:1, 4) nor an object (7:7; 8:1) but, as in Isaiah 6:1, the Lord himself (9:1). Formulas and key words are not repeated from the other visions.

Yet 9:1–4 is connected to the cycle both thematically and formally. Its five conditional sentences with five places where the Israelites will not be able to hide (9:2–4a) correspond to the five visions. The first four (Sheol/heaven; Carmel/sea) are paired just like the first four visions, and the last stands on its own. The fifth vision brings the message of the report to a climax: the inexorable fate of Israel. The end of the people, avoided in 7:1–6 and announced in 7:7–9 and 8:1–3, is now described in detail. The basket of summer fruit (8:1–2) and the Lord standing at the altar (9:1) could be complementary elements of a single picture, the great autumn festival. So the cycle depicts the onslaught of judgment beginning at the periphery, the fields outside the city (7:1–6), then moving past the (city?) wall (7:7), and finally reaching the temple (9:1) at the heart of the community.

The vision, together with its hymnic conclusion in verses 5–6, is a final expression of the theme of creation and chaos (5:7–9; 8:7–14). The mention of *the top of Carmel* (9:3 = 1:2) and the *flee* but *not . . . escape* motif (9:1 = 2:14–16) frame the book as a whole, while the memorable expression *the sea-serpent, and it shall bite them* (*hannāḥāš ûnĕšākām*) is a direct reference to the Day of the Lord text (*and was bitten by a snake* = *ûnĕšākô hannāḥāš*; 5:19). Most importantly, both 2:13–16 and 5:18–20 revolve around the theme of the impossibility of escape, which is also central here.

## Comment

1. Amos's vision takes place in an unnamed temple. Most probably this was the temple at Bethel, although later readers would have naturally made a connection with Jerusalem. The Lord is *standing beside* [*niṣṣāb ʿal*] *the altar* just as he 'stood beside' (*niṣṣāb ʿal*) Jacob in his Bethel vision (Gen. 28:13). The sacrificial *altar* in the outer courtyard was the place where God met the worshippers who brought their offerings to him. Consequently, it was the object that symbolized and made possible human contact with God (Riede 2008: 187–188). The opening scene is rather reassuring. The Lord is standing by the altar where the officiating priest or king would be (1 Kgs 13:1). He is present with the worshipping community (Soggin 1987: 122–123). Things change, however, once the Lord speaks. The command *Strike the capitals until the thresholds shake* (*yirʿāšû*) signals the start of an earthquake. The addressee is not clear, perhaps an unidentified angelic figure in the vision (cf. Gen. 28:12; 2 Sam. 24:16–17). This may have been Amos's original prediction of *the earthquake* (1:1 *hārāʿaš*) whose fulfilment served as initial authentication of his message. The *capitals* are the decorated heads of the columns that either stood in the centre of the temple, supporting the roof, or flanked the door. Together with the *thresholds* the *capitals* symbolize the whole structure from 'top to bottom'. The threshold in particular was an important part of the temple complex which marked the boundary between the inner realm of the sacred and the outer profane world. Its significance is attested by the existence of a special priestly office, 'keeper/guardian of the threshold' (2 Kgs 22:4; 25:18; Jer. 35:4). In the Levant the temple gate was often the most impressive structural component, indicating its crucial role as a boundary marker (Hundley 2013: 121–122).

Within the framework of Ancient Near Eastern thought, the vision carries a symbolic significance that far outstrips the mere prediction of a natural disaster. In both Egypt and Mesopotamia, the temple, as the meeting point of the divine and the human spheres, had cosmic significance. It was a mirror image of creation, a celebration and actualization of the triumph of order over chaos. Its proper maintenance ensured the stability of the world and the prosperity and security of the nation (Hundley 2013: 41–48, 76–84). A similar worldview may underline some Old Testament texts, such as Psalm 24, where the created world is parallel to the 'hill of the LORD' and the gates of the temple are synonymous with the 'ancient doors' of the heavenly sanctuary. The shaking thresholds of the temple in Amos's vision, then, indicate that the boundaries between the holy and the profane are compromised and the world itself is in danger. Bethel, which once was a 'gate of heaven' (Gen. 28:17), now no longer fulfils this function (Riede 2008: 207–208). The strike against the temple shatters the world of the Israelites and is followed by a cosmic pursuit that will end only with their total extermination.

The translation *shatter them on the heads of all the people* is problematic. It is much better to translate the Hebrew: 'kill those who are at the head of them all, and the last of them I will slay by the sword' (Hadjiev 2007). The words are a continuation of the divine command. The Lord orders one of his servants to shatter the temple and kill the leaders of the community who are presumably inside (Judg. 16:23–20; 2 Kgs 10:21). The rest of the worshippers who survive (because they are in the courtyard?) will be chased and executed personally by the Lord. The impossibility of escape sends the reader back to the opening oracle where the same idea is expressed with some of the same vocabulary (*flee, yānûs* 2:16; cf. 2:14; *escape*/'save', *yimmālēṭ* 2:14–15).

**2–4.** The rest of the oracle develops this theme in full. The shattering of the temple has deprived the world of security and stability. Five conditional clauses name five possible places where those who flee God might attempt to seek refuge. Their parallel structure, governed by the recurring *though* ['*im*] ... *from there* [*miššām*], creates a snowballing effect which impresses upon the listener the futility of flight. The first pair, *Sheol* and 'the sky' (*heaven*, NRSV), depicts the extremities of the universe: its lowest point where the dead go and its highest point where God dwells. The second pair, *the top of Carmel* and the *bottom of the sea*, represents slightly lower points situated along the same axis. In the Ancient Near East the mountain top was often seen as a divine abode and a gateway to heaven (cf. Exod. 24:9–11). The sea, on the other hand, was the entrance to Sheol (Jon. 2:1–6). The fifth place is paradoxically *captivity in front of their enemies*. Even this in-principle highly undesirable outcome will not afford respite. Paradoxically, it is not their enemies but their God whom the people have to fear. On the motif of futile attempts to hide in heaven or in the underworld, see Psalm 139:7–12 (cf. Job 11:8–9).

*I will fix my eyes on them / for harm and not for good*: the idiom 'I will set my eyes on you' means 'I will take good care of you' (Jer. 40:4; cf. 39:12, 'look after' someone). Amos reverses the idiom to express God's determination to bring harm. The repetition of *my eyes* from verse 3 (where NRSV translates *my sight*) adds to the emphasis on human inability to hide. The antithesis between *harm* ('evil', ESV) and *good* links back to 5:15 and the cause behind Israel's current predicament.

**5–6.** The cosmic perspective of the vision is continued and brought to a climax by the final doxology of the book (cf. 4:13; 5:8–9). The *earth*, the *heavens* and the *waters of the sea*, places where the Israelites attempted to hide (vv. 2–4), are under the complete control of the Lord. The opening *he . . . touches the earth and it melts* ('trembles', NJPS) probably refers to an earthquake (see the use of *mûg*, 'melt, totter', in Ps. 75:3; Nah. 1:5), symbolic of the destruction of the temple and the general dissolution of the world. The comparison with the *Nile of Egypt* confirms that the melting of the earth and the mourning of its inhabitants are caused by the return of chaos (see above on 8:8). The final *who calls for the waters of the sea, / and pours them out upon the surface of the earth* is a verbatim repetition of 5:8b. While some ambiguity could be maintained there between the beneficial and destructive actions of God, there is little doubt that here the devastation of the flood and a reversal of creation is intended.

In the centre of all this upheaval verse 6a references the Lord's building activity. What he builds is not entirely clear. *Upper chambers* rests on the emendation of MT *ma'ălôtāw* 'his stairs' (or 'his podium') to *'ălîyôtāw* 'his upper rooms' (Ps. 104:3, 13). Paas (2003: 294–295), however, suggests that the MT should be retained and the 'stairs' taken as the steps leading up to the royal throne, placed in an Egyptian fashion on an elevated platform. The Lord builds heaven and earth into a royal pavilion where he sits as king.[8] The destructive power unleashed upon the world does not undermine the authority of its Creator and King.

*Meaning*

The vehement rhetoric of the fifth vision is designed to convey one message: the end of Israel is going to be an utter and complete disaster from which no-one will be able to escape. This end is presented as destruction of creation, the shattering of the temple and universal death. The personal presence of the Lord dominates the passage but provides little basis for comfort. His omnipresent power is bad news for the victims of his judgment. As King of the world, every sphere of his creation is under his surveillance and control, which means there can be no hope, and no escape.

What is the point of such a thoroughly devastating message? We must reckon with the fact that the text assumed different meanings in the changing circumstances of Amos's audience. The visions report reuses polemically some of the cherished theological concepts of the Bethel temple. Together with the aggressive rhetoric this suggests an origin in the context of heated debates between the prophet and his listeners. The harsh message of judgment aims to shake the audience out of their apathy and scepticism. Thus, the proclamation of the end paradoxically endeavours to prevent that end, either for the whole nation or for a restricted remnant, by

---

8. The term *'ăgudātô* in the following line also presents difficulties and the LXX ('his promise/announcement') struggled with it. The common rendering 'vault', which understands it as synonymous to the vault of Gen. 1:6, assumes that the word means something 'which is firmly held together' (Paul 1991: 280 n. 77). Based on context Andersen and Freedman (1989: 846) argue for 'its supports', i.e. a depiction of the lower part of the structure, while Stuart (1987: 389) suggests 'storeroom'. Paas proposes a papyrus 'bundle', the pillar on which the heavenly canopy of the divine throne rests.

forcing people to own up to their sins and change their ways (Riede 2008: 332–335). After the end of the Northern Kingdom the visions read differently. They were no longer a challenge to the arrogance of people who did not believe such a tragedy was possible. Instead, they showed how the nation had travelled a long path towards disaster: ignoring divine warnings, wasting opportunities to change, trifling with divine forgiveness. The visions also proclaimed to those crushed by defeat and exile that the Lord was just and his power still intact. The desecration of his temple and the plight of his nation did not undermine his royal throne (Jeremias 1998: 159–160). These events were not indications of his weakness but, on the contrary, of his complete and total control of the world.

# 6. THE RAISING OF THE FALLEN BOOTH OF DAVID (9:7–15)

*Context*

Thematically the epilogue of Amos falls into two distinct literary units. The first (vv. 7–10) deals with the partial destruction of Israel; the second (vv. 11–15), with its restoration. The epilogue qualifies the message in the visions of a complete and final end of Israel. The two units are held together by the preponderance of first-person divine speech: *I will destroy* (v. 8), *I will command* (v. 9), *I will raise up* (v. 11), *I will restore* (v. 14), *I will plant* (v. 15). Everything that happens is initiated by God.

The passage picks up several key phrases and motifs from the preceding material that recall Amos's proclamation of judgment. The first subsection (vv. 7–10) underlines its connection to the fifth vision by dense concentration of verbal repetition: *kaptôr* (*Caphtor*, v. 7 = *capitals*, v. 1); *eyes* (v. 8 = vv. 3 [*from my sight*] and 4); *I will command* (v. 9 = vv. 3–4; cf. 6:11); *by/with the sword* (v. 10 = vv. 1, 4); *rā'â* (*evil*, v. 10 = *harm*, v. 4). At the same time, it signals to the reader that we are nearing the end of the book by allusions to a number of earlier passages, most notably the OAN. The rhetorical question in verse 7 connects in inverted order to the beginning and end of the OAN: (1) *Are you not like the Ethiopians to me,* / *O people of Israel? says the* LORD = see 2:11b; *Did I not bring Israel up from the land of Egypt* = see 2:10; (2) *Philistines* = see 1:8; (3) *Arameans* and *Kir* = see 1:5.

The allusions in verses 11–15 also recall the message of judgment but in order to reverse it. These allusions include the following: in verse 11, *raise up* the *fallen* (5:2; 8:14) *booth* (5:26) *of David; breaches* (4:3); in verse 12, the *remnant* (1:8; 5:15) *of Edom* (1:11–12) and *all the nations* (OAN; 6:14; 9:9); the *name* [*of the* LORD] (6:10); in verse 13, *The time is surely coming* (4:2; 8:11); in verse 14, *restore the fortunes* (lit. 'return the returning'; cf. 'return' [*šûb*] his punishment in 1:3 and *passim*; and *you did not return* [*šûb*] in 4:6–11) of *my people Israel* (7:8; 8:2); *they shall rebuild the ruined cities and inhabit them;* / *they shall plant vineyards and drink their wine* (5:11); in verse 15, *out of the land* (7:11, 17). On the historical context of this passage see the Introduction.

### Comment

**7–8.** Two rhetorical questions, both starting with *hălô'* (*Are you not/Did I not*) and separated by *says the* LORD, determine the shape of verse 7. They expect a positive answer, but the force of the first one is not clear to us because we do not know for sure what associations the word *Ethiopians* (*bĕnê kušîyîm*; lit. 'the sons of the Cushites') had for Amos's original audience. Cush was the country to the south of Egypt. The term is used to describe the most extreme south-western point of the Persian Empire (Esth. 1:1; 8:9) and more generally distant lands (Zeph. 3:10). Consequently, one way of understanding the reference would be as a comparison between the Israelites and the most remote people living at the ends of the earth. The Lord cares for all people, near and far, not just for Israel.

Alternatively, the whole verse may deal with migration and deportation. The chiastic arrangement Ethiopians – Israelites – says the Lord – Israel – Egypt invites us to read the comparison of Israel and Cush in connection to the exodus from Egypt, especially since Cush and Egypt are sometimes used as synonyms in the Old Testament (Strawn 2013). Perhaps an unknown Cushite migration is in view in the first rhetorical question.[1] Likewise, we know nothing of the Aramean origins from *Kir*. Only the Philistine arrival from *Caphtor*, usually identified with the island of Crete (the ancient versions identify it with Cappadocia; cf. Gelston 2010: 88), is attested more widely in the Old Testament (Deut. 2:23; Jer. 47:4) and can be linked to the migrations of the Sea Peoples at the end of the second millennium. Beneath the surface, there is a menacing undercurrent to the mention of all these beneficial divine acts. The coming of the *Arameans* from *Kir* is a reminder of their threatened exile to Kir in 1:5. In 1:3–6 the Arameans and the Philistines are coupled together, just like in 9:7, but for exile and extermination. *Caphtor* is the same word as the *capital* (*kaptôr*) struck in 9:1. On *bring . . . up from the land of Egypt* see 2:10. The implication is that God can just as easily take away what he has given.

The rhetorical questions make a shocking point. They deny the special significance of the exodus from Egypt by comparing it to the migrations of other Ancient Near Eastern nations – Cushites, Arameans, Philistines. In the final analysis, Israel is no different in God's eyes from the rest of the nations of the world. Such a controversial statement can be explained only as the impassioned response to an opponent's objection made in the course of a public debate, probably something like *Evil shall not overtake or meet us* (v. 10). Verse 7 attacks the foundations of this assertion. The listeners did not believe in the veracity of Amos's proclamation of disaster (*evil*) because the exodus from Egypt proved that God was on their side (3:2; 5:14); therefore, nothing really bad could happen to them. In 3:2 Amos responds to this kind of thinking by pointing out that the special relationship entails special responsibility. Here his strategy is entirely

---

1. The mention of Cushan of Hab. 3:7 may be a reference to an ethnic group with Cushitic ancestry which had migrated into the Arabian Peninsula (*NIDB* 1.812). In Gen. 10:6–12 Cush is also linked to Mesopotamia, perhaps seen as the ancestor of the Kassites who ruled Babylon in the second millennium (*ABD* 1.1219). Any number of traditions about Cushite migrations may stand behind such opaque references. As in the OAN and 4:6–11 Amos is relying on elements of the cultural and communicative memory of his audience that are not accessible to us.

different: he denies the special relationship altogether. The two sayings originated in two different polemical settings. Perhaps with time Amos became more radical and controversial in the means he employed to dismantle his audience's resistance (Barton 2012: 71–76).

In the literary context of the epilogue, the main point of verses 7–8 is not to counter imagined objections to the prophet but to clarify the limits of God's punishment and Israel's destruction. Verse 8a draws the theological conclusion from the position established in verse 7. As the Lord guides the migrations of the nations, his *eyes* are upon them to *destroy* any *sinful kingdom*. Since Israel is placed on the same level as the rest of the nations, its *sinful kingdom* will likewise be destroyed. Verse 8b introduces a surprising and unexpected qualification. There is one sinful kingdom, the *house of Jacob*, that the Lord is not going to *utterly destroy*. *Jacob* evokes the sinful worship at Bethel (3:13), the 'arrogance' that the Lord hates (6:8) and the experience of judgment tempered by mercy in the first two visions (7:2, 5). The statement in verse 8 opens a new chapter in the life of Jacob, similar to his position at the start of the visions cycle. Jacob is again under judgment tempered by mercy. In contrast to the first two visions, here this mercy is not manifested in the delay and withdrawal of the punishment, but in the limitation of its scope. The fifth vision has asserted that no-one will escape by means of personal effort, but now the Lord states his intention to allow some to be rescued. This is worked out in detail in the following verses.

**9–10.** In the oral context of Amos's preaching the oracle about the *sieve* was another polemical proclamation of the impossibility of escaping God's judgment (cf. 5:18–20; 9:1–4). The sieve lets the grain fall onto the ground and retains larger stones and other impurities to be thrown away. The point of the metaphor is that *no pebble shall fall to the ground*; in other words, the sieve will not let anyone escape but *All the sinners of my people*[2] *shall die by the sword.*

---

2. This phrase is grammatically ambiguous and can mean either 'every single one of my sinful people' (i.e. everybody) or 'every sinner from among my people' (i.e. only some out of the whole), corresponding to the different focus of the oracle in its original oral proclamation and its current literary context (Hadjiev 2008: 666).

However, the current context brings to the fore another dimension of the image. Its new function is to explain how it is possible that the Lord will destroy the sinful kingdom but not utterly destroy the house of Jacob (Hadjiev 2008: 664–667). The Lord will indeed punish every single one of those who disbelieve in the coming of this *evil*. The *sinners of my people* (v. 10) reminds one of the *sins* (5:12) of *my people Israel* (7:8; 8:2), and *evil/disaster* (v. 10) is a recurring theme (3:6; 5:13, 15; 9:4). The shaking (*nûaʿ*) of the sieve (v. 9) uses the same word translated *wander* in the judgment pronouncements of 4:8 and 8:12. However, another group, invisible so far, is beginning to gradually move towards the surface: the good grain that falls to the ground escapes the deadly presence of God and survives the disaster. This group is not explicitly mentioned in the text, but the following passage will force the reader to consider them as well. The passage qualifies the absolute statement of 9:4 that God will exterminate even those who go into exile.

**11–12.** From the ashes of partial destruction (vv. 8–10) suddenly a new age of restoration emerges. The transition is abrupt and unmotivated. There is no mention of repentance, pursuit of justice or Israel's seeking the Lord that can explain the different divine handling of the nation. What follows is an expression of the sheer mercy of God, given to a still-undeserving people.

*Raise up, fallen*: salvation is a reversal of the previously announced judgment (5:2; 8:14). The *house of Jacob* (v. 8), the partially destroyed *sinful kingdom*, is transformed into a new entity, called the *booth of David*. The expression is unique in the Old Testament and its precise meaning is disputed.[3] Two textual clues are worth pondering. First,

---

3. The booth is often taken as an image either of the Davidic dynasty or of the Davidic empire (Glenny 2009: 218–220). The participle *nōpelet* could be translated 'falling', which implies that the hut is still standing but in poor condition, or 'fallen', i.e. it has been totally destroyed. If the first reading is adopted, the allusion would be to the reduced power of the royal house in the time of Amos (Rudolph 1971: 280–281; Paul 1991: 290). The second reading fits most naturally with the fall of Judah and the Babylonian exile (Wolff 1977: 353). Stuart (1987: 398) repoints to 'David's Succoth', a city that serves as a base for military operations in the Transjordan.

the booth is said to have *breaches* and *ruins* which the Lord will *repair* and *rebuild*, a clear allusion to the destroyed walls of a captured city (4:3). This can only be 'the city of David', Jerusalem (Pomykala 2004). Second, the suffixes in the Hebrew text that refer to the booth vary in gender and number. The NRSV obscures this by a uniform rendering – *it/its* – following the lead of the LXX which renders all pronouns as feminine singular, relating them to the 'tabernacle/tent' (*skēnē*). The confusing grammar is not the result of a mistake or corruption but is a deliberate literary device that provides the key to interpretation (Nogalski 2011: 355–356). It forces the reader to recognize that the booth is not to be taken simplistically as a literal reference to Jerusalem but symbolizes a larger, more complex entity:

- I will raise up the fallen booth (feminine singular) of David (masculine singular).
- I will repair their (feminine plural) breaches: refers to the *ruined cities* of verse 14 (feminine plural) represented collectively by the 'fallen booth' (feminine).
- I will raise up his (masculine singular) ruins: refers to David (masculine). Both David and the booth emerge as parallel symbolic representations of the entity which God restores.
- I will rebuild her (feminine singular): refers to the booth/city of Jerusalem. In Hebrew the word 'city' (*'îr*) is also feminine.
- So that they (masculine plural) may possess: there is no obvious grammatical referent to the subject of the verb. The only option is David, understood collectively as representative of the inhabitants of the restored city (Goswell 2011: 256–257).

The prophecy avoids the more widespread expression 'house of David' in favour of the unique image of the *booth* (*sukâ*). The word refers to a temporary shelter made of branches (Neh. 8:15–16), erected by people working in the fields (Isa. 1:8) to provide protection from the sun and rain (Isa. 4:6; Jon. 4:5). It is also used as a synonym of the 'tent' where the ark of the Lord is housed (2 Sam. 11:11). Since this is a term related to agriculture, its main point here is to convey the simplicity of the new community into which the *house of Jacob* (v. 8) has been transformed. It stands in contrast to the rich houses and strongholds of the Israelite elite (3:13–15; 5:11; 6:8; Hubbard 1989: 239–240). The other significant contrast is with the 'booth of your king' in 5:26, the only other place where *sukâ* is used in Amos. There it has cultic connotations and is part of the description of Israel's idolatrous worship. The contrast becomes even more meaningful once we appreciate the fact that the *booth* in Amos 9 refers to Jerusalem primarily as a centre of worship, the city of the temple (Goswell 2011: 250–256; cf. Radine 2010: 199–210). The raising of the booth, then, is a rejection both of the idolatry and of the injustices of the old Israel and an embrace of worship that is acceptable to God.

To sum up, what God restores in the *booth of David* is a worshipping community of people living in their restored cities, symbolized and led by the Jerusalem temple. The Northern monarchy is dismantled (7:9) and replaced by the Davidic dynasty, which, however, no longer refers to the kings ruling in Jerusalem but is extended to the people as a whole and thus 'democratized'. A similar idea is expressed in Isaiah 55:3 where the covenant with David is extended to the people (Isa. 55:1), pictured as Zion (52:1; 54:1, 11–12). Zion in its capacity as a cultic centre has already been depicted in Isaiah as a tent (Isa. 33:20; cf. 54:2) and more specifically as the 'tent of David' (Isa. 16:5).

The *remnant of Edom* stands in parallel to *all the nations*. Edom is used in the Old Testament as a symbol of the enemies of God's people and representative of the nations of the world in their rebellion against God (Obad. 15–17; Isa. 34). The pair Edom/the nations connects the ending of the book with the opening OAN (1:11–12). The *remnant* (cf. 5:15) suggests that the judgment has struck not only Israel but the nations as well. The idiom *called by [my] name* implies ownership (2 Sam. 12:28; Isa. 4:1) and power to rule (Isa. 63:19). The Lord's authority over the conquered nations will be exercised by the unnamed people who *possess* the remnant of Edom, that is, by the new community called the *booth of David*.

The LXX translation of this verse is remarkably different: 'in order that those remaining of humans and all the nations upon whom my name has been called might seek out me, says the Lord who does these things' (*NETS*). LXX transforms a nationalistic promise about the military conquest of rival neighbouring ethnic groups into a spiritualized promise of worldwide conversion to God. This is achieved by three very small changes to the Hebrew text.[4] Its significance for a Christian reading of Amos derives from the fact that the LXX version is quoted in the New Testament (Acts 15:17) which validates and builds upon its theological reinterpretation (see *Meaning* below).

**13–15.** Political restoration is followed by economic prosperity. The *one who ploughs* (October/November) *overtake[s]* the *one who reaps* the harvest (beginning in April/May). This can mean that the seed grows so quickly it has to be reaped well before the usual harvest time, while ploughing is still going on (Hammershaimb 1970: 141–142). It makes more sense, however, to see the overtaking differently, as an image of the abundance of the harvest, not the speed of its growth. The fields have produced so much that the reapers have not been able to collect it all by the autumn when ploughing for the next year has to start (Nogalski 2011: 358; similar is the understanding of LXX, cf. Glenny 2013: 160–161). Likewise, there are so many grapes that those who begin to tread in September have not yet finished in November/December when *the one who sows the seed* goes out. This results in so much *wine* that the *mountains shall drip . . . and all the hills shall flow with it* (see above on Joel 3:18).

The NIV 'I will bring my people Israel back from exile' understands the two words in the phrase *šabtî 'et šĕbût* as coming from two different roots: 'turn' (*šûb*) and 'captivity' (from *šābâ* 'to deport'). The more common translation *I will restore the fortunes*

---

4. The changes are (1) substituting the verb *yāraš* ('possess') with *dāraš* ('seek') which requires the change of only the initial consonant; (2) repointing *'ĕdôm* ('Edom') to *'ādām* ('humans') which requires no changes in the consonantal text if Edom was spelled defectively; (3) ignoring the object maker *'et* (untranslated in English) before the 'remnant of Edom' which allows the new phrase 'remnant of humans' to serve as the subject of the verb (seek), rather than as its object. Gelston (2010: 88) thinks the variant reading resulted from the mistake of the translator who misread *yrš* for *drš*, while Glenny (2009: 224–226) attributes it to theological reinterpretation.

[*of my people*] derives both words from the root 'turn' (*šûb*), literally 'to turn a turning' (*HALOT* 4.1385–1387). The phrase often includes liberation from captivity and return from exile but has broader implications of restoring fortunes to their former state of prosperity and blessing (Job 42:10; Ezek. 16:53, 55). For Israel this means here rebuilding their cities and enjoying the fruits of their economy. The *booth of David* has now reclaimed the title *my people Israel* whose end (8:2) is overtaken by the new beginning. Just as the Israelites *plant vineyards*, so the Lord will *plant* them on the land. The final metaphor adds the promise of enduring security to the picture of abundance. This is a very different kind of security from the reckless illusion of safety entertained earlier by the leaders of the nation (6:1).

## Meaning

The final passage deals with one of the major themes in the book of Amos: the judgment and destruction of Israel. It takes that theme a step further and addresses the question 'Is there any future beyond the absolute devastation?' The rhetorical situation is now different. The reader is moved to a later episode in the divine–human drama after the blow has already fallen on the people. There is no longer a necessity to deal with arrogance, false security and unbelief. In that new situation the epilogue reveals that the destruction will in fact be only partial and will not be the last word. The message of salvation does not provide any great comfort to the elite of the Northern Kingdom because the house of Jacob is completely reconfigured in the act of restoration. It is redefined as *the booth of David*, an allusion to Jerusalem from where the Lord roars at the start of the book (1:2). The broad meaning of the term *Jacob*, used to designate the kingdom of Northern Israel (Isa. 9:8–9), later the kingdom of Judah (Jer. 5:20) and then those who were taken into exile (Isa. 46:3; 48:1), facilitates the transformation. However, this new Jacob is not simply the Southern Kingdom of Judah, a political institution which resembled too closely the kingdom of Israel. It is a community that has been destroyed and remade, its glory no longer that of a royal palace but of a humble farmer's hut.

The New Testament points to the final stages of that transformation by giving the passage a new meaning. In Acts 15:16–17 the raising of the booth of David signifies the dual reality of the resurrection of Christ and the establishment of the church. This is not an arbitrary equation as the cultic overtones of the phrase *the booth of David*, with its reference to Jerusalem and its temple, demonstrate. The resurrected body of Christ and his body the church as a temple of the Holy Spirit represent in the New Testament the fulfilment of the reality of the divine presence on earth that is anticipated in the Old Testament by the earthly Jerusalem. The military conquest of the nations is reinterpreted in spiritual terms, as the advance of the gospel which invites all peoples to seek the Lord in this new universal temple. Thus, a passage that on the surface promises national restoration and material prosperity in actual fact reveals the arrival of the messianic kingdom for all nations, with its blessings of peace, security and plenty.

Printed and bound by CPI Group (UK) Ltd, Croydon, CR0 4YY

25/03/2025

14647342-0001